Black, White
and *Brown*

PARKE | PRESS
Norfolk

The Norfolk 17: The "threat" that kept 10,000 white students out of classes for fiv

Black, White and *Brown*

The Battle for Progress in 1950s Norfolk

by
Forrest R. "Hap" White

Black, White and Brown: The Battle for Progress in 1950s Norfolk
Copyright © 2018 by Forrest R. White.
All rights reserved.

Originally published as
Pride and Prejudice: School Desegregation and Urban Renewal
in 1992 by Praeger Publishers, 88 Post Road West, Westport, CT 06881

All rights reserved, including the right to reproduce this work
in any form whatsoever without permission in writing from the publisher, except
for brief passages in connection with a review.

Published by
PARKE PRESS
Norfolk, Virginia

ISBN 978-1-7323105-0-6

Library of Congress Control Number is available upon request.

Printed in the United States of America

Contents

List of Figures vii

The Resurrection of Jim Crow ix

Acknowledgments xiii

Introduction xiv

Prologue: Norfolk Before 1950 xix

1. Planning the New Norfolk 1
2. Premonitions of Crisis 26
3. First Reactions to *Brown* 42
4. The Bulldozer Era 63
5. Redevelopment Rationales 90
6. Prelude to Confrontation 112
7. In Pursuit of a Mandate 131
8. A Very Massive Resister 148
9. A Second School Crisis 172
10. Conclusion 182

Abbreviations 223

Glossary 224

Bibliography 236

Index 256

About the Author 263

Figures

1. Norfolk's Neighborhoods 33
2. School Sites under Consideration in 1954 45
3. Atlantic City Redevelopment Project 87
4. Norfolk's Dual School System, circa 1954 99
5. Norfolk's Racial Patterns and Redevelopment Areas,
   circa 1958 102
6. From *De Jure* to *De Facto*: School Resegregation
   in Norfolk, 1956-1958 144
7. Impact of *De Facto* Segregation on School Locations 109
8. New School Buildings, 1959 176
9. School Construction Statistics, 1952-1959 177

The Resurrection of Jim Crow
Preface to the Second Edition

Norfolk at mid-century was no different than most other Southern cities: years of Depression and wartime boom had left all of them with an aging and badly overcrowded inventory of housing and massive unmet needs for new schools, streets, parks, highways, sanitation, and related infrastructure, just to support their existing population. Few cities were really well positioned to grow: they were so landlocked and cash-strapped that they would be hard pressed to maintain their existing infrastructure, much less extend it into the surrounding countryside. Their tax bases were just as stressed: prime industrial areas had either been seized by the military or else taken over by wartime industries that now faced an uncertain future. Rotting wharves, crumbling piers, decaying warehouses, and struggling support services helped to highlight that intra-coastal shipping had all but died out and given way to railroads and inland trucking facilities. Their downtown financial and shopping districts were still crowded, but uninviting. Their streets, many of them laid out in the horse-and-buggy era, were too narrow and lacked the parking support facilities necessary for success in the new auto age. The bulk of their housing stock dated to the boom years of the 1920s or even earlier, and much of the in-town housing stock had been badly cut up into multiple apartments during the wartime housing crush.

The situation was particularly dire in the black communities. One of the legacies of Jim Crow was that most jurisdictions had "separate but equal" tax structures, whereby the meager revenues raised from the "colored" districts were the sole support for black schools and communities. Thus most of the "colored" housing districts lacked paved streets, curbs, sidewalks, storm sewers, parks, playgrounds, and other public improvements. These districts had never been able to support badly needed new school construction, and thus, almost every school for black students in the South was a hand-me-down from the white community: crowded, dilapidated, out-of-date, and lacking in cafeterias, libraries, gymnasiums, science labs, and other modern support facilities. This was one reason that the impending collapse of the Jim Crow "separate but equal" legal structure was so threatening. Enlightened community leaders could see it coming: racial barriers had already fallen in industry, the military, and public accommodations, and it was clear that the armada of challenges already headed to court would eventually produce further victories.

The 1954 *Brown v. Board of Education* decision cut at the heart of this arbitrary cultural and civic divide; the era of calm preparation was over, and excited leaders all across the South rushed to outdo each other in proposing a myriad of administrative obfuscations, delaying tactics, and legal bulwarks to protect their hallowed institution of segregation. When change was forced upon them by the courts, Southern school systems faced both trauma and turmoil. Only Little Rock, Arkansas, faced a more tremulous passage than Norfolk, where the white public junior and senior high schools were closed for five months, locking 10,000 students out of the classroom. Yet the gossamer of legal obstructions thrown up by state and local authorities to preserve segregated schools was only the tip of an iceberg of far less obvious municipal machinations and school board shenanigans meant to more permanently divide whites from blacks in Southern cities. While the legal structure of Jim Crow fell fairly quickly to a decade-long onslaught of court challenges, it was this largely unseen and quasi-legal effort that is still successful in preserving *de facto* segregation even today, more than seven decades later.

"Interposition" was what Southern leaders called it: the doctrine that Southern officials had an obligation to use whatever state and local legal authority they could find to block what they felt were unjust actions by the federal government or its courts. And James J. Kilpatrick, then editor of the *Richmond News Leader,* was its most ardent champion and chief publicist. The doctrine had been around since before the Civil War, but suddenly, with the *Brown v. Board* decision of the U.S. Supreme Court, it found new traction. Although the best that Southern leaders in Congress could come up with was the "Southern Manifesto" championed by Virginia's Harry F. Byrd, state and local officials seemed in competition to propose the most outlandish schemes of obfuscation, urged on at each turn by the editorial cheering sections of newspapers like the *News Leader* and Norfolk's own afternoon paper, the *Ledger-Dispatch*.

In many ways, this behind-the-scenes use of school and municipal power represented a new life for Jim Crow segregation. The Jim Crow system of "separate but equal" laws was born during the Reconstruction Era, when the federal government first attempted to extend civil rights to blacks. To defy the new federal decree, Southern leaders used Black Codes, voter suppression, sharecropping, and complex legal machinations to continue economic oppression and second-class citizenship, elements of chattel slavery. When the federal courts began in the 1950s to strike down the underpinnings of the "separate but equal" laws that were the bulwark of this system, Southern states and cities like Norfolk found new, largely unheralded ways to reinforce their sacrosanct color lines and forcefully substitute *de facto* segregation of their schools, neighborhoods, and public facilities instead. So Jim Crow was reincarnated in these extra-legal, largely administrative machinations. The irony is that urban renewal and interstate highways, the two hallmarks of Eisenhower-era progressivism, were used so forcefully to halt progress by dividing communities, reinforcing color lines, removing transition neighborhoods, and otherwise replacing the legal framework of Southern segregation with more permanent structures.

Besides the ferocity of its attack upon urban blight and the fierceness of its resistance to school segregation, a third factor makes Norfolk's experience in the 1950s unique: the behind-the-scenes, quasi-legal effort to ensure segregation—this second Reconstruction—that was so well documented. First published as *Pride and Prejudice: School Desegregation and Urban Renewal in Norfolk*, in 1991 by Praeger Press, Forrest "Hap" White's annotated doctoral thesis revealed the extent of the city's effort to use redevelopment, city planning, interstate highways, school organization, and school site selection to reinforce the falling legal façade of *de jure* segregation. There had long been charges that other Southern cities engaged in similar reconstruction efforts, but for the most part those went unexposed. Few, if any, other cities risked such comprehensive exposure of this dark chapter in our history of the twentieth century. But, although hailed for its narration—"riveting . . . touched with eloquence" and "depth of exposé" (Guy Friddell, *Norfolk Virginian-Pilot*)—White's *Pride and Prejudice* had too much the look and feel of its origin as an award-winning academic dissertation to reach an audience beyond just Norfolk.

White's 1991 groundbreaking study provides a comprehensive template to official resegregation efforts. That's why it was so gratifying when Parke Press called out of the blue to propose a second edition that would transcend the academic feel of the first and reach a wider readership. "A classic," Marshall McClure of Parke Press called it, is a work that deserves far wider dissemination and a new generation of readers eager to find out how the benighted effort to create a color-free society were so thoroughly derailed. *Black, White and Brown* now tells that story the way it should have been revealed three decades ago.

Acknowledgments

This illustrated edition has been made possible with the generous help of Tim Rudziensky of Virginia Images; Troy Valos of the Sargeant Memorial Collection at Norfolk's Slover Library; Peggy Haile McPhillips of the Norfolk Historical Society; the Library of Congress; and encouragement from many others who wanted this story to be told.

※

Introduction

THE TWIN WAVES of boom and bust had broken many times upon Norfolk's shores. Bombarded, blockaded, captured, and even plundered, the city had endured its share of misfortune at the hands of invaders; but Norfolk, too, had suffered even more mercilessly from enemies within, having been razed by the patriots, isolated by trade restrictions, strangled by intrastate rivalries, decimated by yellow fever, terrorized by the armed mobs during Reconstruction, and then very nearly ruined financially by the disarmament that followed World War I. Through it all, however, the promise of prosperity lingered just around the corner. For more than 300 years the ships of many nations had sought refuge in her fine natural harbor. For two centuries the hammer blows of the shipbuilding trade had reverberated across her waterfront, punctuating the bustle of ships' chandlers, sail makers, jack-tars, tavern keepers, and sailors on leave. Merchants, upon surveying this hubbub of activity, dreamed of the day when the harbor would one day compete with the great ports of New York, Baltimore, Boston, and Charleston. It was the pursuit of this dream that brought them the resiliency to overcome the harrowing scars of defeat. Over and over again, Norfolk had bounced back from the crushing blows of misfortune, only to be leveled once more.[1]

In short, Norfolk had been washed by the twin tides of hope and despair as often, if not more precipitously, as the other great cities of America. Approaching the middle of the twentieth century, Norfolk appeared to have as great a prospect of prosperity and as little to fear as any city in the nation: World War II was over, and yet there would be no disarmament; her enemies lay far beyond the reaches of her coastline defenses; the ravages of the Depression had been left far behind; and her merchants and captains of industry were eager to get on about their tasks, hopeful that the time was at last at hand to build the great city of their dreams.

At first glance, Norfolk's history during these postwar years does not seem remarkably different from other American cities.

The boom and bustle of the war years gave way to a momentary respite, and then raged on in the frantic growth of suburbia. The highways zoomed, the buildings loomed, and the babies boomed in postwar prosperity. The civic elite who ruled Floyd Hunter's Atlanta[2] had their counterparts who reigned over Norfolk's growth, a well-being that extended to every segment of the community: merchants found a seller's market; consumers spied an unbelievable selection of goods and services; employers sensed unrivaled opportunities for growth and expansion; workers faced an unprecedented array of career positions; and even the sick, old, and unemployed discovered a growing national consensus that all should share in the spoils of victory.

Two events alone make Norfolk's history at this time remarkable from that of other cities: one, the voracity of its assault upon urban blight, and two, the ferocity of its resistance to school desegregation. The rate at which the federal bulldozers gobbled up its slums earned Norfolk all-American honors and a lasting place in the annals of municipal achievement; the collision between the advocates of integration and the forces of Massive Resistance won the city only a footnote in the history books, and fleeting dishonor on the national scene. Norfolk's reaction to these two issues, and, indeed, their very emergence as historical turning points, may be directly traced to the rise and fall of two distinct *foci* of power—one, economic, and the other, political—irrevocably tied together in a tale of pride and prejudice. It is the story of how boom perverted very nearly came to bust; how the same forces that launched the tide of urban renewal acquiesced, waned, and then finally regrouped to form the last bulwark of resistance against an even greater surge of racial antipathy; and how new blood, untutored and untested in the political conventions of the era, emerged to eclipse both these elements at the seat of municipal power.

Much that is both right and wrong with Norfolk today may be traced back to developments during the formative years between 1950 and 1960. Before then, its citizens were far more attuned to the small-town provincialism of rural Virginia than to the urban dynamism of the great port cities that were its competitors. The leadership, the vision, and the progressive policies that could have brought about such a change never had a chance to rock the *status quo*; they were too finely filtered, processed, and forced out through the sieve of machine politics. It was not until the close of World War II, when Norfolk stood on the brink of economic ruin, that its citizens found the courage to overthrow the political machine that had dominated its deliberations and stifled its advance. Norfolkians now became obsessed with the dream of a revitalized city; they saw at last an opportunity to discard the unpleasant memories of wartime shortages and depression deficits, and they jumped at the chance to advance the kind of leaders who could make this vision come true.

Many factors were responsible for the fall of the old political order, but it was unquestionably civic pride, really unbridled boosterism, that swept new leadership into office with a mandate for reform and rejuvenation. Pride was the magnet that attracted a different breed of leader—financially secure, successful, confidant, and socially superior—to the helm of municipal government; pride was the driving force that cleaned house at city hall, and recruited instead an exciting and vibrant coterie of professionals, planners, engineers, and reformers capable of putting the dreams into practice; and it was pride, along with a heavy dose of optimism and sense of adventure, that helped to transform a once-indolent populace into a dynamic and progressive citizen force. The business and civic leaders who took over city hall were realistic enough to realize that they could not achieve their goals alone without assistance from outside sources, including the federal government. A host of national experts descended upon the city to help draft the blueprints of this dream—a vision that would thrust Norfolk into the forefront of the nascent fields of municipal planning, redevelopment, and urban renewal.

By the early 1950s, however, the impetus for change had waned, and the reformers who had been swept into office by civic pride and optimism lost out to others who owed their allegiance to the old political order, now more flexible and resilient than ever. The dream of a New Norfolk had reached the building stage, and it now took on a different form than had once been envisioned. The planners, reformers, and out-of-towners who had once peopled city hall now gave way to a new wave of bricks-and-mortar men, far more provincial and politically dependent than their predecessors. There was an attempt at first to retain the guidance of the business and civic leaders, but this effort, too, faded with their falling political fortunes.

Time and events had changed considerably since the old political machine last ruled city hall, but its leaders failed to discern the differences, and in doing so, very nearly brought the city to its knees. For them, racial antipathy had always been the cause celebré that rallied supporters and overrode all other more meaningful divisions in the white community. Under the reformers, black leaders had been given an advisory role in planning and redevelopment, and that now made them convenient targets for attacks that would also sting the flanks of the progressives. The social advances of the postwar era were the first casualties as the machinery of municipal government was retooled to conform to racial antipathy. Discrimination at first took the more subtle form of the sort of political tit-for-tat that frequently accompanies the fortunes of the electoral process, but the *Brown* v. *Board of Education* decision accelerated both the rhetoric and the scope of the contest. Virginia's Massive Resistance (movement) to school desegregation soon locked both races into a cutthroat competition with stakes so high that neither side could afford to fold its hand. In this contest, prejudice—the unreasonable adherence to the conventions, traditions, and mores of the past— reigned supreme and soon became the underlying force behind every phase of municipal policy. Even the planners' tools of redevelopment and urban renewal—the hallmarks of the reformers' rule—were prostituted to serve this end.

Prejudice brought Norfolk once again to the brink of ruin: with schools closed, the population divided, neighborhoods threatened, and development stagnated, its future was indeed uncertain. The city that had once been so open to new ideas, innovative approaches, and outside leadership had closed its doors to the rest of the world, and turned inward upon itself, afraid now to face even the slightest alteration in the status quo. This time the voices of pride and boosterism that had once led the city to municipal glory stood silent. Only a handful of public-minded citizens—bit players up to now— dared to oppose the politics of prejudice; they lacked the resources to mount a challenge to the established order; so, instead, they sought to defuse the confrontation. In the end their strategy was successful, and their opposition inspired the major business and civic leaders to finally speak out. Aroused at last, the forces of pride and boosterism stepped in to avert the ultimate conflict, but their move came too late to seize for themselves the mantle of municipal office; it passed instead to those few brave citizens who had initiated the challenge.

Norfolk at mid-century had faced an uncharted sea of opportunity that had induced its business leaders to dream of splendors far beyond the city's grasp; in striving to achieve those ends, they had miraculously transformed this once sleepy little port into a dynamic and modern metropolis. Along the way their leadership peaked, ebbed, and was then replaced by a surge of prejudice that very nearly ruined the city. This rush of events destroyed both the old political order and the newer forces of boosterism; leadership in the future fell instead to a new group of citizens without identifiable cause or calling, certain only that the city would have to live in a world in which neither pride nor prejudice reigned supreme.

By 1960 Norfolk had come to face a less certain future: its grand visions had been scaled down to encompass a lesser reality, but one in which all citizens could share on equal terms; and the city had learned that it could not afford either the economic costs of rebirth or the social toll of racial antipathy. The monuments to this era are many: they are cast in concrete, steel, and glass, but they may also be seen in the trail of bulldozed rubble, vacant buildings, and bombed-out open spaces; the evidence may also be found in the toll of suffering and despair; its record may still be read in this tale of pride and prejudice.

※

Prologue: Norfolk Before 1950

FOUR SAILORS WITH A BARMAID in tow steamed out into Granby Street and launched into a chorus of *Roll Out The Barrel*. A single car cut out of traffic and pulled to the curb, jubilantly sounding its horn over their slurred rendition of the chorus. This mild commotion on an otherwise still August afternoon stirred onlookers from their shaded refuge in the shops and storefronts that lined the street; a few quick words were exchanged, and the news flashed through the gathering crowd. Other cars began sounding their horns in salute, and soon a blaring procession of automobiles was inching its way past the swelling throng. The taverns along Beer Barrel Row began closing their doors as patrons rushed to join the melee in the street. The *Roll-Out-the-Barrel* boys had by now picked up a chorus line of converts that was snake-dancing arm in arm through the stalled traffic. Streamers of toilet paper drifted down from the offices above, the opening salvos in a furious fusillade of impromptu confetti that belied the constraints of wartime rationing. The merrymakers dancing in the streets below were the precursors of one of the most raucous, brawling, celebrations in Norfolk's history. The day was Tuesday, August 14, 1945—V-J Day—and the radio had just signaled the end of World War II. Not since Patrick Henry's army of patriots burned this Tory stronghold to the ground had the nation's domestic military forces had such a grand night on the town. One solemn sailor surveyed the jubilant commotion surrounding him and summed up the frequent lament of his colleagues, "Of all the damned places to be when this thing happened, we had to be in Norfolk."[1]

The following day dawned quietly for the city; half of its population was nursing their worst hangover of modern times. The other half—Norfolk's more permanent residents—faced an even grimmer morning after. The city's streets were empty, its shops, banks, and government offices having been closed for a day of prayer and thanksgiving. Gone were the sailors, the shipyard workers, the snake dancers, the blaring automobiles, and the drunken carousers of the night before; even the taverns and the bawdy houses of East

Main Street were closed for the day. Here and there the white "dixie cup" of a sailor's cap bobbed among the flotsam of confetti and other jetsam of the celebration. A handful of bleary-eyed strangers still ruled this empty roost from perches tucked away well off the beaten path.[2] To Norfolk's more permanent residents this panorama of desertion served as a grim reminder of what the city would be like without its navy. While the war was raging overseas, they had thought only of tolerating this domestic military invasion until they could reclaim the city as their own—they had given little thought to really making a "home" for the transient population. Now that the war was officially over, however, the thought of empty streets and the fleet's departure struck the community to the core, rousing it from its civic stupor, and infusing it with a thirst for fresh leadership and new direction.

Control of city hall had long been in the hands of the city's professional politicians, a group that had always shown tremendous willingness to run the show without external interference. The "Prieur Machine," as the local affiliate of the statewide (Harry F.) Byrd Organization was called, was run by Clerk of Courts William "Billy" Prieur. Time and circumstances over the course of the Depression and the war years had combined to make the Prieur Machine far more powerful than either the perks of office or the patronage of political organization would have indicated. Since they were powerless to influence the deliberations at city hall, and unwilling to risk the ire of the Organization that controlled so many jobs in a hard-strapped economy, Norfolk's business and financial leaders turned their attention instead during the Depression to a more receptive arena, the sphere of civic involvement. Not only did they find great success in these endeavors, well separated from the political operations of the city, they also forged key alliances and learned to build a community coalition of their own that would one day rival the more entrenched political operatives. Through the Community Chest and a number of related charities, the businessmen worked tirelessly to relieve the suffering of their fellow citizens; by means of the National Recovery Administration and its volunteer successor, the Emergency Relief Commission, they also learned to rely on federal support in this effort. Through their own Citizens Crime Commission they studied the harsh economic impact that slums had, not only upon city services, but also upon the lives of their inhabitants.

Prologue: Norfolk Before 1950

xxi

The war years had brought incredible hardships to the citizens and great turmoil to city government. Norfolk experienced a tremendous period of growth at the start of the war, and its population would double, even triple on the weekends, as thousands of sailors, soldiers, and shipyard workers on leave descended upon the downtown area for entertainment. This put an enormous strain upon both the city's municipal services and its aging housing stock; the politicians were so reluctant to provide even essential municipal services for these new, more "temporary," residents that the Navy Department had to step in to build schools, parks, playgrounds, highways, recreation areas, utilities, and a host of other projects. The businessmen forged their own alliance with the U.S. Navy, and, acting as the Norfolk Housing Authority, built several thousand new housing units for the servicemen.

The first postwar problems, however, began to appear almost immediately as the specter of closed stores and empty streets served as a grim reminder of the fact that, in peacetime, Norfolk would again have to stand on its own financial feet: the navy would no longer be willing to foot the bill for some much-needed and long overdue municipal improvement. That prospect was so frightening, that the city council called for a cutback in planned improvement projects and current levels of service.[3] This proved to be the final straw for Norfolk's business establishment: it had endured the national vilification of the city in the media and halls of Congress for its sordid nightlife, but they would not now stand for a self-imposed recession. Area businessmen knew that the city could not maintain its position in the world of trade by depending solely upon merchant shipping and local industries; Norfolk needed the navy, now more than ever, and local merchants turned their efforts furiously into remaking the city into a place where the navy would want to stay, rather than remain known infamously as the world's worst liberty port. The subsequent uproar of merchants and businessmen over proposed municipal cutbacks prompted a dramatic turn of events. The powder keg of civic unrest was finally ignited.

Almost as suddenly as the tides of war began to recede, a new wave of community pride and civic boosterism rose to take its place. The war years that had witnessed a dramatic upsurge in citizen activity to accommodate and alleviate the bombardment of navy personnel[4] now gave way to a new direction in civic involvement. The civic leaders who had gone all-out to beef up the wartime charities to serve the new, transient population were not now content to rest. The club ladies who had knocked themselves out to provide wholesome entertainment for "the boys" were no longer content to sit at home. The volunteers who had staffed the bandage brigades and peopled the U.S.O.s were looking for a new cause. The transient residents who had poured into the city during the war years were now almost as established as the old-timers; they would not tolerate a cutback in the very services and facilities designed to meet their needs. Thus, all of these diverse elements—the civic, the business, the volunteer, and the transient communities—had a hand in forcing the issue of Norfolk's postwar renewal out into the open; all of them urged a dramatic reversal of municipal policy.

Another issue seethed beneath the surface of this desire for change. During the war, crime had become big business in the city. Gamblers, prostitutes, racketeers, and bootleggers had invaded the area—as they invariably do to all boom towns—to cater to the more salacious desires of sailors out on leave and shipyard workers out on the town. Norfolk's finest citizens began to feel that too many of these mobsters and racketeers controlled city hall, replacing their own more legitimate voice with bribes and payoffs. The blatancy with which the city's "other element" conducted its venal activities shocked and enraged the citizenry. It was no wonder that such conduct was the talk of the town, and an open link between the gangsters and the politicians was widely suspected.[5] Norfolkians had long endured the shenanigans of all sorts of wartime carpetbaggers and entrepreneurs, but the prospect that these gangsters and racketeers would continue to control the city's fate in peacetime now became too great a burden to bear, and thus the closing months of 1945 became the winter of discontent for many residents.

Political conformity had bred a closed society in Norfolk—a society afraid to accept outsiders, new ideas, or even dissension among its provincial little community. The city's close proximity to the navy and government workers during World War II had been a positive force that had done much to erase that stagnation. The war years had been a bitter experience in many ways—with the crowding, inconvenience, crime, and hedonism—for both the hometowners and the sailors alike, but in the end, the war had opened the minds of many of the citizens to a world beyond their own parochial realm, while others had found their mission in ministering to strangers from all parts of America. Norfolk had opened its doors to the Navy slowly, cautiously, and even grudgingly, but now a fear was growing that those doors, once closed, would remain forever shuttered.

The next few months would witness some remarkable changes for a city overly conditioned to accept the narrow scope and dreary conformity of its venerable political leaders. The citizens that had so recently focused their attention upon fighting despots overseas would suddenly turn their efforts towards resisting a more home grown version of totalitarianism. The hometown folks who had so recently despised the visiting sailors as an army of occupation would turn instead to welcome them as economic liberators. That bleak specter of closed stores and empty streets in Norfolk's downtown commercial district would prompt a fondness for the profligacy and crowded jubilation of sailor's revelry, and that longing would in turn provide the public mandate for a remarkable chain of events that would sweep this once-seedy little backwater port into the forefront of a national municipal reform movement, bringing as well an era of unheralded progress and prosperity.

The U.S. Navy, along with the Norfolk Housing Authority, built several thousand segregated temporary housing units for servicemen. Library of Congress

Meager revenues raised from the "colored" districts were the sole support for black schools and public facilities in black neighborhoods. Thus most of those neighborhoods lacked paved streets, curbs, sidewalks and storm sewers. Library of Congress

Slums dwellings like these, many of which lacked running water, central heat and indoor plumbing, were torn down in N.R.H.A. Project One to make room for modern public housing units in new garden apartments. Getty Images

1

✼ ✼ ✼ ✼ ✼

Planning the New Norfolk

WHEN BULLDOZERS RIPPED into the wall of a house in the 700 block of Smith Street on December 11, 1951, they marked both a new beginning and a crumbling end. At long last, the city was moving from the quiet haunts of its earlier infamy into the spotlight of national attention. The house that first shuddered, shook, and then crumbled that wintry morning marked the beginning of the first federally financed slum clearance project in the country;[1] it also signaled the passing of a very special style of government in Norfolk, and served as both the legacy and the tombstone of the final retreat from progressive reform in the city.

Those first bulldozers were propelled by a force of civic pride and boosterism that would project Norfolk into the forefront of the Age of Redevelopment before it peaked, and then dissipated altogether. The muffled applause by the gloved dignitaries who had gathered to witness this event faded as the bulldozers tore into the sagging structure. In their eyes, the memories of yesteryear were giving way to a dynamic effort to build the metropolis of the future. Those first bulldozers were the most dramatic and tangible evidence that the dreams of an indolent age were at last on their way to becoming a reality.

That first house stood as well as a sad omen of what would come. As the small crowd gathered, crewmen bound the house in chains and clamped them to the bulldozer designated for the job. At the appointed moment, the machine started and lurched forward, dragging its chains through the underpinnings of the structure. The house shook, but did not fall[2]—a remarkable augury of blight's resistance to eradication. As if to prophesy the unseen forces of the future that would chart the city's course—as if to warn of invisible props that underlay Norfolk's renewal—the house still stood, its underpinnings completely destroyed. Embarrassed crewmen reattached their chains to a more elevated point, reporters and dignitaries chatted idly by, news photographers reloaded for a second shot, and history paused momentarily in the making. The second time the bulldozers lurched, the chain took hold and the frame collapsed in a shower of crumbling plaster, rotting boards, billowing dust, and scattering functionaries.

Norfolk was irreversibly embarking upon a whole new approach to municipal activity, but it was more than just a fervent desire to erase the memories of an unpleasant past that had put the city in the vanguard of urban renewal. It was more than just the aimless longing for the golden dream of "A New Norfolk," more than just the fulfillment of campaign promises. Norfolk had reached this pinnacle of regeneration because a specific group of men had possessed the courage to not just dream, but to act. Theirs was a bold vision, and it was shared by men and women all across the country, but the difference in Norfolk was that they were just the sort of individuals who could make that aspiration a reality. All were committed to the cause, and all were conditioned to success. They had made their reputations, both business and civic, by overcoming long odds; they knew how to gamble for high stakes, but, more importantly, they knew how to win. The individuals who sparked Norfolk's redevelopment were business leaders who wielded the power and prestige to overcome almost any opposition and drag the city into nearly any venture. Certainly the fine points of that redevelopment—the stakes, expense, delay, social costs, and suffering—were as misunderstood by the general public in Norfolk as in any city in the country, but it was here that the city's leading citizens put their reputations on the line behind renewal. And that made all the difference.

The council-manager type of reform government was designed to be a "businessman's rule." The system was intended to take the power out of the hands of the political hacks and give it to the true leaders of the community, and then back them up with the technical and professional expertise necessary to make the very best decisions for the community. City government, the theory went, had become too complex, its myriad services so vast, its management too technical, and its planning too vital to be left to amateurs. That was the ideal, but in far too many council-manager cities, the power had merely passed from one group of parochials to another. In most cities the real leaders, the real opinion-makers, had lost interest in municipal affairs; the result of their abdication was that a group of small-businessmen and petty interests took over instead—a group that was still businessmen, but only second-tier ones; they were capable only of dreaming small dreams, and often failed to comprehend the bigger picture. In most cities, directorship of the taxpayers' multi-million dollar municipal corporation had settled into the grasp of people scarcely off the assembly line—foremen, at best, who could only hold the machinery of government on course until visionary leaders returned to take control.

In Norfolk, however, a peculiar set of circumstances had befallen the city and was forcing a different sort of leader to the top. The previous local leadership had so bungled the prerogatives of power that the "first team" had been forced out of their boardrooms and counting houses to take over. At the close of World War II, Norfolk faced the prospect of folding altogether in the hands of the "little people" who ran most other cities; the lure of wartime profiteering, the power to control the expansion of municipal services, and the opportunity to promote political or parochial interests had been too much for them. The transfusion of new leadership that was taking place in Norfolk's reform movement came from the bluest blood in the city. At last, the real corporate minds hoped to take over the directorship of city government. They understood management on a large scale, and knew that even if they could promote themselves to the city's board of directors, they could not fulfill their aspirations for the city all by themselves; just as in their own private enterprises, they would need an army of specialists, planners, and consultants to plot and carry out their vision. So in addition to dreaming big dreams, they possessed the dynamism, energy, and wherewithal to carry them out.

Even so, any move to snatch control of the city from the political organization that had ruled it for decades would be no mean accomplishment, especially in a Virginia election system that used every conceivable means, including the poll tax and early registration deadlines, to keep the voting population small and manageable. In fact, when the frustrations of the business and civic leaders first began to surface and take on a political bent in the winter of 1945, the poll books for the June election had already been closed, precluding any effort to register new voters who shared this hope of reform.[3] It was the stormy resignation of Colonel Charles K. Borland, Norfolk's long-suffering and usually staid city manager, in "a violent temper" over the city council's proposed cutback of essential services,[4] that proved to be the culminating event. Both his resignation and his parting blast at machine politics took the community by surprise, especially since Borland was just a few months away from becoming eligible for a substantial retirement pension.[5] Talk at a testimonial dinner hastily arranged by the business community soon turned to a political agenda. At first the businessmen sought an audience with local Organization chieftain William "Billy" Prieur, hoping to convince him that a change in city leadership was needed,[6] but when these efforts at appeasement proved futile, the People's Ticket of Richard D. Cooke, Pretlow Darden, and John Twohy was born.

The men who now proposed to take control of Norfolk had two undeniable loci of power: the one financial and the other civic. These were not the ordinary group of downtown merchants hoping to harness municipal spending to keep the central business district alive. There was not a single retailer in the lot; instead they were the heavyweights of the area's business community: bankers, brokers, builders, corporate attorneys, and building-supply dealers. They had more than just a personal interest in Norfolk's rebirth and redevelopment—they had a financial stake in it. They were also the foremost representatives of the city's civic pride and community spirit; throughout the Depression and war years the city's charities had turned to these individuals for leadership, and they had built up their own independent civic following as a consequence.

Although it was left to corporate attorney Richard D. Cooke, automobile dealer Pretlow Darden (younger brother of Virginia's popular wartime governor), and concrete magnate John Twohy to carry their standard, this was a group effort that found almost every substantial business and civic leader in the city aligned against one of the most powerful, well-financed, and experienced political organizations in the state; failure meant great risk and personal sacrifice for all who participated in this coup. All had benefitted from their alliance with the Byrd Organization in the past, and now had much to lose if the selective enforcement, special treatment, and red tape of municipal government were suddenly turned against them. All had relied too heavily in their corporate ventures on the rapid processing of building permits, legal documents, inspections, and applications not to fear a significant threat of intimidation if their new collective venture were to fail. Once committed, they had to succeed, and they threw themselves into the exhausting work of the political campaign with the same vigor, skill, and determination evident in their civic and corporate achievements. It proved to be a hotly contested race—"the hottest political campaign in Norfolk's history."[7]

The "Silkstocking Ticket," as the Cooke-Darden-Twohy group was immediately labeled in the hardball oratory of the Prieur Machine stalwarts, hoisted the "Time For A Change" standard and ran carefully against the lackluster record of the wartime city council. They were determined to run as three conservative businessmen who had close ties to the Byrd Organization, thereby avoiding at least the appearance of challenging Billy Prieur directly. It was a clever strategy, but it meant they had to both outdo the existing administration in conservative rhetoric and out-organize the Prieur Machine on its home turf. As part of that effort, they pledged not to seek reelection, thereby hoping to convince the traditional Organization voter that they only meant to revitalize Norfolk's governmental structure, not found another political dynasty.

Fortunately, the People's Ticket had both the personal credibility and the backing to pull off one of the most dramatic upsets in the otherwise closed conformity of Virginia's political arena. Their election, by a better than 2-to-1 margin in the largest voter turnout the city had ever witnessed, gave them a mandate to bring progressive government to Norfolk.[8] As if to seal their pledge of "business-like government, free from political influence and control," their first order of business was to set about hiring the "best city manager money can buy . . . not to get the best would be money wasted."[9] They turned to Charles A. Harrell, past president of the International City Managers' Association. In addition to having a strong national reputation for long-range planning and careful administration,

Harrell had grown up in Norfolk, started his career in its service, and maintained close ties to the area. Even so, it was the promise of the new city council not to interfere in his administration—rather than the money or the hometown connection—that proved successful in luring him away from his post in Schenectady, New York.[10]

Harrell set busily about the task of rebuilding Norfolk's tarnished national image and cleaning its squalid municipal house. The promise not to succeed themselves lent a sense of urgency to the actions of the new city council: "We knew what we had to do, and we knew we were only there for four short years; so we did it."[11] As part of its campaign promise, the People's Council gave Harrell free rein to bring in an army of professionals and consultants to help chart the city's rebirth. But Harrell went beyond this charge, and skillfully involved as many of the city's critical business and civic leaders as possible into a new hierarchy of appointed boards and commissions that further removed the political functionaries at city hall from the decision-making process.

The task of municipal house cleaning, however, ran into some serious opposition, especially from the well-entrenched forces in the Public Safety (Police and Fire) Department. A fortuitous event, however, helped to break the back of the Prieur Organization in this arena as well. A young captain of detectives, Claude "Bubba" Staylor, who later served as both chief of police and city councilman, took the initiative when the Organization's police chief was out of town to raid Norfolk's "protected" gambling and numbers rackets. Staylor's raid sent off howls of protest, especially when the police chief quickly returned to drop the charges against several of what the newspaper labeled as the city's "most notorious gangsters"[12] for lack of evidence, while more than a hundred of their customers languished in jail.[13] The blatant partiality of this treatment, plus the fact that Staylor had uncovered evidence of bribes and payoffs to more than half the force, helped to unravel a comprehensive scheme of municipal corruption. A special grand jury of the city's business and civic elite used this opportunity to bring down both the protected rackets and the police hierarchy.[14] The Silkstocking Takeover was thus complete, and the Organization's grip on city hall broken.

City Manager C. A. Harrell was not one to delay once he had achieved the circumstances conducive to action. The scandal in the police department and the publicity generated by its subsequent investigation had given him the mandate for reform he sought; skillfully he shifted people to promote his professionals to a larger grasp of power. Although many of the experts who had descended upon the city returned quickly to their previous haunts in industry, commerce, and academia, they left behind the blueprints for progress in their voluminous charts, statistics, and analyses. Knowing that the work of these boards would outlast the electoral mandate of the People's Council, Harrell conspired to shift as much of the burden of charting municipal expansion as he could from the offices in city hall to the volunteer boards and commissions that established the policies. The People's Council exercised such a strong personal pull that others of similar talent were drawn from industry, commerce, professional callings, the arts, and the charities into volunteer service to the city, and this level of civic involvement became one of the most enduring legacies of their reign. By staffing these independent boards and commissions with his own professional advisors, and then feeding them the reports of the hired consultants, Harrell knew that he could broaden his mandate beyond the limitations of the work force at city hall.

The roster of the postwar city council, Redevelopment and Housing Authority, and the Planning Commission read like a listing of local Community Fund chairmen, charitable benefactors, First Citizen Award winners, and civic headliners—just the type of individuals who so rarely get personally involved in running the day-to-day operations of municipal enterprises. These men who had been forced to take over the rebirth and redevelopment of Norfolk were the true opinion leaders in the community. They had the power, the prestige, and the respect to personally dispense with the types of objections that hamstrung so many similar dreams of rebirth across the country.[15]

Harrell's plan worked better than anyone could have expected. Not a single community leader ever refused the council's call to volunteer service,[16] and the city's boards and commissions began calling for new ventures that would have been unthinkable just a few years earlier. Norfolk's citizens soon began to discern the fruits of their labor: a municipal airport, water treatment plant, modern bus system, a bridge-tunnel link to Portsmouth, new superhighways to the downtown, and a host of other new highway and municipal ventures. Only a portion of C. A. Harrell's program was cast in concrete; the rest was set in careful planning and legislation. As part of the city's new housekeeping system, Harrell advocated a vast upgrading of the municipal statutes regarding property. The business and civic leaders who peopled the various volunteer boards and commissions took the lead in recommending revamped zoning ordinances, new building codes, stronger health and safety ordinances, and one of the nation's first enforced minimum housing codes.[17] It was an ambitious program that would never have passed without their support. The new ordinances would require major renovations to half the houses in the city; had the recommendations come from bureaucrats, instead of established community leaders, the public would have quickly suspected that partisan motives or selective enforcement were involved. Yet here were Norfolk's First Citizens, the leaders of its charities, financial institutions, industries, and businesses calling for an uplifting that began with their own bootstraps.

The Norfolk Housing Authority, born of the navy's need for wartime dwellings, had been among the first to catch the spirit of rebirth. The Authority was determined not to die out with the end of the war; it knew how much the city still had to accomplish to provide adequate housing for its citizens. "Redevelopment" was added to its title for the first time at the close of the war, and now the new Norfolk Redevelopment and Housing Authority began to revise its calling. Instead of just serving as the navy's link to additional housing, the N.R.H.A. hoped to provide the means to eliminate much of the city's crime- and disease-infested slums.[18] It began to formulate a plan that included two phases: phase one entailed the renovation of more than 1,000 wartime housing units to accommodate civilian public housing tenants; the second phase included an aggressive proposal to build 1,890 more public housing units in order to clear the path for slum removal. The Authority's sales pitch was accompanied by the release of a graphic pictorial publication, *This Is It*, designed to sell both the human and the economic elements of the plan. The N.R.H.A. did not mince its words: the booklet was clearly designed to sell public housing as the essential first step to the rebirth of the rest of the city:

> A 1937 study showed that the city was spending $5 for every $1 collected from real estate taxes and other income from five slum areas. Public housing cuts these service costs to a

minimum. Public housing reduces the subsidy that taxpayers contribute every year to perpetuate nineteenth century hovels which injure the value of nearby property, impede the city's growth, and threaten the whole population with crime and disease. . . . The citizens of Norfolk will not, we believe, be satisfied with anything less than the complete elimination of every unfit dwelling in the city. Year by year, house by house, the reconstruction must go on until the combined efforts of the Norfolk Redevelopment and Housing Authority and private builders enable every family to enjoy a decent home.[19]

It was an argument skillfully designed to appeal to the business and civic leaders that the commissioners felt comprised their natural constituency; indeed, even under the wartime administration of the Prieur Machine, the former Housing Authority had been the sole prerogative of the business and civic elite that now constituted the Silkstocking Takeover. Now that the People's Ticket was in power, the Norfolk Redevelopment and Housing Authority became the showpiece of the new administration. Not only were the commissioners the very pillars of the city's new businessmen's elite, these men, by virtue of their very extensive civic and charity work, had also gathered a constituency that was far larger than just the Silkstocking group they seemed so adequately to represent. Of the seven commissioners who had helped to formulate the N.R.H.A.'s postwar program, five had headed the Community Fund, four had been named First Citizen, and all seven had actively studied the dreadful conditions of Norfolk's aging housing stock. All had hung their heads in shame when Nathan Straus, a federal housing official rounding out his tour of 137 cities, remarked of Norfolk's blight, "I have travelled all over the United States, from one end to the other, but I have never seen anything as bad as this."[20] All seven commissioners were convinced that the unsafe health and sanitary conditions that existed in the slums posed a very great danger to all the citizens of Norfolk,[21] and they seized upon this rare opportunity to convert the navy's wartime projects to civilian use as public housing.

It was more than just shame, however, more than just crime, taxes, health, property values, and housing conditions that motivated these men. All had lived through a most peculiar period in the history of Norfolk's growth: crisis proportions of wartime conscription had strangely welded the entire citizenry into an active and cohesive civic force.[22] As members of the wartime Housing Authority, they had seen how quickly the people of Norfolk could respond to alleviate the most intolerable hardships. The sense of shared emergency had made the city vibrant and alive; it had carried over into a postwar boom that was unique for the city; it had provided the impetus for the reform movement that was the first tenet of their faith; and finally, it had awakened the citizens to the fact that for a community united, all things were possible. If they could once more promote the sense of shared emergency, once again cultivate enough civic shame to prompt action, then, the commissioners believed, they could translate these forces into a renewed impetus for growth in general and a personal mandate for redevelopment and, specifically, public housing. Theirs was an ambitious plan, and they knew that citizen support was essential to its adoption.

A series of timely events, however, helped to underscore the need for public housing, careful community planning, and quick municipal action. The Brambleton section of the city had for some time been convulsed with racial turmoil when several blacks sought to defy the community's strict standard of segregated housing. During the war years the vast influx of families into the city had put a premium on housing space in the few small areas of the city reserved for blacks. More than half of the black families in the city had been forced to either take in boarders or double up, just as in the white community, but in the black neighborhoods, this meant two or more families living in a one- or two-room apartment. There had been almost no private housing built for blacks in more than a decade and a half, and Brambleton appeared to be the ideal site for black expansion: it was a small (1,100 homes) white community bounded on two sides by black developments, and isolated by industrial properties and the Elizabeth River on the other sides. Once the first few black families began to push across the traditional dividing line between the black and white communities, whites responded with attacks, threats, broken windows, and minor acts of vandalism.[23] After a series of stormy city council sessions, an interracial committee was appointed to study the situation. The council had hoped that some way would be found to guarantee "the separation of white and Negro homes in the area,"[24] but the city's black newspaper, the *Journal and Guide*, refused to let the issue drop. The aggressive attacks of the editors helped to convince the white community that further violence would occur unless something was done:

> It cannot be emphasized too strongly, and it is worth repeating again and again, that the housing situation affecting Norfolk's Negro citizens is not only acute, but desperate, while, by a fair comparison, no such problem faces the white population. The housing predicament with which this community is confronted cannot be resolved by the simple expedient of viewing it as a racial matter. It is based upon an elementary human need and its amelioration must be on this basis alone. It is an age-old story of the law of supply and demand. Norfolk's Negro population has grown by some 25,000 in the last few years, but little new housing has emerged to shelter this population increase . . . while, on the other hand, construction of new white units has been over 5,000. Even assuming that private capital were available and homes [for blacks] could be built, under present restrictive conditions, where could the necessary land be found?[25]

The black and white communities remained at odds, and the interracial committee appointed by the city council failed to devise a new color line in the Brambleton area. The turmoil did not cease with the first few incursions, and soon the breakdown of time-honored color lines began to affect other blocks in the Brambleton section. The situation failed to stabilize, and soon entire neighborhoods were in flight. The *Journal and Guide* continued to intimate that further incidents would occur unless the city began to take some quick measures to provide housing for blacks. The fact that the *Journal and Guide*'s threats of racial strife were reprinted for the white community in the *Virginian-Pilot* helped to build the momentum for public intervention—some step that would alleviate the housing crisis for blacks, yet also work to preserve the separate status of white neighborhoods. Thus, the N.R.H.A.'s push for public housing struck a core of need recognized by both blacks and whites, and public support for the proposal began to build rapidly.

By 1948 a solid consensus in the community had been achieved:

the Norfolk Redevelopment and Housing Authority had been angling for two years for official endorsement of its slum removal program; during that time the events in Brambleton and its surrounding neighborhoods had been simmering; Public Health Director Dr. John Huff had sounded repeated warnings regarding the epidemic dangers of crime and contagion in the city's slums; and opinion in the black community had coalesced around the single, dominant theme of their housing crisis. The city council was at last ready to take official action, but the nature of their commitment was, as yet, still undiscernible. The council was, however, quick to agree upon two points: the city faced a "critical shortage of housing meeting the minimum health standards in Negro and some low-income white areas," and that "this condition is a matter of concern to all other Norfolk residents, regardless of their own pleasant living surroundings."[26] For more than ten years a succession of city councils had agreed that it was "time to do something," the situation was "acute," the housing shortage was "serious,"[27] so the debate this time focused upon what official actions, other than following earlier councils in encouraging private developers to enter the normally unprofitable low-income housing market, could be taken to alleviate the crisis. One councilman recommended that the city "should be among the first in line"—those words would prove prophetic—for new federal redevelopment funds then under consideration by the U.S. Congress.[28] The suggestion touched off such a response that the city council, already saddled with an enormous array of capital projects, was prepared to embark upon "a pure gamble"[29] and appropriated $25,000 for the N.R.H.A. to study the prospects of slum removal even before such a program was either legally or financially feasible!

The council's gamble for federal support was not an idle gesture to ameliorate an increasingly worsening situation; it was a carefully calculated risk. World War II and the Depression had left the core of most other cities in a condition comparable to Norfolk's; it seemed only a matter of time before the federal government cleared the way for such action. Norfolk, however, had every intention of leaping into the national limelight as the first municipality to embark upon a program of redevelopment; grabbing the headlines of urban renewal seemed the city's best opportunity to shake its sleazy wartime reputation and focus attention instead upon all phases of its postwar renaissance. Publicity, however, was only half of the quotient: Norfolk, more than any other city its size, had seen clearly how federal funds could provide the needed transfusion for massive community expansion. For almost a decade the city council under the Prieur Machine had refused to embark upon any municipal project or extend any public service unless the navy dangled the carrot of federal funding as an incentive. Federal funds had aided in the construction of more than 3,400 dwellings; had upgraded numerous municipal facilities, including schools, parks, playgrounds, highways, recreational centers, water and sewer projects; had poured millions of dollars into the area's economy;[30] and had helped, with both these new facilities and the multiplier effect of federal investment, to immeasurably increase the standard of living for all the citizens of Tidewater.[31]

The Norfolk Redevelopment and Housing Authority had already sought to allay fears that its actions would be competing with the private market by challenging the city's builders to begin their own redevelopment programs. *This Is It*, the N.R.H.A.'s official promotional tract, recalled earlier objections to its plans and sought graphically to explain how the city could embark upon a mammoth rebuilding effort, even under existing legislation, and not expend any local funds. The commissioners knew firsthand that federal funds had provided the impetus for the city's economic expansion over the past decade; all were experiencing, along with the rest of the city's business leaders, the fruits of a local boom that had been financed largely with federal support. There was thus little reason why Norfolk should not be first in line for federal dollars as soon as the funds for urban renewal became available.

The N.R.H.A. hired planning consultant Charles K. Agle to study Norfolk's downtown slums and develop a master plan for a major urban renewal project. His report was a shock even for natives who had long known that housing conditions around the downtown area were deplorable. Methodically he studied each block and hovel to reach his conclusions: "large scale redevelopment is the only chance the city ever has had to accomplish a drastic modernization of its heart."[32] Map after map, table after table, showed the same concentration of irreversible blight choking the central business district: blocks where every structure needed major repairs, where almost all of the houses dated back to the nineteenth century, where there were 13 or more fires over a two-year period, where there were 17 or more arrests in the previous months, and where there was a heavy concentration of tuberculosis.[33] As in many other cities, the streets of Norfolk's downtown area were the descendants of cowpaths and carriageways upon which a gridiron street pattern had been imposed.[34] All of the major highways that linked the suburbs to the downtown area terminated a mile short of the central business district, discharging their traffic into a complex maze of back alleys and clogged feeder roads.[35] The feeling was almost universal in the business community that unless the city took some strong steps to increase traffic flow and provide parking, property values and retailing in the downtown area would collapse.[36]

The Agle Report was a sobering eye-opener in other respects. In addition to just reporting the slum conditions that cried out for renewal, it also attempted to confront all of the potential obstacles to successful redevelopment. It was in this regard that many citizens found the report most shocking. Few individuals realized how very profitable slum properties—even in an area as blighted as Norfolk's central ghetto—could be to its owners, and some of the city's finest families were shown to have heavy investments in slum housing. The report showed that even under rent control, an average slum dwelling with an assessed value of $400 could achieve contract rents of $142 a year per room, out of which very little besides the $10.80 per year real estate tax bill had to be paid for maintenance and upkeep. One example, pointed to as typical of the inflated value of slum housing, sheltered 32 families in a rickety, wood frame building that had only four sinks and four toilets; it brought in $4,500 a year in rent and paid out only $98 in taxes.[37] Another complex (the Tidewater Apartments) provided an even more notorious example of slum profiteering: there were 152 single-room units that netted the owners $23,400 a year in rent. There were no baths or showers; instead, the only facilities for cooking, cleaning, washing, drinking, and sanitation were six cold-water privies consisting of a single faucet and toilet. The total tax bill for the complex was less than $600 a year[38]—a highly profitable investment!

Thus Norfolk was compelled by a number of powerful motivators to become the first city in the nation to qualify for federal funds the following June, when President Truman signed the U.S. Housing Act of 1949 into law. The act granted municipalities both the legal authority and the necessary funding support to buy up such properties. Before the act was passed, the city could rely upon its powers of eminent domain to purchase private property only if were reused for "public" purposes, such as land for schools, highways, and parks, but additional public investment in a deteriorating neighborhood would have been foolish. Before this new power of redevelopment passed to cities, nothing in the municipal arsenal would permit cities to buy up private property, tear it down, and then resell it to other private residential, commercial, or industrial developers—the essence of urban renewal. The act empowered cities to buy up large quantities of slum housing for a "fair" price—roughly 60 percent above their assessed value, or less than two years' rent on most buildings—and to acquire the rest through condemnation proceedings.[39] The Agle Report had predicted that "the future of Norfolk for the rest of its history will be fixed by the action of the next ten years;"[40] it might just as well have added that the legislation and supporting federal funding would be the city's only real chance to have much of a future at all.

At last assured of both federal funding and community support, the Norfolk Redevelopment and Housing Authority forged ahead with its program—the first urban renewal initiative in the country. N.R.H.A. Project One bore a striking resemblance to the blustery, full-speed-ahead approach of its sires; it proposed to bulldoze 120 acres of blighted land to make way for broad highways, light industries, new commercial districts, civic improvements, schools, playgrounds, and a giant convention hotel. It also bore the mark of City Manager C. A. Harrell's balanced approach of careful planning and community concern: almost all of the 1,800 families uprooted by the bulldozers would be relocated in modern, sanitary public housing units, and many would eventually move back into their own neighborhood, once it had been rebuilt at public expense. No one doubted the legitimacy of the undertaking: the slum properties cleared represented some of the most squalid, festering hovels in the nation;[41] the municipal projects undertaken were those seen as most essential to salvaging the central business district; and the land cleared for renewal was critical to the city's efforts to restore its flagging real estate tax base. Before demolition even began, however, the N.R.H.A. rushed to completion several hundred new public housing units on vacant land in order to absorb the first wave of redevelopment refugees.[42] Each time the bulldozers poised to bite off another chunk of blighted land, the N.R.H.A. rushed to completion new housing projects to absorb the relocated residents. Indeed, this was all part of the careful, humanistic approach of the Silkstocking Takeover that promised "to alleviate as much as possible the hardships which are the by-products of such a project."[43]

Partly because this was the first redevelopment project in America, and Norfolk was aware that the rest of the nation was watching, and partly because the city had been so long prepared for this endeavor, N.R.H.A. Project One was a masterfully planned and conceived undertaking; certainly it was one of the most-studied proposals ever advanced by a municipality. Ever since Colonel Borland's Citizens Crime Conference of 1937 exposed the financial and human cost of slum life, the city's business elite had dreamed of downtown renewal. The N.R.H.A.'s own study in 1946 *(This Is It)* and the 1949 Agle Report had added depth and dimension to the vision. It took five years to complete N.R.H.A. Project One, but the enormity of its carefully planned success was apparent to all. In the end, the project offered something for everyone: broad new thoroughfares provided downtown merchants with their first really modern link to the rest of the area; a new light industrial zone on Tidewater Drive was attracting so many private investments that it was prompting its own multi-million dollar construction boom;[44] new businesses were already moving into the redeveloped commercial areas; backers of a major new convention hotel (the Hotel Norfolk) were examining a corner site in the project;[45] and the former residents of some of the most dilapidated dwellings were able to reclaim their old neighborhoods, now completely rebuilt as planned communities. More importantly, the whole city was caught up in the boom psychology that accompanies such a dynamic undertaking, and the spin-off effects could be seen in hundreds of other unrelated expansions, investments, rehabilitations, and modernizations.[46] Urban renewal proved to be the spark that kindled the entire business community into action, and Norfolk raced to blot out the sorry memories of its sordid past.

A more complete description of the size and scope of N.R.H.A. Project One is necessary in order to comprehend its full impact. The project included one 80-acre section that is bounded by Virginia Beach Boulevard on the north, Lincoln Street on the east,

Brambleton Avenue on the south, and Monticello Avenue on the west. It then extended east along Brambleton Avenue to include a broad strip surrounding Tidewater Drive—roughly 127 acres. New York's Stuyvesant Town was then the biggest housing project in existence, but it was a little more than one-third the size of Project One; New York had forty times the population of Norfolk in 1950, but less than twice the slum clearance acreage contained in Norfolk's undertaking.[47] Land acquisition cost $5.7 million, of which the U.S. government paid two-thirds ($3.8 million). Norfolk's $1.9 million share was not a cash loss; it was worked off instead in land set aside to build new schools, a recreation center, fire and police stations, utility lines, and street improvements, which the city would have built anyhow. The project generated an additional $18 million in public expenditures—more than half of which came from the state or federal government for public housing and highway costs—and $15.6 million in private construction.[48] The total cost to the federal government for building the 3,000 public housing units planned by the N.R.H.A. was close to $30 million[49]—a sizeable multiplier in any economy.

The business leaders who sired N.R.H.A. Project One saw redevelopment as more than just a means to eradicate blight, relieve deprivation, and cure downtown traffic congestion; they were focusing as well on a more serious situation that struck deep at their own sense of financial security. Norfolk had too many of its economic eggs in one basket; its huge naval installations made the city essentially a one-industry town[50]—an enterprise that was virtually exempt from real estate, personal property, and other local tax assessments. After World War I, Norfolk paid a heavy price for this over-reliance when disarmament left the nation with a one-ocean navy that, after the outbreak of war in Manchuria, sailed away for duty stations on the West Coast. A brief inspection of the waterfront gave ample evidence of the fact that coastwise shipping—once the economic staple of the area—had been almost completely absorbed by rail and trucking facilities. Other than shipbuilding and coal export, the city had no other private industry of any magnitude[51] and, in fact, suffered a severe shortage of available industrial land. A few million dollars clipped from a naval appropriation by an errant congressional committee could well send the area into an economic tailspin.

After the end of the war, the city's economic leaders had given serious attention to attracting new business as a hedge against such congressional capriciousness, but they had achieved little success. City Manager C.A. Harrell had already recommended an aggressive plan of annexation, or, he warned, "the city would die by inches."[52] In spite of his insistence, annexation under the state of Virginia politics at that time proved to be both a costly and a risky course, although one to which Norfolk was deeply committed. Even if they could acquire vacant land through annexation, however, the city's business leaders still had to face the harsh reality that Norfolk could not hope to serve as a major industrial hub because it lacked a cheap source of power.[53] A plan to attract light industry into newly developed sites close to the heart of the area's financial and commercial district— a scarce commodity in any community—was the city's only hope for a competitive alternative. For this reason, a major redevelopment project that entailed massive clearing of land close to the downtown financial district was seen as the one best hope for the area's continued financial success. More than a third of the land cleared in N.R.H.A. Project One was thus dedicated to developing prime industrial and commercial sites with both rail and major highway access.[54] The catch was that in order to be able to provide new land for these kinds of critical business and industrial uses, the majority of the land cleared under redevelopment powers had to be "residential" in nature. Federal law at the time also mandated that after redevelopment the majority of the land must continue as residential property. Thus cities, like Norfolk, could clear a slum, but they had to balance residential, industrial, commercial, and public uses in the type of carefully planned undertaking exemplified by N.R.H.A. Project One.[55]

Finally, N.R.H.A. Project One was successful at alleviating a part of the housing shortage for poor blacks. Not only did it create 3,000 new public housing units, it proposed to divide these between the project site and newly acquired vacant land on the outskirts of the downtown area. This was in keeping with the housing pattern in the rest of Norfolk at the time: black neighborhoods were spread across the city, instead of just concentrated in a single downtown district, as in most Northern cities.[56] Since only 1,800 families would be moved out of the project area during demolition,[57] this represented a significant net gain in housing for blacks. The fact that the new black housing area would be carefully isolated by broad new thoroughfares that would serve as solid color barriers was also viewed positively by whites fearful of encroachments into nearby neighborhoods. In addition, a new recreation center, police precinct, fire station, and the first elementary school (Young Park) built for black students[58]—the others were hand-me-downs from the white community, a standard practice in the South—were included as part of the project. Because the new school, park, and recreational facilities were designated for use by blacks, the city hoped to relieve some of the pressure to integrate white facilities in adjoining neighborhoods.[59]

City Manager Harrell also saw redevelopment as a panacea for many of the city's other municipal needs. Throughout his tenure as manager, Harrell placed a strong emphasis on neighborhood needs: upgrading schools and residential streets, decentralizing police and fire facilities, and building new parks, playgrounds, community centers, and recreation areas. N.R.H.A. Project One also bears the imprint of his careful approach to community planning. Besides meeting the obvious commuter transportation needs of the area by building two additional highway approaches to the downtown area, the project represented the city's first full attempt to create a planned public community for its black residents. Although surrounded by the updated highway system, Young Park, a 752-unit public housing project (named for P. Bernard Young, Sr., founder of the *Journal and Guide* newspaper), would be built upon a neighborhood street concept virtually inaccessible to through traffic. Population density would be reduced from the pre-redevelopment levels of 50 families per acre to only 20. In addition, the phased development of the area was designed so that every family would have a place to go as the project gained momentum[60]—a goal that was far easier to work out on paper than put into practice, especially since a number of families and single individuals were ineligible for public housing.

As part of his concept of professional community planning, City Manager Harrell was taking active steps to prevent future slums from developing in the ring of older middle-class housing which separated the downtown area from the newer postwar subdivisions on the outskirts of the city. Roughly one-third of the city's residential structures could be described as in danger of slipping from relatively good housing for its era into the dilapidated state that precedes a full-fledged slum[61]—all of it in this middle-class ring that included all or portions of the city's first streetcar and automobile suburbs. The tremendous influx of people attracted to Norfolk during the war—Norfolk's population increased by 48 percent, or almost 70,000 people, between 1940 and 1950—placed a premium upon existing houses, and many of the homes in these areas either took in boarders or were cut up into multi-family dwelling units. The transient nature of this new population and the slapdash quality of the remodeling jobs left deteriorated dwellings in even the finest neighborhoods.

The major weapon in Harrell's arsenal against blight was the newly-formulated minimum housing code, which was not scheduled to go into effect until January 1, 1954. Housing codes were still a relatively new concept when Walter Hoffman (later, a federal judge) and his committee of lawyers and building officials had to put one together for Norfolk; in fact, fewer than a dozen other cities across the nation had begun experimenting with code enforcement as a way to prevent blight. Housing codes specified "livability standards" for dwellings, rather than concentrating on the more limited coverage afforded by fire, building, and health codes. Examples of provisions in Norfolk's new code included at least one window per room, running water inside the building, a flush toilet connected to a sewer (but not necessarily inside the dwelling), adequate means of garbage disposal, and a safe form of central heating with a flue to the outside of the building—none of them extravagant standards by any measure, but all representing a distinct improvement over the conditions that existed in many semi-blighted areas. The Norfolk code writers were obviously setting their standards on the low side of "livability" because they realized that strong enforcement would be the key to its effectiveness as a slum deterrent.[62] As a tribute to the wisdom of the code writers, almost 2,500 dwellings were rehabilitated during the first two years of the code's operation; only 173 buildings were vacated as a result of enforcement, and most of these were reoccupied later after completion of the required renovations.[63]

The small crowd of dignitaries and city officials who gathered outside the hovel at 755 Smith Street that wintry morning in 1951 had come to cheer the revitalized spirit of a New Norfolk as much as to applaud the singular event they were witnessing. The New Norfolk was as blustery, bold, and bullish as its sires in the city's business establishment; it was as compassionate and humane as the civic leaders and charity workers who attended its birth; it was as levelheaded, pragmatic, and professional as the planners, designers, and consultants who fussed over its infant developments; and finally, it was as careful, concise, and well directed as the city manager who tutored it. In electing the Silkstocking Ticket, the voters had opted for a change from the cautious, humdrum course plotted by the wartime city council; they got more than they had bargained for. In 1946 the people had been swept up in the vision of a New Norfolk; by 1951 they were witnessing the bricks and mortar, the concrete, steel and glass, of its realization. A revitalized redevelopment and housing authority was plotting eradication of the city's blight; a new port authority was bent on reclaiming the glory of its past; new zoning laws and subdivision regulations extended the promise of orderly expansion; annexation initiatives held out the assurance of continued growth; revamped building, health, housing, and fire codes served as an omnipresent guard against gradual deterioration; a massive capital improvements program was rapidly solving the needs for more parks, schools, water, sewage, street lighting, traffic control, and transportation facilities; construction was already underway on a new bridge-tunnel link and a modern airport terminal; new highways promised an end to the city's isolation;[64] and everywhere there was evidence that the citizens themselves had caught the spirit of these ventures and were embarking on their own fix-up, expansion, rebuilding, and modernization campaigns in thousands of smaller endeavors.

For many, N.R.H.A. Project One represented the high-water mark of the city's effort not just to tear down the old and build the new, but to do it with such style and vision that it would capture the attention of the nation, and thereby erase some of the taint of Norfolk's earlier infamy. It marked a sharp contrast between the foot-dragging of the wartime city council and the foot-racing of the Silkstocking administration. Buoyant of spirit, newly confident, and optimistic once again in outlook, Norfolk's citizens were finally prepared to face the future without trepidation. Project One represented as well a remarkable diversity of personalities, a fortuitous display of insight, and a timely turn of events. Foremost among these was the leadership and vision provided by Charles L. Kaufman and the other citizen elites who served as commissioners of the Norfolk Redevelopment and Housing Authority. Profiteering from blight and overcharging the poor were as widespread among Norfolk's slumlords and a certain segment of its real estate community as anywhere in the nation;[65] in many instances the profits were collected by families and individuals that had almost parallel standing in the community. But the commissioners of the N.R.H.A. had the sheer force of commercial and financial persuasion to stare down opposition from even the most well-connected property owners. Their standing in the community was so high that these individuals were able to launch the city boldly and irrevocably into what was in most of the other council-manager cities of the nation a torturous and easily sidetracked course.[66]

The silkstocking People's Ticket of Richard Cooke, Pretlow Darden, and John Twohy, in combination with a loose voting alignment with independent Councilman Rives Worsham,[67] possessed much the same kind of community power and prestige. By ripping political control of city hall from the grasp of the Prieur Machine, they restored faith in municipal government—a step that was necessary before any progressive measure could be taken with citizen support. The people of Norfolk would never have stood for the impositions provided by the revamped building, fire, health and minimum housing codes if they had feared indifferent or selective enforcement for political gain; neither would they have stood for either the cost or the inconvenience posed by massive municipal construction initiatives if they had doubted the motives behind these efforts; they would never have granted their city the power to acquire private property and destroy it in preparation for eventual resale to other private investors—the very essence of the redevelopment process—if either end of urban renewal had been controlled by ring politicians.

The People's Ticket maintained dignity and devotion to principle in spite of the controversy that raged about them. Nobody doubted their motives or questioned either their integrity or their purpose, but a group that embarks on so many unparalleled municipal endeavors must inevitably make enemies and provoke opposition. The city council chambers reverberated with the hubbub of both civic support and fierce opposition throughout the brief tenure of the People's administration, but the council plunged onward despite the controversy, always careful to explain each step of the undertaking to those who would follow. This was the true mark of their partisan independence, for no political group could have long endured the intensity of the public debate, the level of criticism, or the unpredictability of popular support posed by each new initiative. Even so, the People's group had the courage to persevere and risk being judged only by their accomplishments.

City Manager Charles A. Harrell was the right man at the right time to carry out the initiatives of the People's City Council. He represented absolute incorruptibility and professionalism at a time when both were sorely needed at city hall. Twenty years after his reign as manager, Norfolk was still completing the final phases of the ambitious program he had set forth. More than any other single individual, Harrell understood the true potential for municipal planning and government. He was responsible for snatching the operation of city hall from the grasp of short-sighted governmental functionaries, and then tutoring both citizens and municipal workers alike on what could be accomplished. His was a vision of greatness for city government that would be hard to forget, even long after he had passed from the local scene. Harrell brought the best technical and professional minds in the county to study the city's problems and to help chart its growth; many of them decided to stay and lend a hand in achieving the realities promised in their reports. Harrell made Norfolk City Hall one of the most desirable locations in the country for aspiring public servants: not only was the city continually at the forefront of the newly developing fields of municipal planning, urban renewal, and code enforcement, but the People's Ticket also promised that these new powers would be used exclusively for municipal services, free from the taint of political interference or partisan purpose that was apparently so prevalent elsewhere. Harrell dared to empower the citizens—both the sparkplugs of its neighborhood leagues and the dynamos of its civic and business elite—to help plan and promote municipal endeavors. He inspired the best from his own employees, and was able to restore a sense of pride and accomplishment to city offices. Harrell's vision, backed up by the proposals of numerous citizen groups and consultants, provided Norfolk with the basis for a master plan for city growth and development—a step that put it almost two years ahead of other areas in the competition for federal urban renewal dollars. Other writers have bemoaned the lack of unity and leadership that plagues most council-manager cities and precludes, for the most part, decisive action; thanks to City Manager C. A. Harrell and his close connection and cooperation with the People's City Council and its corporate elite, Norfolk suffered no such disability. In fact, Norfolk, because it had such leadership, thrived in the area of urban renewal precisely because it had truly achieved such a professional and nonpartisan atmosphere. Because politics was mixed in with their administration, most other council-manager cities failed to achieve the level of consensus that was possible to sustain such activities—a level of unanimity that was ordinarily only possible in the highly partisan strong mayor cities.[68]

Lawrence M. Cox, the executive director of the Norfolk Redevelopment and Housing Authority, headed a promising staff of planners and designers who moved quickly to seize their opportunity before the momentum for progress dissipated. "Hustling young Larry Cox," as he was described by one trade magazine,[69] was ambitious and demanding enough to get results. The relocation program, as well as the total design for Project One, set a standard for the rest of the nation. Cox had been head of the N.R.H.A. almost from its founding, and over the years, especially during the hectic war effort, had developed a capable staff that was both loyal to him and fully committed to redevelopment. Close collaboration between Cox, the city council, the commissioners, and the business community helped to push N.R.H.A. Project One off of the drawing boards and into reality.

The support of Norfolk's two major daily newspapers, the morning *Virginian-Pilot* and the evening *Ledger-Dispatch* (later the *Ledger-Star* after a merger with the *Portsmouth Star*), was also instrumental in advancing both the cause of the Silkstocking movement and the accomplishments of its administration. The two papers, although fiercely competitive, were owned and published by the same family group; together they served as the spokesmen for the city's business elite, and the accolades of triumph from the newspapers for the latest ground-breaking or achievement frequently sounded brassier than any possible press release. The support of the papers, especially the more progressive *Virginian-Pilot*, was critical to the People's efforts to win election, maintain momentum through the police scandal, and promote its program of redevelopment, code enforcement, and bonded indebtedness. Reporters for both papers were insiders to both the events and the intrigue at city hall, and this access to the decision-makers, as well as the fact that a reporter in this era kept a fixed beat for years, gave them a stake in protecting their sources.[70]

Finally, the spirit of adventure and self-sacrifice that prevailed among Norfolk's citizens helped enormously in clearing the hurdles inherent in redevelopment. The People's Ticket had been elected in 1946 with an overwhelming mandate for progress, and the citizens waited patiently through the initial stages of planning and development. Seizing control of city government took more, however, than winning a single election, yet the citizens did not lose faith even during the darkest hours of the police scandal—an event which could have easily wrecked all hope of progressive activity in most administrations; in Norfolk, instead, it helped to assure success. The people were prepared for action, and they watched patiently as each new step unfolded. Norfolk's growth during the war years had been enormous, and municipal services had suffered greatly under this additional burden, but the people never lost faith that City Manager Harrell and the Silkstocking members of the city council would eventually catch up to that growth with their own ambitious program of expanded municipal services.

Other cities that were similar to Norfolk found their own plans for growth and redevelopment stymied because their citizens lacked either the vision or the spirit of sacrifice to participate in progress; not so with Norfolk. Redevelopment, especially of the magnitude that had been planned, called for enormous personal hardships from many individuals, especially from those who could least afford to suffer more, and yet they bore their discomfort, and for the most part, bore it in silence. The People's Ticket and its attendant push for progress truly represented the efforts of a rejuvenated body politic; the bulldozers that ripped through the sagging walls of that first Smith Street structure and the adjacent areas in N.R.H.A. Project One represented the high point in the momentary blaze of glory that characterized Norfolk's Silkstocking Takeover.

✳ ✳ ✳

2

✳ ✳ ✳ ✳ ✳

Premonitions of Crisis

NORFOLK REDEVELOPMENT AND HOUSING AUTHORITY Project One would take five years to complete, but even before the bulldozers ripped through that first house on Smith Street, the men who had charted the meteoric rise of Norfolk's corporate stock had already retreated to the plushness of their boardrooms and counting houses. The individuals who had so carefully planned and nourished its inception were already fading from the scene. Each new ground-breaking or ribbon-cutting ceremony marked the passing of the old order: the planning phase was over, and now it was time for the builders. The Silkstocking Takeover had run into a snag: as part of their promise to clean up city government and make it more responsive, the People's Ticket of Cooke, Darden, and Twohy had promised not to seek a second term; now the very events that served as tributes to their triumph stood as tombstones to their passing. The Silkstocking Ticket was unable to propagate successors, and the spirit of renaissance and reform that had vaulted it to victory had, by 1950, dissipated, and then dissolved completely.

At first, as their term drew to a close, the reform movement sought to find others who would carry their banner,[1] but none of the city's business or financial leaders was willing to again risk openly opposing Billy Prieur or his political machine. The sense of urgency and shared emergency that had brought the reformers to power had passed; the Outs had become the Ins in the kind of political perversity that always hastens the doom of such reform movements;[2] and dramatic change had become altogether too commonplace in Norfolk. Business was booming, and the citizens were no longer forced to turn to the corporate community to avert financial ruin. Local prosperity, aided by the Cold War state of military readiness, had lulled the citizens into a false sense of contentment, fully prepared to count their blessings in the privacy of their homes, untouched by and undemanding of municipal government.

When their search for successors came up dry, the People's group again sought an audience with local Byrd Organization chieftain Billy Prieur, hoping to find some middle ground that would continue their legacy of progress within the more limited confines of machine politics. Finding compromise candidates was no easy matter, especially because Prieur would not agree to anyone who had played even the slightest role in the Silkstocking Takeover. Eventually the political negotiators were able to agree upon one man who emerged at the top of everyone's list of potential contenders.[3] W. Fred Duckworth was an ideal choice to head the Harmony Ticket that would emerge from these back room discussions: because he was a relative newcomer to Norfolk, he had no close financial, civic, or personal ties to the Silkstocking crowd. On the other hand, he possessed the type of managerial skills necessary to head up Norfolk's complex municipal organization. Duckworth had been brought to the area from rural North Carolina in 1936 by the Ford Motor Company to manage its South Norfolk plant, one of the few major industrial concerns in the area not directly owned by the People's reformers. Several years later he left that position to manage the area's War Production Board, a post that expanded his circle of community contacts. After the war he started his own car dealership, Cavalier Ford,[4] a project that received Silkstocking financial support. Even though he was not a Norfolkian, the People's group was impressed by his managerial acumen, his considerable array of skills, and the extent of his commitment to his adopted city.[5]

The People's group was not as pleased with Duckworth's two running mates, both of whom were chosen less for their accomplishments than because nobody could find solid grounds to scratch them from the list. Lawrence C. Page had served on the city council just before the war, but had shown the good sense to excuse himself from office before being branded for its wartime failures.

Although he was a real estate broker, he had no close ties to the powerhouses of the People's group, and since he had also run as a Republican for the U.S. Senate against Organization scion Harry F. Byrd, Sr.,[6] he was obviously no longer associated with Prieur's crowd. N. B. Etheridge, an independent garage owner, was a political unknown without any apparent ties to either the Organization or the Silkstocking crowd. For the People's forces, the Harmony Ticket of Duckworth, Page and Etheridge represented a marriage of necessity, rather than a bond of trust between these two disparate political groups.[7]

Shortly after the bulldozer ripped through the wall of that first house on Smith Street, City Manager Harrell, the one man who more than any other had been responsible for the rebirth and rejuvenation of Norfolk, departed abruptly to accept a similar position in San Antonio, Texas. At the time, the most common explanation for his departure was that he and Duckworth, the new mayor, had clashed bitterly over who would run the operations at city hall.[8] Clearly the City could not endure two chief administrators pulling in opposite directions, and Duckworth, with his "bulldozer drive and directness," was bent on running the City from the mayor's office, a marked contrast to the free-wheeling independence granted C. A. Harrell by the People's City Council.[9] For his part, Harrell had always indicated that he would resign before surrendering his judgement to partisan considerations;[10] the arrival of Duckworth and the Harmony Ticket, however, meant that the Organization was again advancing a foothold in city hall. When C. A. Harrell left, with him went all hope of continuing the municipal reform brought about by the People's group; soon his police chief and a number of other key administrators who had been instrumental in carrying out his program also departed with indications that they had been fired by the new city council.[11] Mayor W. Fred Duckworth was the perfect man to step in now and fill the gap in leadership left by Harrell's departure: he offered a continuation of the progress and prosperity without necessitating any further decision or dissension on the part of the citizens. He was an unusually able leader, and if the decorum of democracy was somewhat abridged under his tutelage, the voters did not seem to mind very much. The Planning Stage had passed, the Builder had taken over, and the people seemed to approve unquestioningly the fruits of his labor, giving credit equally to the planners and builder alike. Duckworth was above all else a bricks-and-mortar man, and he presided daily over the construction of the New Norfolk. As the building blocks of its bright facade were laid in place, nothing, not even the heavy storm clouds of racial disunity building on the horizon, seemed capable of diverting that progress.

The Prieur Machine made no attempt under Mayor Duckworth to return to the corrupt and profligate practices of its wartime administration; its members had been absent long enough from the seats of power that they were content to settle for positions, without demanding authority. Although hardheaded, and occasionally dictatorial, Duckworth had no problem adapting to the programs begun under the People's group. He continued Harrell's administrative innovations, merely rerouting the technical advisors through the mayor's office. Although he was decisive and extremely aggressive, like Harrell, he never moved until satisfied that all the conditions were favorable. C. A. Harrell's departure threatened the continuance of the Harmony coalition, but Duckworth stepped in to take personal control of city government, and so assuaged some of the fears of machine politics.

During the Duckworth era, Norfolk was run almost exclusively from the mayor's office: it was there that city council made its decisions during private pre-sessions before the regular public meeting, and those not in attendance were told later how to vote. He throve on consensus, and minor differences between council members at the public sessions took on major proportions in his mind. Although protective of the Byrd Organization's interests, Duckworth would not brook incompetence. He rose quickly to the top of the local Organization and soon, along with Prieur, dominated its decisions as well. This combination of elected authority, political power, administrative expertise, and driving personal force was devastating to City employees who faltered or got out of line.

Duckworth did not have to bargain for acquiescence from the People's group; he won it through strength. The Silkstocking crowd respected Duckworth's ability and integrity, or at least they feared crossing him without a guarantee of victory. Although more political than they had been, Duckworth's program did not differ perceptibly from their own: they saw that city hall was still well run; there was little evidence of corruption; business leaders were still consulted; the authority of the expert consultants and advisors was still intact; and the framing of Harrell's blueprints was well underway. All in all, the business establishment had few complaints, although plenty of reason to feel uneasy: such power, concentrated in one man, if misdirected, could prove disastrous. The citizens, too, seemed relatively content with Duckworth's administration, and councilmanic contests during this time produced very little in the way of a challenge to the Mayor's preeminence. This was truly the "Era of Good Feeling," as one local historian labeled it,[12] for even the corporate and civic leaders who had wrested control of the city's growth from the courthouse ring politicians now breathed as well the chloroform of prosperity. Business as usual prevailed at city hall: "the reformers had grown tired, the regulars had taken over, and things would have to get pretty bad before the reformers would stir again."[13]

The U.S. Supreme Court's decision in the *Brown v. Board of Education* case struck like a thunderbolt through the false sense of local optimism that prevailed in May of 1954. By the time the citizens of Norfolk looked up to discern the dangers ahead, they found the state's political leaders scurrying in panic for punitive structures and hastily contrived extra-legal shelters as a means to divert the raging force of racial discontent that had been building for centuries in the backwaters that surrounded the city. It was clear from the outset that Norfolk would not be allowed the freedom to pursue its own independent course, separate from the rest of the state, even if its leadership were so inclined. The very fact that Duckworth was now so entrenched at the throttle of municipal control meant that Norfolk would follow the dictates of the statewide Byrd Organization.

Norfolk, one of the most liberal cities in the South, now ironically became the main battlefield upon which the fate of Virginia's Massive Resistance Plan would be decided. Vast segments of its population had little use for those racial codes and institutions, both written and unwritten, that were primarily Southern. The storm-whipped waves of Massive Resistance would break as well over Arlington, Charlottesville, Prince Edward County, and Warren County, but these would be small-scale tests of its veracity when compared to a city Norfolk's size. At the time, Norfolk had a population rapidly approaching 300,000, and was earning new status as the state's largest city. More than one-third of its population represented the liberalizing influences of its naval or NATO (North Atlantic Treaty Organization) forces; the rest benefitted in their day-to-day contact with these and other representatives of vast national and international interests. Under the able leadership of C. A. Harrell and the People's group, Norfolk had forsaken its obligatory glance to Richmond for guidance, and instead looked to the rest of the world for approval.

The many varied opportunities of government service in the area had made Norfolk a mecca for Southern blacks hoping to improve their lot in life. The desegregation of the military forces that had taken place under President Truman meant that blacks could rise to positions of leadership in an integrated society that existed just on the periphery of Norfolk's own. The lure of steady employment in the area's shipyards and rework facilities prompted a continual stream of job-hunters that started even before the hostilities had even begun. Whereas most blacks in Norfolk were of relatively low economic status when compared to their white neighbors, a black middle class was growing at a faster pace than elsewhere in the South. Although most of the major trade unions had not yet been cracked, the door of opportunity to nondiscriminatory positions in government and war-related industries had just been opened, and opportunities in the private sector would become available as soon as black citizens had achieved success in these endeavors.

All in all, the history of race relations in Norfolk had been good, especially under the even-handed municipal management of C. A. Harrell and the Silkstocking crowd. Only 27 percent of Norfolk's 300,000 citizens were black, a segment "large enough to provide leadership, but not so large as to be believed to threaten established patterns."[14] But to Duckworth, the black leadership had already proven itself a thorn in the side of municipal unanimity, and Duckworth was not one to overlook even the slightest irritant. Even though black council challenger P. B. Young had posed no real threat in the 1952 race, Duckworth was apparently miffed that the black community had opposed his own "harmony" slate. There were other, more serious signs of a growing challenge in the black community, far more significant than the periodic offering of token opposition candidates. By 1954, blacks were growing increasingly antagonistic to the Mayor's housing, development, recreation, and municipal finance policies. The Supreme Court's decision in May of that year only made that dissension more readily visible to the general public.

Ever since the first blacks began moving into the white section of Brambleton in the mid-1940s, a succession of city councils had been incapable of halting the demise of traditional barriers to integrated neighborhoods. The tub-thumping of the Organization's wartime city council gave mute sanction to a wave of white violence and vandalism that temporarily halted the spread,[15] but the election of the People's Ticket in June of 1946 gave new impetus to that transition. The People's group tried to maintain an air of orderly calm and reasonableness; their approach was to talk out differences with committees comprised of members of both races. In the atmosphere of calm that prevailed under their reign, traditional racial barriers in Brambleton fell quickly. Brambleton had always led a somewhat tenuous existence as the sole white community in the zone of the city dominated by blacks, and its white residents had relied heavily on the combination of natural, geographic, and traditional barriers to keep it that way. Once the color barrier at Corprew Avenue had been breached and violence had subsided, the area fell quickly to growing pressure to provide homes for the emerging black middle class. In 1949 Ruffner Elementary was opened for the diminishing white population of Brambleton, and the Stonewall Jackson School was turned over to the black school system.[16] The John Goode Elementary School, ironically named for Norfolk's Confederate congressman and president of the Constitutional Convention that stripped blacks of the power to vote[17] was shifted to the black school system in 1950. Two years later in 1952, Ruffner was reassigned to the black system as a junior high school, thereby signaling the final defeat of the last white holdouts.[18]

Once the color line had been successfully breached and finally broken in the Brambleton section, it fell more easily in other parts of the city as well. Norfolk in the 1950s, like many other older Southern cities, was unlike its Northern counterparts: it did not have a single, central black ghetto surrounded by a ring of white suburbs.[19] Instead, Norfolk contained a number of small white communities, most of which had their own sections for black housing (*see* Figure 1). Successive annexations had brought these communities within the city boundaries, but the result was that Norfolk's black population occupied, in addition to a central slum area, a number of isolated black communities that existed next to whites in the Atlantic City, Lambert's Point, Granby (Bollingbrook), Sewells Point (Titustown),

Figure 1 – Norfolk's Neighborhoods

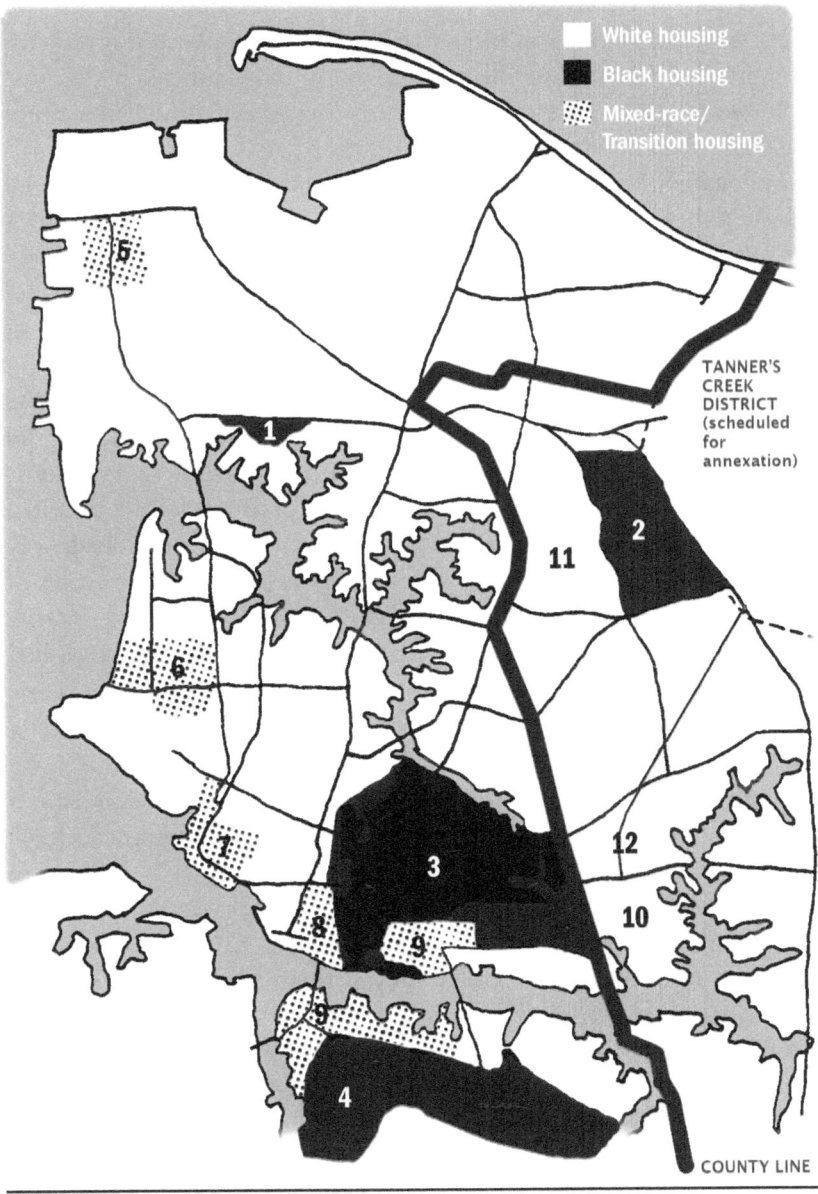

1 Titustown/Carney Park	5 Benmoreell (Navy housing)	9 Brambleton
2 Oakwood/Rosemont	6 Lambert's Point	10 Broad Creek Shores
3 Uptown/Project One	7 Atlantic City	11 Coronado
4 Berkley/Campostella	8 Downtown	12 Broad Creek (Navy housing)

Source: Norfolk Chamber of Commerce, 1954, pp. 10-12

Tanner's Creek (Oakwood), Berkley, and Campostella sections of the city.[20] There was some pressure to expand the color lines in these areas, but the traditional proximity of blacks and whites in the city had forestalled the white exodus that had taken place in Brambleton, Chesterfield, and in some areas of Berkley.[21] Thus, there was little danger of open racial conflict when the Supreme Court's desegregation decision was handed down in 1954: the city's traditional residential patterns, its history of good race relations, opportunities for advancement in the military and government service, already-integrated military housing, and the increasing desegregation of the city's private charitable, health, religious, welfare, and educational boards[22] seemed adequate to surmount any submerged hostilities.

Increasingly, however, local attention began to focus on the working class neighborhoods of the Tanner's Creek District of old Norfolk County, scheduled for annexation into the City on January 1, 1955, as a result of Harrell's earlier initiatives. Portions of the area had unpoliced cesspools of crime, prostitution, gambling, and debauchery that operated under quasi-official auspices just beyond the reach of City enforcement; other areas held vast tracts of substandard housing without adequate plumbing or water. The condition of the area had already prompted bickering on an otherwise harmonious city council over the unexpectedly high cost of annexation versus the necessity to find new space for industrial and suburban expansion.[23] By the summer of 1954, Norfolk County officials had all but washed their hands of the area until the City took control. The Tanner's Creek District thus existed in a state of limbo: county officials refused to maintain costly municipal services in an area they would soon lose, and the City of Norfolk had not yet acquired title or authority to deal with its problems. Norfolk's eleventh-hour hesitations over the exorbitant asking price only served to increase the area's sense of isolation from governmental authority. For this reason, residents began to grow accustomed to the idea of handling matters on their own without any official intervention.

By midsummer, the area's sense of helplessness and isolation was further increased by the breakdown of color barriers in the formerly all-white Coronado section. Coronado was a small (300 homes) community of white, middle-class wage earners across from all-white Norview High School. Since a large number of its families were military, the area had a more rapid turnover of ownership than would be otherwise expected. Thus, Coronado, with its plentiful supply of middle-class housing, city improvements, and high rate of turnover, was a natural target for black expansion. Only narrow Widgeon Road separated white houses from the black neighborhoods of Oakwood, Oakwood Park, and Rosemont.[24] Although most of the homes in these traditional black sections were little more than tarpaper shacks,[25] new black developments in Mamie Homes, Incorporated (150 homes), Chesapeake Manor Apartments (332 units), and Chesapeake Manor Gardens (389 homes), all built since 1950, made the northern boundary of Coronado a haven for black middle-class families, many of them displaced by N.R.H.A. Project One. The black community faced a severe shortage of available middle-class housing, and the long waiting lists at all of the properties north of Coronado had put a premium on housing there.[26] Moreover, a number of black leaders complained that most black neighborhoods "were generally denied city improvements"[27] such as curbs, gutters, parks, playgrounds, paved streets, and sewers that were already available in Coronado.

Trouble began when a black couple was viewing a house in the black section on the north side of Widgeon Road; a white navy housewife spotted them, walked across the road, and asked them if they wanted to buy her house. Because of the huge demand and short supply of middle-class housing for blacks, this first navy family received a higher price than a white buyer would have offered. Other navy families followed suit, and soon panic gripped Coronado's more established white residents. At about this time the market in Coronado for sale to white buyers all but disappeared; the white banking establishment, realizing the inevitable, refused to finance white buyers in Coronado, and the Veteran's Administration appraisals were dropped as they "generally do go down in areas where Negroes are moving into what was once all-white territory."[28] Once the pattern had begun, white homeowners found it impossible to reverse: they were trapped by powers beyond their grasp.

The harassment of black buyers began innocently enough: two elderly white ladies had allowed a bundle of papers to blow out of the car window; other passing motorists stopped to help them retrieve the papers. When residents learned that the phenomenon of stopped automobiles lining both sides of the street had frightened off a prospective black buyer, the idea of neighborhood caravans began "to show that it was a white neighborhood."[29] The idea caught on immediately; although a number of homes had been sold to black buyers, the caravans proved successful in keeping blacks from moving into their new homes. As word spread, outsiders began to join in the caravans, and soon random acts of violence, especially aimed against unoccupied dwellings already sold to blacks, became commonplace. Bricks and bottles were hurled as missiles, a "No Nigers (sic) wanted" sign appeared, the pipes to one house were ripped out, a bomb was thrown at another, a dozen white youths attacked the car of a black couple, another house and automobile were bombed, bullets were fired into black homes, and soon armed caravans of whites and blacks began roaming the area looking for trouble.[30] The prospect that the present rate of property damage, if not halted, would escalate into human tragedy became more and more evident.

Blacks in and around the Coronado area were clearly terrified by the racial turmoil they confronted. The Norfolk County Police, still the legal authority in the Tanner's Creek District, were not much help in calming their fears. Although the County Police came promptly when called, they engaged in only minimal defensive patrolling. Often they stood among crowds of jeering whites and were indistinguishable from the taunters. County officials were understandably eager to play down the extent of the threat that existed in Coronado, but one officer's characterization of the site of a bomb blast, "the hole appeared to be that left by a dog trying to bury a bone,"[31] only aroused black citizens' fears that little was being done to protect them. Black leaders turned first to the Norfolk City Council for help,[32] and then to the governor when their pleas for assistance were denied. Duckworth refused to provide police protection for black families because the City would not acquire jurisdiction until January 1, 1955; Governor Thomas Stanley was powerless under state law to commit the State Police or National Guard unless the local governing body first requested aid. The fact that former city council challenger P. B. Young carried the request to the Governor over the protestations of the city council, further enraged Duckworth.[33] After a month of escalating violence had passed since the request for assistance, the *Virginian-Pilot* stepped in with some harsh words of criticism for the Mayor and his city council:

> The leadership in the Norfolk City government has been short-sighted in deciding not to show any interest in

Coronado. . . . It does not make good sense for a city to use its authority one mile beyond the city limit to make a numbers racket raid, such as was made Thursday by Norfolk police, but to withhold its influence and authority from a problem which has potentially much more tragic consequences than a numbers game. It would be better to provide too much law enforcement than what may tragically prove later to have been too little and too late. The hoodlum elements ought not to be left in any doubt as to what confronts them if they continue to make an unpleasant situation worse.[34]

In desperation, the black leaders finally approached their old contacts in the Silkstocking crowd who, although no longer in control of any governmental authority, still possessed enormous financial power and corporate authority. The *Journal and Guide* summed up the resultant beefed-up county patrols this way: "The powers-that-be Downtown, after caucusing with the Uptown [black] leaders, brought pressure to bear upon county officials, and the tragedy that could have been Coronado was averted."[35]

A serious breach between the city's black community and its white political leaders was growing, and the fact that P. B. Young and others had effected, with Silkstocking backing, a successful flanking maneuver around the Council only made matters worse. Duckworth and the Organization appeared to oppose any further expansion of the black population within the city, and they severely chastised anyone who strayed beyond the acceptable boundaries. The City government had done all that it could do legally to block a group of black developers from acquiring a large tract of land off Broad Creek Road (*see* Figure 1, page 33); the white leaders were strongly opposed to any development that allowed blacks to settle along the city's major approach route from the suburbs (now Virginia Beach Boulevard). Once they saw that the deal could not be prevented, the City Planning Commission stepped in to prevent residential use by blacks, and zoned as much of the tract as possible for industrial and commercial purposes.[36] When black leaders persisted in attempting to develop the remaining acreage into an attractive subdivision (Broad Creek Shores), the City employed its powers of eminent domain to buy up the remaining 40 acres as a buffer zone, ostensibly to be used as a park or school site. Black leaders were enraged and could see "no other apparent valid reason for seizing the land, other than to prevent colored home owners from locating on it,"[37] and threatened to call for a referendum to block the ordinance from taking effect.

Newly appointed Councilman Roy B. Martin, Jr., rose with the Organization's response, a proposal to "study" the question, with an eye towards amending the section of the City charter that allowed referendums. The black community had proposed the petition drive in order to effect some sort of compromise with the City,[38] but since the previous race had been one of the "no-contest" elections for which Duckworth became famous, they were able to collect 2,488 signatures in less than two days, more than enough to force a vote. At last, with the day of the referendum fast approaching, the Organization agreed to a compromise; it was wisely unwilling to test its strength at the ballot box in what was seen by many whites as an illegal and arbitrary use of power. The City agreed to take only 24 of the original 40 acres in the site, and leave the other sixteen acres, already platted and under contract, for development as Broad Creek Shores. The City's chief concern, that (white) Ingleside Elementary School remain widely separated from black housing, was met,[39] and the blacks were able to keep a large tract of waterfront property, carefully separated by the City's acquisition and natural geographic barriers from nearby white communities, for expansion. Councilmen Page, Abbott, and Ripley dissented because it included paying a premium price to the black developers for the City's share of the original tract. The final ballot produced one of the few split votes ever recorded on the Duckworth city council,[40] and ensured the Mayor's bitter enmity for cracking the façade of his previously united front. The black community left the Council chambers congratulating themselves for their victory, unaware that Mayor Duckworth, a sore loser at the game of power politics, was already plotting their demise.

At the height of the Broad Creek Shores controversy, the City had appointed a three-man committee to study "the need and desirability of obtaining additional sites for use in constructing private homes for our colored citizens."[41] At the time of its appointment, the Land Committee, or "Kaufman Committee," as it was called in the black community, had been a part of Mayor Duckworth's efforts to resolve the impasse short of granting land in the Broad Creek area to black developers. Recognizing the city's "desperate need" for additional suitable sites for black houses, the mayor turned to the Silkstocking crowd in an attempt to solve the dispute peacefully. The three most powerful representatives of the old People's group remaining in the city's government—N.R.H.A. Chairman Charles Kaufman, and Planning Commissioners Henry Clay Hofheimer II and John S. Jenkins—were appointed to the committee. Privately the committee was charged with finding additional space for black expansion in areas that would not threaten white neighborhoods or segregated schools; no one wanted a repeat of the racial strife that characterized Coronado.

Initially the committee received a hostile reception from the black community because of its association with the mayor's position on Broad Creek Shores, but gradually the reputation for fairness and the high esteem in which its members were generally held won over some support and cooperation. The editors of the *Journal and Guide* apologized for their initial inhospitality, terming it "a natural reaction to an unnatural determination on the part of city council."[42] Even after careful study and consultation with black leaders, however, the committee failed to find appropriate sites for new development; indeed Norfolk's desperate need for space for all types of expansion was the driving motivation behind its costly annexation initiatives.

Instead, the Land Committee proposed to undertake an extensive redevelopment project in a portion of the new Tanner's Creek District that included Oakwood, Lincoln Park, and Rosemont —a 370-acre site that had more than 1,000 dwellings, all of them already occupied by black families (*see* Figure 1, page 33). Oakwood began its existence as a shantytown on the outskirts of established all-white settlements before the turn of the century. For as little as $50 a black family could purchase a small tract of land and then scrounge enough scrap lumber, tarpaper, and materials to build a shack. Eighty-five percent of the homes were substandard; few had adequate sanitary facilities; and even fewer could ever be rehabilitated to comply with existing codes.[43] Even the *Journal and Guide* recognized that the area contained "some of the worst imaginable slums," and applauded the committee's decision.[44] The committee proposed a massive redevelopment and reclamation project that would rebuild the community to accommodate 2,500 families—an addition of 1,500 units—in individual homes, semi-detached houses, and garden apartments. Like N.R.H.A. Project

One, the plan included playgrounds, an elementary school, and a small shopping center.[45]

The proposal was well received by members of both the black and white communities; "inasmuch as the site proposed for reclamation has been occupied by colored people for the past sixty-five years, the segregation factor does not enter the package."[46] In point of fact, no other alternative existed for the area. Most of the homes would have to be condemned and torn down anyway under existing health, fire, safety, and building codes, and the City would be unwilling under current spending formulas to extend sewer and water lines to the area, pave streets, or provide sidewalks, streetlights, and gutters. The N.R.H.A. sought to allay the fears of Oakwood residents by promising to give a "liberal" appraisal for existing homes, relocate those homes sound enough to save, provide financing for new homes, give residents priority in site selection, and even trade comparable land for redeveloped sites.[47]

Kaufman and the N.R.H.A. were surprised to hear the strength of Oakwood's opposition to renewal. Most residents knew they were too poor to afford the new development, even if their current substandard dwellings were generously appraised; they lived in Oakwood because there they could survive on little or no regular income. "We old people can't buy new homes," said one resident, "If you take our homes, we'll just be out in the street."[48] Because they had heard horror stories from other blacks who had been resettled during N.R.H.A. Project One, homeowners were understandably unwilling to wait in the line for a unit in Norfolk's already overcrowded public housing; instead they wanted to stay where they were, as they were. This strong anti-redevelopment sentiment forced a critical re-examination of the project by Norfolk's black leadership. Attorneys J. Hugo Madison and Joe Jordan objected that the project tended to perpetuate residential segregation.[49] Others began to question the advisability of crowding an additional 1,500 families in an area that already held more than 1,000. Most stated they would oppose it until the current residents were given sufficient guarantees, written or otherwise, to sway a majority of local support. Thomas Young, president of the *Journal and Guide*, and Rev. W. L. Hamilton, pastor of Shiloh Baptist Church, Dr. Lyman Brooks, president of the Norfolk Division of Virginia State College (now Norfolk State

University), and other black leaders who maintained links to the Silkstocking crowd still favored the project, but the growing split in the black community over the City's use of its redevelopment and housing powers was quickly pushing younger, more activist leaders to the fore.[50]

The Oakwood Redevelopment controversy was an important episode in the history of the period for a number of reasons. First, it marked the emergence of an important coalition between Mayor Duckworth and the remnants of the People's group still in power. Both groups were committed to continuing the city's informal practice of segregated housing and eager not to repeat the horrors of Coronado. Mayor Duckworth may have been rebuffed at his premature attempt to forestall a Broad Creek Shores settlement, but with the Silkstocking crowd and the Norfolk Redevelopment and Housing Authority firmly in his camp, further efforts would be both more calculated and more successful. Oakwood represented the willingness of the People's representatives to harness the powers of redevelopment to ensure segregated housing developments. More importantly, it also indicates the most natural target for the next phase of redevelopment activity; Oakwood was a *bona fide* slum, ready-made for a redevelopment project: few of its homes could ever hope to pass the City's minimum housing codes, and blight and dilapidation were evident throughout the neighborhood.

Finally, Oakwood points to a growing split in the black community between the older, business-oriented leaders like P. B. Young, Rev. Hamilton, and W. T. Mason, and the younger, more aggressive activists like Joe Jordan, Victor Ashe, and J. Hugo Madison. The next round would be fought in the courts, and the younger leaders had neither the inclination to compromise nor the bargaining skills possessed by their elders. Oakwood proved that these younger leaders were gaining a ready audience willing to hear the message that new tactics were necessary to defeat the state and local forces arrayed against them. The more established black leaders still commanded enormous respect in both the black and white communities, but all their powers of amelioration would be needed to avert future strife between their charges and the forces of the Organization.[51]

※ ※ ※

3

✻ ✻ ✻ ✻ ✻

First Reactions to *Brown*

THE INTENSITY of the school desegregation controversy may best be seen within the context of the ongoing power struggle between the black and white communities; in both instances, Norfolk's pattern of residential segregation, because it brought black and white neighborhoods within close proximity to one another, was the cause of friction between the races. Even so, the initial reaction in Norfolk to the Supreme Court decision was decidedly calm. School Superintendent J. J. Brewbaker's response was typical: "We must accept these decisions and give them considered judgment and not let our emotions get in the way.... We will do everything we can from an intelligent point of view." He then went on to forecast "very little mixture" of races due to the residential "lines" within the city. Councilmen Ezra Summers and Roy Martin expressed the political sentiment: "Norfolk will probably be less affected than any city in the state because of the geographical set up here [that includes] well-defined residential districts." The *Virginian-Pilot* pointed to the bulwark of *de facto* segregation that stood against integration encroachments:

> In Norfolk and other Virginia cities where Negro and white schools are built largely in conformity with the white and Negro patterns of residence, where the Negro population is distinctly in the minority, and where the two races respect

each other, adjustment to the new order will be gradual and not likely to produce deep change for a considerable time. The majority of Southerners, and the best of Southern leadership will strive to work out their civilization in accord with the constitutional requirements.[1]

Newly elected Governor Thomas Stanley, fresh from his narrow victory over Republican challenger Ted Dalton, reacted calmly as well. He contemplated "no precipitate action" and stated that the "views of leaders of both races will be invited" in approaching the problems created by the court. Stanley's pronouncement was met with a hail of abuse from Southside Virginia, the string of counties and small towns which formed the state's tobacco belt south of Richmond. Because many areas of the Southside had majority black populations, racist sentiment and opposition to school integration there was stronger than elsewhere in the state. Under pressure from the Southside, the heart of the Byrd Organization's constituency, Governor Stanley soon adopted a more militant posture: "I shall use every legal means at my command to continue segregated schools in Virginia." Former Governor Bill Tuck expressed the Southside's sentiment,

> There is no middle ground, no compromise. If the other [areas] won't stand with us, I say make 'em. . . . If you ever let them integrate anywhere, the whole state will be integrated in a short time.[2]

A new political group, the Defenders of State Sovereignty and Individual Liberties, was then being formed in the Southside to feed the venom of the state politicians who promised to oppose integration at all cost. The Defenders did not represent the night-rider, confederate-flag-waving brand of resistance found farther South, but as a statewide organization, they gave backbone to all politicians who similarly pledged unyielding opposition to integration in any form.[3]

In spite of the hysteria that characterized the Southside in general and the leadership of the Byrd Organization specifically, the reaction on the part of Norfolk citizens remained one of tranquility. A sampling of letters to the editor revealed that by a two-to-one ratio the writers expressed "a calm, rational attitude towards desegregation and/or a strong disapproval of the public stand of Virginia officials." A local group for interracial cooperation concluded that "There exists in this area of the South a body of moderate, informed, thoughtful, educated, and earnest public opinion which would accept desegregation easily. Extremist opinion is always noisy, and people who are against anything shout louder than those who are simply acquiescent."[4]

One predictable response from Norfolk officials was the immediate halt and quiet reassessment of the City's school building program and redevelopment efforts. The Oakwood Plan was set aside for almost a decade, but the postwar baby boom had brought the need for classroom space to crisis proportions all across the state. For this reason, Governor John Battle had set aside $75 million in state funds for school construction during his four-year (1951-1955) term. The localities had previously been held responsible for all such construction—a fact that put Virginia's school system at the bottom of any listing of quality or funding effort. In 1950 Virginia had the lowest percentage of high school attendance in the nation, the next-to-the-highest percentage of high school dropouts before graduation, and the next to the smallest percentage of school-age children in school, but the state had never before done much to help its localities meet their pressing needs.[5] Norfolk, in the waning days of the People's administration and City Manager C. A. Harrell's tenure in office, jumped at this chance to receive state funding, and embarked upon an aggressive $13 million school construction program that included new buildings and improvements to both the black and white school systems alike.[6] This program included the first new school buildings for blacks in the city, the others having been hand-me-downs from the white community.[7] Four new schools (Bowling Park, Young Park, Diggs Park, and Lindenwood), three of them built in part with federal funds under the redevelopment effort, had been added to the black system prior to the *Brown* decision,[8] and other funds were spent on additions or improvements to existing black schools.[9]

At the time of the *Brown* decision, the school system had several projects under consideration which were now jeopardized by the explosive new issue of desegregation. In addition to Oceanair Elementary, which was already in the planning stages, three other sites were under active consideration for new schools (*see* Figure 2): a

Figure 2 – School Sites Under Construction in 1954

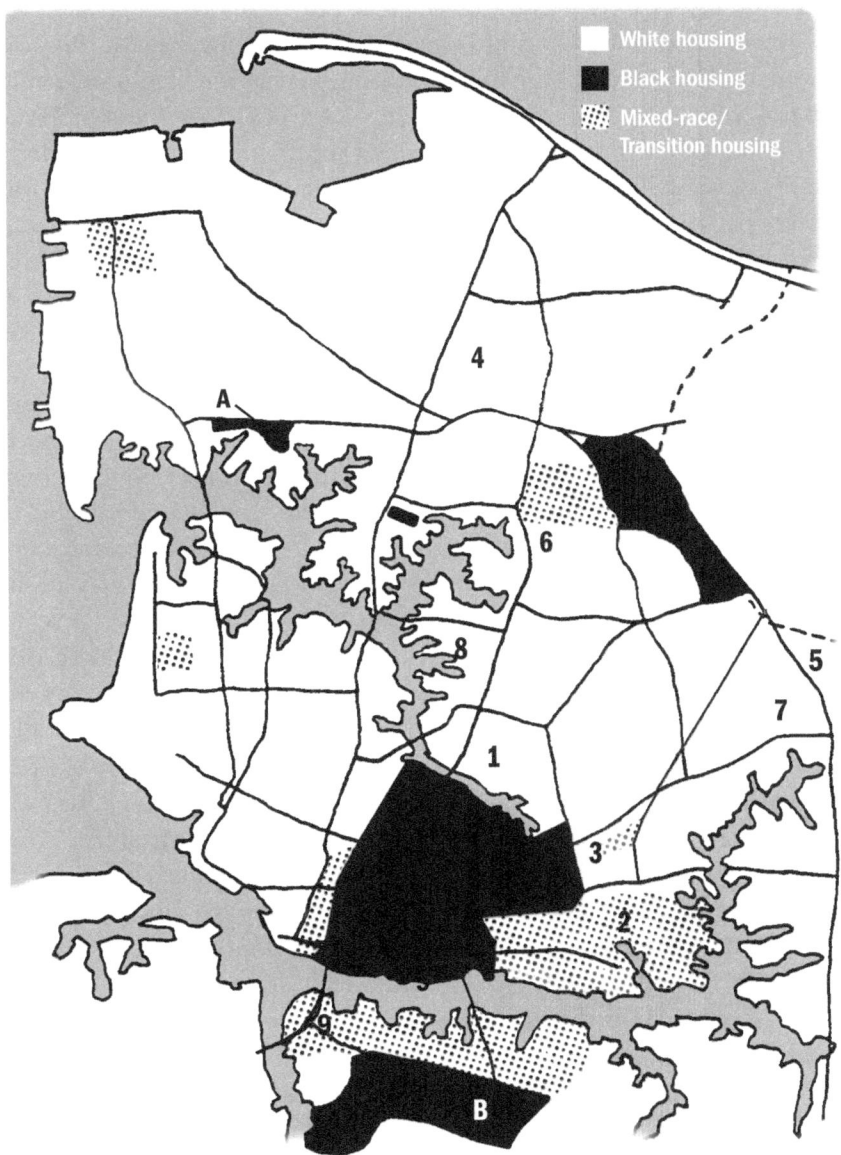

BLACK SCHOOLS
A   Titustown Elementary site
B   Southside (Campostella) Jr. High site

WHITE SCHOOLS
1   Maltby Avenue site
2   Ingleside Jr. High site
3   Atterbury Road site
4   Cottage Toll Road site
5   Military Highway site
6   Norview Jr. High site
7   Lansdale Jr. High site
8   Lakewood Jr. High site

"Southside Junior High School" for blacks in the Berkley/Campostella area; a large parcel of land in the Ballentine area was supported as a replacement for the aging Lafayette School (white); and a site just west of Titustown Elementary, an aging school for blacks near the naval base, was proposed as a replacement facility.[10] All three projects now faced new scrutiny, apparently as a result of the *Brown* decision, and the school board's intention to continue building new schools for blacks seemed to dissolve: "Southside" (Campostella) Junior High was not built for almost a decade; the Ballentine tract was sold to a private developer; and, even though an addition was built on a portion of the third site, Titustown Elementary was never rebuilt as originally intended.

In addition to these, the City Planning Commission was helping school officials select five other sites in the Tanner's Creek district scheduled for annexation, where there was an "urgent need" for two new junior high schools and three 700-pupil elementary schools. The Norfolk School Board proposed building one of the junior high schools on additional land around Ingleside Elementary, and a 33-acre tract in the Sherwood Forest area was being considered for both an elementary and a junior high school; the other tracts included a 20-acre site in the northern portion of the city, a 12-acre tract in the east near the airport, and an 8-acre site north of Norview High School.[11] New school construction had, however, been halted as a result of the *Brown* decision,[12] and there quickly followed a period of quiet reassessment. In spite of the urgent need for new facilities, only the Norview site was found acceptable. Ingleside Junior High School was never built, apparently because the site was too close to Broad Creek Shores and other black housing developments (*see* Figure 2, page 45). Although the board did decide to build an elementary school on the Sherwood Forest tract, the site was also apparently too close to black housing to win approval for a junior high; the northern tract, site of a city plant nursery, was found to be unsuitable for development (three decades later it became Northside Park); the eastern site was rejected because it was in the path proposed for Interstate 64; and the smallest site, the 8-acre tract north of Norview High, was used to satisfy the critical need for a junior high school (Norview).

Because of the urgent need for new school buildings, there followed a furious period of planning by the board. School board files indicate that a number of plans were considered by the school administration over the next few months, but the board advanced only those that could clear all of the possible political objections. Gone was any focus on rebuilding aging black facilities; also abandoned were any sites that might prove to be too close to nearby black communities. When construction plans for 1955 were finally announced, School Superintendent J.J. Brewbaker assured the City Manager that:

> Desegregation will have no effect on this building program. With the exception of the addition to Oakwood [an elementary school for blacks], all other construction is for and needed for white children.[13]

In a carefully worded press statement, the board indicated that it was preparing to meet the new threat posed by *Brown* with "reasoned planning."[14]

Even so, finding suitable sites for badly needed junior high schools in the Tanner's Creek District proved to be a difficult task. In addition to the rejected Ingleside and Sherwood Forest tracts, plans to locate in the Lansdale and Lakewood areas were also submitted to the city council for approval.[15] The board even went so far as to hire architects to design Lakewood[16] and Lansdale Junior High schools. In the end, after much behind-the-scenes maneuvering, the Council scratched these sites from an extended list of projects, and instead converted Willard Elementary into a junior high.[17] Even though a consultant had indicated that the city's school population would increase by more than 4,000 students per year for the next few years[18]—the equivalent of five new schools a year—Norfolk elected to move slowly and deliberately, even if this meant badly overcrowding some existing facilities and adding a double shift at others.[19] Instead of launching an aggressive new building program as originally envisioned, the board opted to adopt a safer course, and moved instead to add new wings to its most overcrowded existing facilities.[20] One of the schools marked for immediate construction was a combination elementary-junior high for black pupils in the Oakwood area, the residential neighborhood of a large number of plaintiffs in the suit filed by the National Association for the Advancement of Colored People (N.A.A.C.P.). In a letter to City

Manager Thomas Maxwell, Superintendent J. J. Brewbaker hinted at the need for the combination school:

> Negro junior high pupils attend Jacox, which is approximately seven miles from the section in which they live. The nearest junior high is Norview.[21]

Reporter Luther Carter went even further when he surveyed the proposed building program in light of the desegregation suit: "One obvious effect of a combination school would be to accommodate some Negro junior high pupils who might otherwise want to attend Norview Junior High, a white school and by far the closest junior high to the Oakwood-Rosemont area."[22] The board also pressed its case to build "Southside" (i.e., Campostella) Junior High School to accommodate the growing black population in the Berkley area.[23] Again, reporter Luther Carter noted the changing racial composition of the city as a motive for the proposed facility: "School officials have noted a pronounced tendency for whites to leave Berkley, and for Negroes to move in."[24]

In fact, Norfolk had made tremendous progress under the Battle funds and $13 million building program advanced by C. A. Harrell and the People's administration. By 1953 the Norfolk School Board could say for the first time that the cost of educating a white pupil and a black pupil in the city's schools was equal.[25] Before Harrell, the City's effort was determined by a complicated formula that was weighted heavily upon the percentage of total revenues received from black and white taxpayers. By 1950, however, the City was actually paying more to its black teachers (with both more degrees and more seniority) than to its white ones, having raised the salary of black teachers some 62 percent since the Prieur Machine's wartime city council dominated school spending.[26] In fact, Norfolk was cited by Senator Sam Ervin of North Carolina for its efforts to improve its black educational system. In an article Ervin wrote for *Look* magazine defending continued school segregation in the South, a picture of Norfolk's newly constructed Young Park School (built in part with federal redevelopment funds) bore the caption: "New Negro schools, like this one in Norfolk, Va., attest [to] efforts of [the] South to meet [integration] problems in its own way."[27] In spite of this momentum, the impact of the *Brown* decision and the overreaction of the state's political leaders forced the City to halt its school construction plans[28] at the very time it was most in need of new classroom space, as a result of both annexation and the baby boom.[29] The *Ledger-Dispatch* summed up the attitude of those in charge of school construction:

> In recent years Southern states have been making great financial outlays to put Negro schools on a par with those for white students . . . however, once the court's rejection of separate-but-equal theory became known, there was no longer any great pressure on local officials to continue the special and costly attention to [the] Negro school building programs.[30]

In spite of the official "go slow" attitude of the city council, the school board began to take its first few cautious steps toward compliance with the spirit of the *Brown* decision. First, it advanced a proposal to create a biracial study group to recommend possible courses of action. The move was endorsed by the Education Association and the Council of Parent Teacher Associations (P.T.A.),[31] but opposed by the N.A.A.C.P. leadership. One black leader broke the deadlock with his endorsement, "There is no harm in studying and bringing integration about in an orderly manner." Next, the school board voted down Virginia's model 30-day notice-of-termination clause in its teacher contracts, a step recommended by the state's political leaders as a way to prepare for the possibility of closed schools.[32] Gradually the school board's commitment to keep schools open and to comply with the spirit of the Supreme Court decision began to win it both accolades from the international press and a few denunciations from Southern writers. Typical of the positive reaction was this statement from the *Roanoke World News*:

> [The Norfolk School Board has supplied] the first official word of calm in Virginia's heated integration debate. In so doing it has broken the solid front of opposition to the Supreme Court's decision and decree.[33]

Norfolk School Board Chairman W. Farley Powers appeared somewhat embarrassed by the sudden notoriety and stated:

> I do not want to get into any controversy [with the rest of the state]. We might make some preliminary moves [to keep schools open], but we must abide by state law.³⁴

School Superintendent Brewbaker was equally aware that Norfolk's progressive attitude marked it in some sections of the state as a "hotbed" of liberalism because:

> We have been conscious that a change [from segregation] is inevitable. We have not been trying to think up ways to circumvent the ruling.³⁵

Indeed, the rest of the state appeared to be preoccupied with thinking up legal angles to somehow block the eventuality of the Supreme Court's ruling. *Richmond News Leader* editor James J. Kilpatrick happened upon the century-old doctrine of "interposition"—whereby a state supposedly has the right to "interpose" its own authority between an unjust action of the federal government and its local political subdivisions—and the interposition craze was begun. The state's official reaction was the Gray Plan—named for State Senator Garland Gray—that provided numerous ways for Virginia to "interpose" its authority and so block integration. The plan called for a state pupil placement board that would take over the pupil assignment duties of the local school boards; special tuition grants to parents of school children who attended private schools, parochial establishments, or public schools in another jurisdiction to escape desegregation; and an amendment to the compulsory attendance laws that suspended them in areas where public schools were desegregated. Few politicians and only the *Virginian-Pilot* of all the state's newspapers opposed the Gray Plan. Provisions within the plan that would have allowed local subdivisions to desegregate on a local option basis if the federal courts persisted were scrapped by the legislature when Senator Harry F. Byrd, Sr., leader of the statewide Byrd Organization, pointed out the need for all local governments to stand together in "massive resistance" to the dictates of the Supreme Court. In response, the Virginia Legislature proposed the Stanley Plan, which required the Governor to close any school under court order to integrate, and cut off all state funds from any school district which tried to reopen in spite of the governor's interposition.³⁶

While the rest of the state was reeling under the bombast prompted by the Gray Plan, Kilpatrick's doctrine of interposition, the Stanley Plan, and Harry Byrd's Massive Resistance, the citizens of Norfolk had another plan with which to contend: the Summers Plan. Under Duckworth's rule, Ezra Summers was the closest thing Norfolk had to an independent voice on the city council.[37] In July 1955, Summers introduced a surprise proposal whereby the city could achieve integration if it ever came under a court order: the first step would be to have every parent in the school system, both black and white, fill out an intention card which indicated whether or not they wanted their children to attend an integrated or segregated school. The school board would then determine how many schools it would have to operate on an all-white, all-black, or integrated basis, and then assign each pupil to the school of his parents' choosing. One of the unwritten elements of the Summers Plan was the hope that few white parents would choose to send their children to integrated schools; those who did would be punished by isolating all the "troublemakers" in the same school; if white parents did not choose integrated schools, then schools would not be integrated. Local politicians extolled it as "in keeping with the Supreme Court's decision" because it allowed every child to attend the school of his or her choice.[38]

Obviously the Summers Plan added little positive thought to the discussion of the day, but it does indicate the political mood of obfuscation and deceit that ruled. There were people in Norfolk who understood the *Brown* decision and its ramifications, but by and large they refused to believe that Norfolk schools would have to be integrated or that public schools would have to be closed. They placed too much faith in the hands of local and state politicians who could promise them a plan, any plan, no matter how ill-conceived and contrived, to circumvent the ruling.[39] The true leaders of public opinion in Norfolk, the business and civic elite who had earlier ruled the city, had been so effectively removed from the political process by the Organization that they were quiet while this irrationality gripped their city. The school board, too, was all but ignored as the public rushed to seize each new political panacea.

Undaunted by the political bombast of the period, the Norfolk School Board went quietly about its business, hoping to keep a low profile and thus avoid confrontation with the Organization leaders who dominated city hall. Taking a page from the old People's book, the board went ahead with its plans to appoint a biracial committee to recommend action; then it commissioned an exhaustive study of the board, its policy, practices, and the future needs of the Norfolk school population. Local politicians pointed frantically to the need to stand toe-to-toe in Massive Resistance with the rest of the state—as one local legislator did with this rhetorical outburst concerning the Southside counties with their heavy concentrations of black population,

> Their house is on fire. They want us to send fire trucks to help them. I think it is our Christian duty to help put out the fire for them [by opposing integration].[40]

Even so, the school board resisted these impassioned pleas with great aplomb. School Board Chairman Paul Schweitzer pointed to how Norfolk's situation differed from the Southside's:

> There are only thirty percent Negroes in the Norfolk school system . . . geographically located so that they are well taken care of in their present schools. If we adopt a gradual plan of integration, there would be so little you wouldn't notice it.

School Superintendent Brewbaker echoed this theme:

> There would be few Negroes in white schools because of existing "residential segregation." . . . We are all in favor of segregation. . . . It is just a question of what is the best plan. . . . I'm not in favor of integration, I'm in favor of carrying out the Supreme Court decree with the least harm to pupils . . . and to the schools.[41]

Other school officials pointed to the Navy, NATO (headquartered in Norfolk), and government service as liberalizing influences that had exposed many Norfolk students to a variety of cultures without undue harm. One principal stated that more than a third of his students had already attended integrated schools elsewhere without problems.[42] In fact, when Norfolk Catholic High School was integrated by the Catholic diocese following the *Brown* decision, the event passed without comment from the press or protest from the public.⁴³

The school board's air of official calm had bought a year of grace from legal pressures to integrate; its members had hoped to use that year to prepare the public for calm compliance with the desegregation dictates, but time and events had conspired against it to block this intention. Unlike its counterparts in other parts of the country, the black community in Norfolk had not rushed into court to force immediate integration of the schools; instead, local black leaders had followed the more temporizing course of petitioning the school board to desegregate.⁴⁴ Of course the threat of court action lay behind that petition, but it was an important first step towards finding a peaceful solution to the desegregation controversy. The school board unfortunately could not respond in kind: too much had transpired in the year since that initial petition had been filed, and the state and local political leaders had moved to block any authority it might have had to comply. The Broad Creek and Coronado controversies had bred a climate of racial mistrust and resentment—a feeling that cut off all previous channels of communication between the races. Unfortunately, and without its choosing, the board was now caught up in a larger political confrontation in which neither side could accept defeat. Similarly, any opportunity it might have had to defuse the crisis with token gestures was now gone. The year of grace had passed, and only the courts could decide the outcome.

In the mounting atmosphere of racial tension that now prevailed, the local chapter of the N.A.A.C.P. began to step up the firepower of its assault upon the city's racial institutions. Accordingly, in May 1956, almost two years to the day after the Supreme Court's landmark ruling, attorneys Victor Ashe and Hugo Madison formally abandoned the petition process and filed their school desegregation suit in the U.S. General District Court, Eastern District of Virginia.⁴⁵ Their suit reflected the changing mood of the black community: a majority of the petitioners were from the still racially tense Oakwood and Coronado sections of the Norview area; most of the rest were from the transitional neighborhoods of Atlantic City and Broad Creek, where racial boundary lines were not yet clearly drawn.⁴⁶ In spite of this late start, litigation in Norfolk quickly proceeded, and was soon two or three steps ahead of that in the rest of the state. Part of the reason for this fast pace was Federal Judge Walter Hoffman's no-nonsense approach to litigation in his court. Even though he was a Norfolk native and law partner of Organization stalwart State Senator Edward L. Breeden, Hoffman was rapidly earning a reputation as a distinguished and independent jurist who would not brook the obfuscation and delaying tactics common elsewhere. For their part, the local N.A.A.C.P. attorneys pressed vigorously on the case, obviously encouraged by the fact that Hoffman had already struck down segregated barriers in the city's parks[47] and public transportation systems.[48]

The school board closely followed this judicial trend, and proceeded cautiously under the assumption that Norfolk's schools would soon be under court orders to integrate. The board appeared in its pronouncements to be fully prepared to operate a desegregated school system under such auspices. The city's political leaders, however, were cognizant of the fact that integrated classrooms, no matter how slight their impact might be upon the functioning of the local school system, were diametrically opposed to the policies of the state:

> Norfolk is already looked upon with suspicion by some sections of the state; if we are forced by federal courts to be the first in Virginia to integrate, it would be held against us by the rest of the state for the next twenty years.[49]

Norfolk faced the real possibility that the state would shut down its schools indefinitely to avoid integration, just as it had closed nearby Seashore State Park when ordered to desegregate it.[50]

Since there had as yet been no shred of sympathy for Norfolk's predicament, the school board sought a closed-door audience with Mayor Duckworth, the city council, and the city's legislative delegation; its members hoped to develop some plan of action that would protect the city from political reprisals from the rest of the state. Norfolk's only real hope in this regard lay in taking the final decision to desegregate out of the hands of the local school board and passing the onus back to the state for resolution; thus, if the state government could be forced to take the blame for ordering desegregation of Norfolk's schools, then there would be no reason for imposing economic sanctions or exacting legislative retribution against the city for complying. To Norfolk's political leaders the threat of reprisals from the rest of the state was very real, and one that they feared more than the authority of the federal courts: the confrontation at Little Rock had not yet taken place, and no one knew just how forcefully the federal government would move to back up court orders to integrate. On the other hand, the city's desperate wartime financial experience provided ample evidence of just how devastating the consequences of reduced state funding could be to its economy. Simply put, the city's plan was to ask the state to "interpose" its own sovereignty between the federal courts and the school board. To Norfolk's leaders the logic was clear:

> We can't put a window in a school without the state telling us what size it must be, and on a matter as far reaching as segregation, the state should be willing to stand up to it. This is clearly a matter in which the state should tell us what to do.[51]

The meeting broke with the resolve that the City would request a special session of the General Assembly in order to assure timely enactment of the necessary legislation. Public pronouncements of Norfolk's interposition plan were highly touted by members of the state legislature and city council in attendance; almost immediately the school board began to back away from the inflammatory language emanating from the closed-door session. Members of the board felt that interposition really meant "imposition"—that the plan only gave the rest of the state a chance to impose its more conservative, provincial philosophies upon the errant liberalism of its urbane sister city—and that shutting down the Norfolk school system was a step the rest of Virginia might be willing to take, especially if Norfolk were to bear the consequences alone. This was a move the board meant to resist at all cost: its members had been charged with the responsibility of running the largest school system in Virginia, and this meant keeping schools open under any circumstances, even if the rest of the state disapproved. Members of the board, therefore, attempted to soften the impact of the city's interposition plan by stating that Norfolk was merely seeking "the advice and guidance" of the Legislature. They recognized that they were unable to act alone in the face of court-ordered desegregation, but spokesmen stressed that the board "wants to conform to state policies, but the continued operation of public schools here is of utmost importance."[52]

The school board's reluctance to back Norfolk's interposition plan publicly was the first sign of a coming confrontation between the appointed members of the board and the elected officials that made their appointments. Unlike the city council, the members of the board were not responsible to any particular partisan constituency, and not dependent upon popular reelection for continuance; they were thus free to choose the course they felt best for the community without all the posturing and puffery of the politicians. Partly for this reason, researchers all across the South were reporting that appointed school boards dealt far more moderately with the desegregation crisis than their elected counterparts.[53] In Norfolk, the city council had a particular reason to mistrust any evidence of independence emanating from the school board: in the past the Council had used the board as a convenient dumping ground for business leaders from the People's ranks who still deserved special recognition because of their high standing in the community. The school board had always been a relatively powerless body, and Council's strict control of the budget served as a powerful check on even the most errant body. Previously there had been little danger in stacking the school board with key business leaders closer to the People's persuasion—membership on the board carried high status without any of the spoils potential of the City's housing, planning, zoning, or various inspection appeals boards—and the city council felt that a display of strong business support for public education was important for the city. Finally, the Council had sometimes employed the tactical strategy of blaming the school board for community ills when it came time for reelection, and had thus always sought to avoid placing any of the Organization's faithful in such a role. It was this scapegoat role that most concerned the city council now: they feared that the public pronouncements of the school board indicated a willingness, however reluctant, to serve as a whipping boy for the state by accepting desegregation if it was ordered. Thus the move to embrace the philosophy of interposition may be seen as a timely ploy to subvert the authority of local boards, and make sure the power to resist desegregation was in the hands of more partisan operatives.

In spite of the school board's apparent willingness to accept court-ordered desegregation, it nevertheless pressed vigorously its legal efforts to resist such an eventuality. In private the board may have been willing to defy the state's authority, but in court it argued forcefully that public school segregation was a valid exercise of the state's police powers to protect its citizens. The board also advanced the argument that it was an agency of the state and thus subject to the same privileges, protection, and immunities as the state. Further, the board contended that the N.A.A.C.P. had filed the suit against the wrong party: technically the board lacked the legal jurisdiction to establish and maintain a school system on its own, and merely served as advisors to the city council, against whom the suit should have been brought. The board's final argument, however, carried a little more weight: the court lacked jurisdiction in this dispute, it contended, since only people duly qualified for admission to the public schools and whose request for transfer between schools had been denied could legitimately prove harm.[54] This was a telling point, since, unlike the *Brown* cases, which had been brought on behalf of black children who had been denied the "equal opportunity" to attend the school of their choice, the Norfolk case had been brought by leading blacks who petitioned the court to end a perceptible public wrong; none of the petitioners could show a personal harm.

The members of the school board knew, however, that they were merely buying time with their legal arguments, and that the N.A.A.C.P. would return to court in a few months with the right defendants and the proper mix of plaintiffs able to prove injury by rejection of their transfer applications. The board's legal maneuvering had bought enough time to forestall school integration in Norfolk for one more school year;[55] its members knew it would take this long for the board to receive, deliberate, and then ultimately reject the petitions. The board's spirited defense was enough to keep the state politicians off its back temporarily; in the meantime, it had begun to develop a plan which might take some of the pressure off of the N.A.A.C.P. desegregation suit. The school board approached the city council with a request for an additional $15 million building program, much of it earmarked for adding libraries, cafeterias, music centers, resource areas, multi-purpose classrooms, and other facilities to existing black schools.[56] school board member Ben Willis was candid enough to comment on the sudden upgrading of black schools: "The better their [i.e., the black] facilities, the less pressure their argument will have."[57]

One of the schools marked for immediate construction was a

combination elementary-junior high for black pupils in the Oakwood-Rosemont section, where a large number of the N.A.A.C.P. plaintiffs had been located. *Virginian-Pilot* reporter Luther Carter sensed the impact of the desegregation suit on the proposed building program:

> The School Board has indicated that when all appeals against the federal court order have been exhausted, it will attempt to minimize its effect by using a plan for gradual desegregation. [The Oakwood-Rosemont combination school] would appear to be in line with this policy. Superintendent Brewbaker also indicated that eventually a combination junior and senior high might be needed in the area [to further ease desegregation].[58]

As part of its overall plan, the board proposed rushing its Southside junior high school (Campostella) to the drawing boards to accommodate the growing black population in that portion of the city.[59]

The school board's proposed building program was not meant as another legal gimmick to head off desegregation; instead it indicated a thorough acceptance of the reality that such a court order was imminent; the board was merely trying to soften the impact of shattered traditions. Theirs was a moderate approach and, as such, it put the board in opposition to most of the state's senior political leaders who believed that the day of integration could be forestalled forever. There was some hope as well that by giving the black community their own top-quality schools, even in the remote areas far removed from their existing, segregated schools, the school board would be relieving some of the pressures to integrate from that quarter. The certain appeal of such a sensible plan was not, however, apparent to local politicians. Councilman Ezra Summers, ever the most vocal of an otherwise closed-mouthed city council, issued a strongly worded statement supporting the Virginia's Massive Resistance efforts and advocating a "go-slow approach" in local school building programs "until the integration disputes are settled." Summers' insistence that the matter "should be studied more carefully"[60] dealt a death blow to the school board's construction plans. The rest of the city council was more diplomatic in their rejection; instead they asked the board to revise its plan "to what we can afford" in light of the precipitate rise in school bond interest rates now being extended to school systems threatened by desegregation. Then, as a final slap at the board, the city council made preparations to go ahead and borrow money at those same inflated interest rates to construct other capital improvements that might attract additional state and federal funding.[61] Armed with surveys indicating that 97 percent of the city's parents and 93 percent of other adults favored increasing school funding,[62] the school board made a strong case, but it was still rejected outright. The inference was clear: the city council had higher priorities than granting money to black schools to forestall court-ordered desegregation.

There was nothing inherently wrong with the school board's plan: it had been based upon the soundest and most moderate judgement of the time; it relied upon professional growth surveys indicating that the schools and improvements would be needed anyway, even if the school system was permitted to remain segregated. What was wrong was that the board's plan had come too late; the City had just paid an exorbitant price to annex a large section of Norfolk County, and the city council could legitimately point to the fact that it had a pressing financial need to extend full municipal services to this area as soon as possible.[63] This was reason enough to block a costly school building program that was, at best, a stopgap effort to defuse the desegregation crisis and, at worst, a reckless gamble to lure potential black plaintiffs away from the N.A.A.C.P. suit with the promise of building and expanding their own segregated neighborhood schools. Norfolk had already made a precipitate effort in the last decade to offer equal, although segregated, facilities for both races, and the City could ill afford the school board's new building proposal, the councilmen argued, especially if integration could be averted through other, less costly means.

Politically as well, the board's move came too late: the calm racial attitudes that prevailed in Norfolk in the summer of 1956 had, by the winter, taken a nasty turn, and the city's white residents were giving ample evidence that they were no longer willing to buy off the black community with promises of separate but equal facilities. A shift in the stance of the city's legislative delegation was the best bellwether of this changing attitude. In the summer, the bulk of the delegation had stood behind the school board's efforts to keep the schools open, even if desegregated. The legislators went so far as to vow to fight the governor "in opposition to any measure designed to deprive Norfolk's schools of full financial support."[64] A year later they would back down from this moderate posture and declare that they held only minor differences with the governor; they disagreed on the tactics of how best to fight court-ordered desegregation, but the local legislators were in full accord with the governor that integration must be fought with every legal means available.[65] In another year they would go full circle from opposition to support of Massive Resistance to integration.[66]

One reason for this apparent shift in public opinion was the growing impact of the N.A.A.C.P. legal victories: in the spring of 1956 Norfolk's public schools were but one target in the scatter-shot legal approach of the local N.A.A.C.P. to achieve integration. By the fall, however, N.A.A.C.P. court action had forced all of the area's parks, recreation centers, and public transportation facilities to either desegregate or close indefinitely. The public school system now stood as the last bastion against a fully integrated society, and the N.A.A.C.P.'s unrelenting legal effort to crack this barrier caused increasing bitterness in the white community. A feeling was growing that Norfolk needed more time to adjust to the changes that had already taken place, and that continuing the battle to desegregate the schools only made racial moderation more difficult.

It was inevitable in the growing climate of racial antipathy that new groups would emerge to capitalize on this force and direct it to serve their own needs. Although the Defenders of State Sovereignty and Individual Liberties had emerged first in the racially explosive Southside as an effort by small businessmen to combat desegregation in that area, the Defenders were gaining increasing acceptance in all parts of the state. The Defenders were not hood-wearing vigilantes, like their counterparts in the White Citizens' Councils further south; instead, they had made every effort to establish in Virginia a legitimate and gentlemanly interest group, and one that carried a great deal of clout with the leadership of the statewide Byrd Organization.[67] Locally the Defenders had established a storefront headquarters to test public opinion, and, having found it favorable, now planned to mount major challenges to the city's legislative delegation along Massive Resistance lines.[68] One other event at the same time indicated an escalation in both the rhetoric and expertise of race politics. Just as the city's business and civic elite were kicking off their traditional fall Community Fund drive, Norfolk was inundated with hate pamphlets aimed at one of its beneficiary organizations. After a hasty series of meetings, the business community was forced to drop the Urban League from the drive for its supposed support of "race-mixing." Although the local origin of the pamphlets was unknown (the Defenders disavowed any responsibility), the pamphlets were traced back to a wing of the Christian Nationalist Party, renowned experts on "rabble-rousing and sensational hate-mongering."[69]

The emergence of these two groups, their apparent successes, and the mounting hostilities directed at the N.A.A.C.P. were giving rise to a climate of political desperation. All around, racial barriers were falling under the onslaught of litigation, and with them were crumbling institutions of long-standing importance in the white community. The hate groups were preparing to fan the flames of racial unrest into a dangerous political force. The school board had been rebuffed in its efforts to moderate the desegregation dispute with an exorbitant building program aimed at lessening the impact of desegregation. The city's legislative delegation had once stood firm in their opposition to closing Norfolk's schools; now they were backing away from that stance, and instead were preparing to vote for legislation that would turn over the control of the city's schools to the very state politicians most inclined to shut them down. The liberalizing force of the People's group was nowhere to be seen; they had been beaten back to their boardrooms and counting houses, and emerged only to take part in lackluster deliberations on relatively unimportant boards and advisory commissions. Even the old war horses of the Prieur Machine had accepted a diminished role in governmental affairs; they had been nearly crushed in the People's *coup*, lost interest, and had resigned themselves to a backseat position as the price to go along for the ride. The entire city looked instead to the one person who had emerged as the strong man in all municipal deliberations.

Of all the major politicians in the city, only Mayor Duckworth had been truly silent on the desegregation crisis. At first the public assumed that the school board and the Organization's legislative delegation accurately represented his thinking, but the vacillation of the local legislators and the dispatch with which the school board's building proposal had been dismissed gave rise to the belief that there was some middle ground between the two, and finally led to speculation that the mayor, too, had plans to save the city from integration. By this time Duckworth was firmly in control of the City and able to direct its growth towards attainment of his own ends, and, since he had spent so much time erecting the edifices designed by C. A. Harrell and the People's administration, he was impatient to get on with the task. Like Harrell, Duckworth had a vision of a New Norfolk, but unlike Harrell and the Silkstocking crowd, Duckworth had shown little commitment to the city's past and even less compassion for its people. He saw himself as a manager, both of the city's politics and its physical plant. His attachment was thus to the city's structures, its administration, political organization, and efficiency—the bricks and mortar of growth. It was a subtle distinction, but one that would not be lost in the years ahead.

4

✻ ✻ ✻ ✻ ✻

The Bulldozer Era

As the city's chief politician and highest elected official, Mayor W. Fred Duckworth remarkably had not yet spoken out on the subject of school integration. Most people supposed that, because of his political association with the Byrd Organization through its local affiliate, the Prieur Machine, his personal sentiments rested with those who preached resistance at all cost, yet he had endorsed none of the myriad scenarios of resistance that had already been proposed by Governor Stanley, Senator Byrd, Councilman Summers, the Defenders, the Gray Commission, James J. Kilpatrick, and others. He had never directly employed the rhetoric of interposition, and he had been strangely tolerant of others who attempted to relate the city's position. In an administration that prized closed-mouth unanimity, it was remarkable to witness the school board left free to pursue its own moderate course while councilmen like Ezra Summers veered off in more extreme tacks. Most observers conceded that Duckworth was, at least, opposed to undertaking the school board's building and modernization program, but even in this regard there were those who felt that his resistance was temporary, and that he was only withholding his approval as a bargaining chip in some grander design: As yet the City lacked the clout to force the black community into accepting any such proposal as a token victory short of desegregation.

By the winter of 1956, Mayor Duckworth had achieved

the promise of his 1950 Harmony slate: He had united business acumen, professional expertise, and political astuteness into a single, concentrated focus of power that carefully balanced the concerns of both the business community and the Prieur Machine. His new political force, and this was by all rights a personal victory, was obeisant to neither the Silkstocking Crowd nor the Organization, although it took its cues from both camps. Duckworth had found in action and accomplishment the common ground that united these two once opposing forces. The only real challenges to his administration had come from the black community: P. B. Young's councilmanic candidacy, the setback at Broad Creek Shores, the desegregation of Coronado, the racial unrest in Brambleton, and the court challenges brought by the N.A.A.C.P. The mayor, however, had gained the near-unanimous backing of the city's banking, business, civic, and political leaders, and in the six years since he had come to power, not a single effective voice had been raised in opposition to his authority; he and his councilmanic running mates swept to election victory year after year against only token, gadfly resistance from the white community.[1] One measure of the depth of Mayor Duckworth's support may be read in the West Side voting precincts, the traditional stronghold of the Silkstocking establishment, where the mayor and his slate were now running up electoral majorities that ran as high as ten to one.[2]

A number of reasons existed to explain Duckworth's enormous personal success. Foremost among them was the fact that both time and events had been good to Norfolk, and as a result, the city was enjoying a period of unparalleled growth and prosperity. The citizens were proud of all that had been accomplished since the war, and the controversy and conflict that had characterized the planning stages under the People's government were now forgotten as the reality of annexation, redevelopment, new highways, tunnel connections, and related facilities began contributing to the city's rapid expansion. Just as the careful, cautious, consensual approach of the People's group had been perfect for the planning stage, Duckworth's forceful dominance of city policy was ideally suited to the current building phase. City government functioned smoothly, almost too smoothly, under Duckworth's firm leadership, and he seemed to control every phase of municipal operation. No longer were city council meetings the long, drawn-out affairs that had characterized the People's sessions; instead Duckworth's council hashed out controversies, arranged compromises, and made all the real decisions in private "pre-sessions." Then, after all potential differences had been ironed out, the Council would emerge for its public meeting, a performance that ran as smoothly as if every member had a script: Rarely was there a dissenting vote, unnecessary discussion, or less than unanimous approval of even the most far-reaching policy decisions.[3]

In council-manager cities like Norfolk, the mayor is granted very few official powers beyond those of the other members of council; Duckworth, however, had added a considerable repertoire of unofficial executive and legislative authority to the traditional ribbon-cutting capacities of a weak mayor. Although lacking in official veto, budgetary, or appointment powers, Mayor Duckworth had parlayed his position as presiding officer into unquestioned authority over the city council. Both his private "pre-sessions" and the smooth and polished public performance of the Council helped to heighten the sense that he alone was firmly in control. Moreover, the City's appointed boards and commissions were no longer functioning as a vibrant source of citizen input and participation in the city's decision-making process; Duckworth had a strange habit of dropping in on the boards, "suggesting" a desired course of action, and then hanging around until he was satisfied that his instructions had been enacted.[4]

In a city that traditionally experienced rapid turnover of both its top elective and appointive officials, Mayor Duckworth quickly emerged as one of the few stable personalities in the administration of municipal affairs. By 1956 almost all of the City's department heads, appointed board members, and legislative delegation had been replaced since the People's reign, and only Duckworth and Vice-Mayor George Abbott had served more than four years on the city council.[5] Ironically, both the People's group and the Organization councils that had preceded them had shied away from placing even the informal powers of Norfolk's weak mayoral position into the hands of a single individual like Duckworth for too long: The office had shifted from Richard Cooke to Pretlow Darden at midpoint in the People's tenure in order to better promote the appearance of popular democracy that they craved.[6] The Prieur Machine had followed a similar practice, but political considerations figured foremost in their decision to rotate the seat frequently: History had shown that the increased exposure of the office made an incumbent mayor the most vulnerable candidate at election time. Mayor Duckworth, however, apparently experienced no such qualms about either elective vulnerability or charges of authoritarianism. By 1956 he had held the office of Mayor longer than any other person since the council-manager form of government had been instituted in 1918,[7] and he gave no indication of a willingness to surrender his authority at any time in the near future.

Duckworth held far more than just the policy-making functions of municipal government within his grasp; in a very real sense he managed the day-to-day activities of city hall as well. Because of two resignations, an unfortunate death, and interim appointments, he was already operating under his fifth city manager since he had taken office six years earlier. For this reason, the City's department heads had learned to function smoothly under the constancy of his leadership, channeling their information directly to the mayor's office in a route that circumvented the authority of the city manager and the rest of the city council. In this skewed hierarchy, the manager served as little more than the mayor's chief adviser, a role which both irritated and exasperated the incumbents. In these circumstances Norfolk was lucky to attract Thomas F. Maxwell to the post. Even though Maxwell possessed many talents that would ordinarily have entitled him to higher status, he suffered one debility that would limit his rise beyond Norfolk's functionary position: Maxwell was a binge alcoholic who could only survive in a closed and protective society like Norfolk's, where the periodic abandonment of his position made very little real difference to the operation of the city. Maxwell, however, was a wizard with budget policy, fiscal planning, money management, and federal grants, and this made him both invaluable to the mayor and an important municipal asset as the city passed through its building phase of postwar growth.[8]

Thus, in spite of the lack of official authority traditionally associated with his position, Mayor W. Fred Duckworth functioned as a strong mayor in an otherwise nonpartisan, professional, council-manager city; if all this power concentrated in one public official and a handful of advisers disturbed the citizens of Norfolk, they gave little indication of such unrest. Occasionally a newspaper editor would level a mild rebuke at the mayor:

> The Administration in which Mayor W. Fred Duckworth has been the leading figure, has shown both good and bad

points in its career. Its early weaknesses were a tendency to settle many questions at the euphemistically named "informal sessions" and a tendency to take sometimes too lightly the recommendations of qualified administrators and especially appointed commissions and agencies.[9]

Most citizens, however, apparently regarded such indelicacies as the natural consequence of having a strong-willed and effective leader at the helm. The mayor's very personal style of leadership and his extremely hierarchical chain of command served in marked contrast to the spirited popular debate that characterized the People's regime. A surfeit of popular advice and consent had seemed to bog down the People's government in the planning process; the mayor's "bulldozer drive and directness"[10]—the words themselves would prove prophetic—cut quickly through the preliminaries, and the people did not appear to mind if a few of the niceties of democratic decision-making were bulldozed in the process. Indeed, the major accomplishment of the Duckworth administration to date was "its ability to undertake large programs" and bring them swiftly to their conclusion,[11] and, as long as he continued to focus the broad powers of city government towards obtainable objectives, the citizens seemed to care little if he wielded those powers somewhat dictatorially. Although no one knew what course Duckworth proposed to follow if the city's schools really faced the threat of court-ordered integration, most assumed that he would act as dramatically as he had already done in almost every other field of municipal endeavor.

Two examples of the City's planning process under Mayor Duckworth help to illustrate both the enormous control of the mayor and the shifting emphasis of developmental priorities under his administration. The primary emphasis of city planning under the People's government had been the modernization and revitalization of Norfolk's downtown commercial center—the "New Norfolk" of which they boasted. Considering the size of the city, Norfolk had never had much of a real downtown business district, and even in the People's era, merchants in the area's fragile commercial strip were already feeling the press of competition from more residential shopping centers. Originally Norfolk had been a city built around its waterfront, but hard times had befallen its shipping-support industries since the demise of sailing ships and intra-coastal shipping, and the business quarter had shifted two blocks away from the rotting wharves and crumbling warehouses that bespoke the heyday of its seaport existence. The once prosperous and active waterfront area had fallen almost completely into disuse, and the city's remaining commercial strip gave ample evidence of its former residential origins: The classic lines of Georgian and Victorian houses rose above the polished marble and glass facades of first floor businesses; narrow streets and winding alleyways were clogged with the traffic they were never designed to carry; church spires stood in lonely vigil over neighborhoods without residents.[12]

Because the downtown commercial center was already struggling to overcome its competitive handicaps, further expansion in the commercial sector was not practical; instead, the People's planners looked to development of the downtown's noncommercial advantages as the only hope for its crowded, misplaced businesses. For this reason, they looked to expansion of the city's cultural and waterfront potential as a way to keep customers in the vicinity of downtown shops.[13] At the time, redevelopment laws forbade the taking of commercial or industrial areas,[14] even those that were abandoned and delinquent in tax payments,[15] and so the planners were forced to seek municipal expenditures that would stimulate private construction. For this reason they turned their attention to two theme-oriented extensions to the downtown, both of which combined a minimum of needed public spending as an inducement to attract private development efforts.

The first proposal focused on a Cultural Center to be located just to the northwest of the existing downtown commercial strip. Major cultural attractions already existed with the Norfolk Museum (now the Chrysler Museum of Art) at one end and the city's Center Theater/Civic Auditorium complex at the other end of the designated area; in addition, the Planning Commission had convinced the Library Board to relocate its main branch to new facilities to be built in the center. The area already possessed an urbane and international feeling, enhanced by the classic lines of the Georgian and federal architecture of the neighboring Ghent and Freemason Street areas. The nearby Smith Creek Marina and the Hague Yacht Basin, with its footpaths, bridges, and waterfront park, were popular havens both for boaters who followed the Intracoastal Waterway and others looking for a respite from the fast pace of urban living. The Commission hoped to build on this recreational quality of the area by relocating the Confederate Monument, the city's obeisance to its Southern heritage, to a minipark to be constructed in the middle, hoping that it would serve to attract lunch-hour picnickers and pedestrian traffic to the area. A second benefit of the minipark would be that it would help to rechannel traffic into the downtown area in a more acceptable pattern; at the time, five of the city's main downtown commuter streets—Llewellyn Avenue, Olney Road, Duke, Boush, and High (now Virginia Beach Boulevard) streets—met in the middle of the proposed Cultural Center and wound their way tortuously into the main downtown commercial district.[16]

The Planning Commission hoped to use this new Cultural Center, replete with its parks, library, museum, theater, marina, and modern traffic connectors, to attract other similar cultural enterprises to this common area. The planners hoped that trade delegations and emissaries from the North Atlantic Treaty Organization countries would relocate into a consulate's row in the area, thereby continuing the international flavor already imparted by the Hague and nearby Ghent neighborhood. The Commission was attempting to encourage some of the city's leading charities and civic organizations to seek adjacent sites, and its members were confident that once the Cultural Center began to take shape, a major convention hotel would buy a site in the area. The Silkstocking businessmen and the various boards and commissions associated with the planning of the center were trying to use their contacts to convince the city's major enterprises to relocate their headquarters in the vicinity. The city was even reserving a site next to the museum and proposed library for an aquarium or naval museum.[17] Plans for the Cultural Center were ambitious, but they seemed realistic enough considering the constraints of the period; the planners had every reason to believe that local businesses, restaurants, specialty shops, and sidewalk cafés would be attracted by the combination of public and private construction, fleshing out a new vitality to an area just outside of the narrow confines of the existing downtown commercial strip.[18] The public funds required to support the undertaking were not large, and those earmarked for library construction and street improvements were necessary regardless of the success of the rest of the project. Enthusiasm for the plan was especially strong during 1951 and 1952, while C. A. Harrell was still manager, and before the People's movement had wholly lost its advisory role in municipal affairs.

At about this time, planners were also attempting to develop a parallel proposal to improve the city's deteriorating waterfront area; they knew that here, too, a similar combination of public expenditures for parks and promenades, plus the right kind of private investment, could attract a contingent of outdoor cafés and specialty shops. A number of proposals were being bandied about, including designs for a seawall, amphitheater, small boat marina, high-rise luxury apartment buildings, new City Hall/Civic Center complex, naval museum, private housing developments, *cordon bleu* seafood restaurant, seafood market, and bazaar.[19] The most promising proposal for waterfront development came from the Norfolk Port Authority, a creation of the old People's City Council. Members of the Authority hoped to unite many of the aspects of earlier proposals around a single, two-staged development designed both to attract new investment and to encourage improvement of existing properties. Phase One focused on the construction of a huge concrete pier that would extend far enough out into the main shipping channel to accommodate the loading and unloading of even the deepest draft vessels. Space along the pier would be rented out to shipping and freight forwarding concerns, and on the shore, as Phase Two, a large quay would be built broad enough to accommodate both drayage and specialty shops, travel agents, seafood vendors, a produce market, restaurants, and outdoor cafés.[20]

Plans for both these projects—the harbor quay and the Cultural Center—advanced just as rapidly as they would have under the People's administration; the city's volunteer boards and commissions proceeded in a vacuum as if they had the same power and responsibilities as before. The Port Authority began to buy up property at the foot of Commercial Place and West Main Street and to aggressively line up prospects for space on the quay among the local merchants and out-of-town investors.[21] The City Planning Commission was moving just as aggressively to line up prospects for its own development at the other end of the downtown area: The Salvation Army, Union Mission, IBM, and other leading corporations and charities were already moving into new facilities in the Cultural Center. Thus, by the time the city council was approached for approval, both projects were well off the drawing boards and fast becoming a reality.

No official reason was ever given for the rejection of either proposal; in fact, the Council seems never to have docketed the items or given them public audience. In spite of widespread enthusiasm and the editorial endorsements of the *Virginian-Pilot* and *Ledger-Dispatch*, both projects were accorded a low-profile, back-burner status that was unusual for such full-blown and well-planned undertakings. The only official action that was ever taken on either project concerned the Library Board's request to relocate the main library to a new site in the Cultural Center: For four years the Council delayed consideration, and then finally announced in August of 1956 that the Cultural Center was "a long-range undertaking [that] has been accorded a lower priority" than other city projects.[22] It was a heavy blow to all who had hoped for an East Ghent commercial revival, and even though portions of the project still survived independent of the others, the idea for a Cultural Center in downtown Norfolk was dead. The Port Authority, too, was forced to abandon its plans, and later settled for less expensive arrangements far removed from the downtown area.

Thus, by the winter of 1956, every major program of renewal or revitalization left over from the People's administration had either been fully activated or quietly put aside; the powers that controlled city hall had shifted dramatically in the decade since the rise of the Silkstocking Ticket. No longer were the city's volunteer boards and commissions, or the business and civic elite they represented, a power in the planning and decision-making process; just like the Norfolk Redevelopment and Housing Authority and the Land (Kaufman) Committee, which were then planning the Oakwood Redevelopment Project, they were operating in a vacuum without political authority.

The appearance that the city ran so smoothly under the mayor's direction was no accident; Duckworth had made a special point to eliminate any opportunity for factionalism or opposition on the city council before it could emerge. Councilmen and city managers came and went at city hall so rapidly during this era that one could easily see why Mayor Duckworth, even if he had not been a forceful leader, would be quickly recognized as the only stable force in the city's administration. Councilmen were chosen from the broad ranks of independent but small-time businessmen—insurance agents, wholesalers, real estate brokers, and shopkeepers—who were successful overachievers in their calling, but who exhibited no remarkable capacity for independent action. None came to city hall with any special following from either prior municipal experience, volunteer service, or through leadership in the business or civic community, and each owed his advancement entirely to Duckworth and those around him.

    The circumstances behind an individual's selection to elective office at this time remain clouded, partly because the unofficial nominating process was shrouded in enough secrecy to preserve both the political viability of the chosen and the continued domination of the selectors. Just as his own 1950 Harmony Ticket had been engineered by some considerable behind-the-scenes maneuvering, Duckworth and those around him apparently never trusted the election process to elevate men of good standing and high ability to the city council. Two old standbys of the Byrd Organization were employed in Norfolk to tightly control the nominating and elective processes: first, the official slate of Duckworth-endorsed candidates was held in secrecy until its announcement at the last moment before the filing deadline, thereby eliminating those Prieur Organization hopefuls who had been passed over in the unofficial nominating process. Secondly, those who ran for elective office were not always those who served: Mayor Duckworth and those around him perfected the Organization's "planned incumbency" scheme whereby a trusted incumbent would stand for reelection and, once elected, mysteriously resign so that a carefully selected successor could fill the slot without risking the perils of popular election; the newcomer would then have the advantages of an incumbent's experience and exposure when he stood for reelection in his own right two years later. Advancement by appointment had become a time-honored tradition in Virginia—most of the state's senators, congressmen, and other top officeholders had advanced at least once in this manner— and it quickly became a hallmark as well of Norfolk City government: thus in 1953, newcomer Roy B. Martin, Jr., was selected to fill the seat vacated when Councilman James M. Williams resigned; Lewis L. Layton similarly took over in 1956 when incumbent Robert F. Ripley stepped down shortly after winning reelection;[23] and Linwood F. Perkins was appointed in early 1957 when Councilman Ezra Summers died in office.[24] Norfolk was so obviously bypassing the popular election process that the *Virginian-Pilot* targeted the Duckworth administration for their lack of political decorum:

> It is a sounder procedure to give the voters a little advance notice before selecting a successor to a man they elected to office. Settling the whole problem behind closed doors is not good procedure even if the result, in all other respects, is satisfactory.[25]

Most observers conceded that Duckworth had the final word in the unofficial nominating process that selected candidates for municipal office in Norfolk. This was no mean achievement when one considers the enormous control exerted by Billy Prieur and his Organization during their heyday, but Prieur had apparently lost interest in municipal affairs since the near-demise of his political machine during the People's administration. Instead, like many other of his contemporaries in the statewide Byrd Organization, he had resigned himself to a lesser role. Local experts point to Prieur's acceptance of an increasingly moderate and independent-acting "Young Turk" legislative delegation as a sign of his lessening involvement in the candidate selection and election process.[26] The Young Turks were so named because they were mostly men in their early thirties, who, although members of the Organization, sometimes refused to back the old Byrd hierarchy. Most were war veterans or urban legislators like Norfolk's own Walter Paige, Theodore Pilcher, Toy Savage, and Jack Rixey, who bucked the Organization establishment to support issues of urban concern or racial moderation. In one sense they well represented Norfolk's urbane constituency, and were thus good selections, but in another sense, the Billy Prieur of the 1930s would never have brooked such independence.

All across the state the Organization was in decline, and, especially in its urban areas, was giving way to new leadership groups such as the Young Turks or Mayor Duckworth's businessmen's coalition. Billy Prieur, who had always preferred the seclusion of the back room to the spotlight of public recognition, was now apparently content to accept a partnership role with Duckworth that placed the mayor in the limelight. No one is really sure who held the upper hand, if indeed either party dominated the arrangement, for both men had powerful egos, and neither would have allowed himself to play a secondary role. It seems more probable that Duckworth and Prieur, both conservatives, were in basic agreement on most major matters, and that each held his own unchallengeable dominion.

Prieur controlled state and federal patronage; Duckworth, on the other hand, controlled municipal policy without interference from Prieur.[27] The Prieur Machine seemed to have evolved away from the corruption that existed during the boom period of the war years, and, once battered by the municipal housecleaning during the People's era, now seemed content to concentrate on the less important "favors" of government that kept its machinery alive: patronage, purchasing, permits, enforcement, and promotions, especially in the more political Police and Fire Departments.[28] With a strongman at the helm of government, Prieur and the Organization seemed both unable and unwilling to challenge the authority of the mayor, thus giving him free rein to direct basic policy as he wished.[29]

If the people were worried that all this power, both political and governmental, was concentrated in the office of their mayor, they gave little indication of such concern. By and large, those advanced by Duckworth and his advisors to both political office and appointive positions were men and women of good character who were probably more representative than the selections of the Silkstocking crowd. If a special danger existed in establishing Duckworth as a benevolent dictator, it would come from one of several quarters. First, the mayor might lose touch with the public will; he had made so many of the City's decisions without public input that he might now discover that he had lost the ability to listen. Second, because the people had been so silent, there was a danger that if a small and vocal minority ever became well organized, then the mayor might overreact to its pronouncements. Also, the mayor's famous temper might intrude upon his otherwise sound judgement. Already city hall was abuzz with rumors about individuals, even respected members of the city's business and professional society, who had dared to oppose the mayor or one of his programs, even in a minor way, only to find their livelihood threatened.[30] Stories also existed about how even senior City officials who had attempted to question a Duckworth decision had been publicly humiliated by the mayor in a tirade of verbal abuse.[31] These, however, were only petty examples of an even greater danger; so far no one knew just how far the mayor might go in a fit of pique to destroy a political opponent or some other, greater threat to his administration. Earlier in the decade, blacks had experienced a pattern of mayoral revenge for their political deviation, and the Broad Creek Shores controversy had shown that the mayor was not above employing his official powers to punish his opposition, but these actions only hinted at the even greater dangers that lay ahead now that Mayor Duckworth had achieved full domination over every phase of municipal operation.

Finally, in spite of all his power and demonstrated skills, Mayor Duckworth had not yet put his authority to work on any of his own programs. The People's Council and City Manager C. A. Harrell had left behind a very precisely planned and carefully orchestrated program of action, and Duckworth's success in bringing those plans to reality had brought him much well-deserved popularity and unparalleled economic stability to the city. Now, however, the People's program was past—Norfolk Redevelopment and Housing Authority's Project One was concluding; the last units of public housing were under construction; the bridge-tunnel connector to Portsmouth was open; the ambitious annexation program was complete; hundreds of new classrooms had been added to the school system; new water and sewer works were already on line; revamped health, housing, sanitation, and building codes were being enforced; and the area was going through the greatest building boom in its history.[32] If the mayor had an agenda of his own, it was a secret as closely guarded as the names of his running mates in the next councilmanic election. Now that all these projects were complete, and the People's follow-up phase of development had been rejected, Norfolk was about to enter a new stage of growth that would carry Duckworth's distinctive and, as yet undiscernible, stamp.

Now at the peak of both his political and municipal power, Mayor Duckworth was at last preparing to launch his own program of development, only this time there was no fanfare, no minority advisors, no citizen involvement, and no prior publicity. That was not his style; Duckworth moved in a more deliberate and purposeful manner, unhampered by either the open accessibility or the frenzy of participatory democracy that had seemed to bog his predecessors down as much in the form as in the substance of government. The Duckworth style involved instead both the acquisition of power and the display of its use, and he had done well in both regards, having constructed the base for unparalleled personal control from the blueprints left over from the Silkstocking reformers. Now, however, the last of the People's programs was either completed or put away forever: The Cultural Center, harbor quay, and Oakwood redevelopment project had all been tabled, and the city's priorities under Duckworth would shift away from developing its assets and turn toward destroying its liabilities. Chief among the liabilities was the impending school desegregation crisis, now bottled up in the federal courts on a string of technicalities that could snap at any moment. Since Mayor Duckworth had not yet spoken out on the desegregation issue, few residents could have guessed that in the coming months he would attempt to deal so directly with the crisis, using the powers of city government to oppose the threat of forced integration as if it were just another political rival. The stakes in such an undertaking were frighteningly high—the desegregation controversy was more than just a collection of human opponents; it would become the major force of change in the nation for the next decade. At the time, however, few people could discern how powerful that force would become, and all across the Commonwealth political leaders were hastening to erect paper barriers and legal obstacles to divert the onslaught of desegregation. Duckworth alone emerged with a plan carefully contrived to construct more permanent breastworks, and had this effort succeeded, it probably would have been imitated all across the nation. Still, few men anywhere in municipal government were in a better position to hazard such a venture: Few men could match Mayor Duckworth's record of municipal accomplishment, partisan consensus, and personal leadership. Even so, the risk was just apparent enough that the mayor saw fit to hedge his bets in secrecy and couch his plan in the guise of the priorities of the old People's group. This was a masterful stroke: No matter how comprehensive the endeavor, if it failed, he would be able to step clear from its liabilities and disavow the complicity of his involvement.

Redevelopment leapt suddenly to the forefront of municipal policy, just as it had during the heyday of the People's administration, and events began to move rapidly—too rapidly for the citizens to fully comprehend either their significance or their comprehensiveness. In December 1956, the Norfolk Redevelopment and Housing Authority announced the commencement of two new undertakings, both begun after the mayor had forcefully suggested their initiation.[33] N.R.H.A. Project Two would clear just over 37 acres of blighted housing in the Lambert's Point section of the city,[34] providing much-needed growing room to the Norfolk Division of the College of William and Mary and Virginia Polytechnic Institute (now Old Dominion University), enabling it to break out of the narrow confines of its two-year preparatory and trade school curriculum. The second project proposed to bulldoze 90 acres in the Atlantic City portion of Norfolk,[35] the chief beneficiary of which would be Norfolk General Hospital, another popular, landlocked public institution. Before the project could even be approved, an additional 45 acres were added to accommodate long-standing plans left over from the days of the People's administration to improve adjacent health, highway, and tunnel facilities.

In marked contrast to N.R.H.A. Project One and the Oakwood Project proposed by the Silkstocking establishment, no housing, either public or private, was planned in either Atlantic City or the Old Dominion (N.R.H.A. Project Two) Project, even though the combined area of the two new developments was more than twice the size of the People's N.R.H.A. Project One—the Atlantic City area alone contained close to 1,000 dwellings. As a matter of fact, the N.R.H.A. was just beginning to embark upon another venture which would destroy an additional 2,600 dwellings that would have been ideal to ease the relocation of refugees from these two new redevelopment initiatives. By annexation, Norfolk had acquired Broad Creek Village, a 468-acre wartime housing project still occupied by the families of government and military workers. In spite of strong protests from the Navy,[36] the N.R.H.A. planned to raze those dwellings to make room for a mammoth industrial park, thereby compounding further the relocation problem.

Bulldozers were still roaring through the dwellings in the Atlantic City, Broad Creek, and Old Dominion projects when the N.R.H.A announced a fourth venture, the Downtown Redevelopment Project. In a carefully concerted attack, the N.R.H.A. swept bare more than 200 acres in the oldest part of the city.[37] The central focus of the assault was Norfolk's notorious East Main Street "sin strip," where once a vast array of bars, honkytonks, flophouses, amusement palaces, tattoo parlors, and burlesques had entertained "the Fleet" and brought disrepute to more legitimate downtown businesses. More than 400 commercial structures would fall in this massive attempt to wipe out a repugnant merchandising industry, and another 485 residences would be razed without the addition of any new public housing units for their evacuees.[38]

With the initiation of these four nearly simultaneous endeavors—the Atlantic City, Old Dominion, Broad Creek, and Downtown Projects—the city was destroying a sizeable share of its developed land—more than 800 acres were scheduled for clearance—in exchange for new opportunities for growth. This new phase of redevelopment was unquestionably the mayor's: Although none of the four projects were new ideas to his administration—all four had been kicked around, along with numerous other proposals, among the various planning and advisory commissions—the enormous scope of this undertaking was entirely Duckworth's invention;[39] the size of the projects, the coordination of the endeavor, the speed with which they were initiated, and even the rationale for such dramatic action, all derived their impetus from his character. In pure size, this new phase in redevelopment was staggering: The four projects encompassed an area ten times the size of N.R.H.A. Project One, which itself was twice the size of any development that New York or any other city had attempted.[40] More than 20,000 people, almost a tenth of Norfolk's population (based upon census tract data), would be forced to flee the bulldozers in this new phase of demolition. More than 4,000 residential structures, many with several apartments, and more than 500 commercial structures would be razed in the unprecedented scope of these combined endeavors.

The speed with which all four projects were undertaken was almost as startling: Less than nine months lapsed from the announcement of the Atlantic City Project to the time that demolition work actually began in earnest; the N.R.H.A. began tearing down structures in Broad Creek almost as soon as it took title to the land from the Navy. By marked contrast, Project One had been almost three years in the planning phase before the city council had made the first appropriation, and then another full year passed before demolition work actually began. Also, by comparison, no formal plan existed for what would be done in the areas once they were cleared. Although the official explanation for all four projects was that they were desperately needed to provide room for industrial expansion, downtown development, and growth of the city's education, transportation, and health facilities, no blueprints or scale models of such enterprises were put out for public display. Either the mayor felt no need to "sell" the projects in this way, or else he really did not have any firm commitments yet for new hospital wings, educational structures, industrial firms, or commercial ventures. N.R.H.A. Project One was one-tenth the size of the new proposals, and it had still taken six years to complete, even though it was vastly overplanned in comparison.

In spite of the fact that plans for redeveloping the projects were at best only loosely formulated, the Duckworth administration had good reason to rush them off the drawing boards and into the demolition stage as quickly as possible. The rationale behind this apparent impulsiveness was not based upon any immediate demand for cleared land, for, indeed, the mayor had never placed a very high priority upon the drudgery and precision of community planning; his forte was quick and dramatic action, and the single-mindedness with which the N.R.H.A. pursued condemnation in these projects was no exception. Ironically the mayor, who had achieved his reputation by building to the People's specifications, would now turn to rapid demolition of property before new plans for its use could be fully drawn, but the simple truth remains that new construction lagged far behind in the list of municipal priorities. The new focus was upon clearing land where existing uses were seriously threatening the continued prosperity of the city. It is easy to see why the sleazy bars and honkytonks, the festering slums, and the seedy business houses scheduled for removal in the Downtown Project were undesirable land uses, but why would a city suffering an acute shortage of adequate and sanitary housing units suddenly turn to destroy more than 3,500 units with decent plumbing? Why, too, would a city desperate for low-cost housing, especially for its black residents, suddenly propose to bulldoze more than 4,250 such units without planning any additional housing, either public or private?

Each of the projects poses an interesting contradiction to sound planning practices. Broad Creek Village, for instance, was unquestionably ideal for future industrial development, but it would take years to fill the 468-acre site. In the meantime the area was occupied by 2,600 individual family homes, all less than fifteen years old and all equipped with modern sewage and sanitation facilities. Although the homes had been built by the Navy during the war as demountable units, prefabrication was becoming more and more the rule in new home construction. Uncertainty about the future of the village had undoubtedly contributed to its decline, but the area still showed signs of health and usefulness as a solid working-class community. Broad Creek Village had served a very unique and successful purpose as a settlement of wartime government housing, but shortly after the Korean War, the Navy sought to sever its relationship as landlord and turn that function over to public housing agencies like the Norfolk Redevelopment and Housing Authority. Since N.R.H.A. Executive Director Larry Cox had indicated his opposition to operating Broad Creek Village as either low-income or public housing,[41] area residents were bitterly opposed to the N.R.H.A. takeover. Because the property was technically in a portion of Norfolk County still slated for annexation by the City, residents fought vigorously to have the Navy turn it over to either the county or to some sort of tenant-sponsored mutual ownership organization. The N.R.H.A. publicly persisted in its desire to demolish the entire tract, and this bitterness between the tenants and the new landlord helped to speed the deterioration of the village once the N.R.H.A. actually took over management. Angry residents blamed deterioration on the N.R.H.A. for its failure to perform simple maintenance duties, but the condition can just as easily be traced back to the residents themselves, who, because of uncertainty over the area's future, failed to continue the same level of upkeep as they had when the future of the project was secure under federal auspices.[42]

Hurricane Hazel struck in 1954 just as the N.R.H.A. was taking title to the property, but the debate over which agency had responsibility to repair the damage, including more than 30 carloads of missing shingles,[43] soon became a moot point. Once the N.R.H.A. assumed control, it began closing off sections and preparing the houses for demolition. The sight of barricaded streets, vandalized properties, and boarded-up buildings helped to panic the residents into agreeing to rezoning the property for industrial use in the hope that they were buying time. They thought that once the property had been rezoned and its fate secure, the N.R.H.A. would institute a program of gradual removal as development prospects solidified.[44] Their hopes, however, were short-lived; within three years most of the residents had been driven out.[45]

Regardless of which element deserves blame for the demise of Broad Creek Village, by the time the bulldozers actually began to roll through the area, blight had become rampant. What had once been valuable and relatively new housing units—all had two to three bedrooms, hardwood floors, deep sash windows, modern plumbing fixtures, and sturdy interior constructions—had degraded quickly into a full scale slum with vandalized and deserted buildings, piles of rubbish, and the look of despair that generally characterizes areas slated for demolition. In its heyday during the war and the years immediately following, when its survival had been certain, Broad Creek had been an ideal working-class community: It had almost no crime, the neighbors looked out for one another, shared a sense of purpose, and felt compassion and kinship with one another—in short, it exhibited a remarkable sense of community and spirit. By the end of the war it had lost its appearance as a military camp, and residents worked feverishly to tend their gardens, improve their dwelling, and save up enough to purchase their own unit. Although out in the county, Broad Creek natives felt that they had their own little city: It had its own schools, churches, parks, playgrounds, stores, and commercial areas; for more than 5,000 people it was "home," and for many their first real home. No wonder that its residents fought so bitterly against the proposal to tear the structures down; they could not believe that with all the newly annexed farmland, Norfolk could not find a better place for industry than on top of their homes.

Ironically, more than 30 years after Broad Creek Village was razed, many of its original "slum" dwellings still stand in other parts of the city: Some of the residents refused to have their units torn down, bought them from the N.R.H.A. for a couple of hundred dollars, and then paid to have them moved to other sites.[46]

Broad Creek Village was not, however, the only area where residents blamed the Norfolk Redevelopment and Housing Authority for hastening decline by spreading rumors of destruction. When Norfolk leaders first began talking, back in 1949, about large-scale renewal of the aging neighborhoods on the fringe of the downtown area, Atlantic City was one of the few predominantly white areas mentioned in the early speculations.[47] Founded around the cotton mill, Fort Norfolk, the seafood industry, and small boat marinas, Atlantic City had been one of Norfolk's first suburbs, predating Ghent, its richer cousin across the Hague (Smith Creek), by almost a decade. Since Atlantic City contained the industries that supported the "carriage set" who lived in Ghent, most of its dwelling units were working-class row houses or multi-family structures. These lent themselves easily to overcrowding and exploitation by nonresident landlords during the critical housing shortage that prevailed throughout World War II and the years immediately following, but these conditions were found in even the city's finest neighborhoods. As rumors of its redevelopment spread, however, those same property owners were understandably unwilling to undertake major repairs or improvements, and the area took on many of the appearances of a "blighted" neighborhood.[48] Even so, however, Atlantic City should have been just the sort of neighborhood that the newly revamped health, housing, and building codes were supposed to rehabilitate. Much of the housing scheduled for removal in the Downtown Project had unquestionably deteriorated beyond repair: Census tract studies indicate that more than 80 percent of the units had inadequate plumbing facilities, 96 percent were built before 1920, 94 percent were without any form of central heating, and the median contract rent in 1949 had been only $14.51 per month.[49] The Atlantic City Project, however, proves a sharp contrast: In 1949, at a time when the severe housing crisis in the community had precipitated subdividing many older homes into multi-unit apartments, almost a quarter of the Atlantic City homes were still single-family, freestanding houses; another fourth were duplexes, a popular building style in many older neighborhoods; and close to 20 percent of the homes were less than thirty years old. In addition, more than 70 percent of the units had adequate plumbing (two apartments that shared a bathroom, a common practice in the city, were downgraded in the census as having inadequate plumbing). More than half the units had central heating, and the median contract rent was $34.86, twice the value of the structures torn down in both the Downtown Redevelopment Project or N.R.H.A. Project One.[50] Undoubtedly, a number of structures had deteriorated beyond rehabilitation, even by today's standards in which restoring older, central-city homes has become fashionable, but many of the deficiencies noted in the census were not only in keeping with existing city codes, but they were also common practices during the local wartime and postwar housing crises.[51]

Ironically, Atlantic City was chosen by the Norfolk Health Department for a major code-enforcement initiative precisely because of the overall quality of its structures and the fact that they were so salvageable. Since federally funded redevelopment projects required that the locality rehabilitate one living unit for each unit torn down, Norfolk had adopted one of the first comprehensive minimum housing codes in the country. Because Norfolk was only the second city in the nation (the other was Baltimore) to attempt large scale enforcement of its code, the Health Department was looking for a neighborhood that was good enough to salvage, but not so bad that code enforcement efforts would make little difference. After careful analysis of the 1950 census data and preliminary field work, the Health Department chose Atlantic City for the first concentrated housing code enforcement effort in the nation. When the staff of the Health Department met with N.R.H.A. Executive Director Larry Cox, they were told that the City had no plans to begin any redevelopment activity in Atlantic City for "at least five to ten years," and that were other areas of the city rated a much "higher priority."[52] According to the former Director of Environmental Health G. D. Monola, who led the code enforcement project, the only badly deteriorated section of Atlantic City lay along the site of today's Brambleton Avenue. Because this area had mixed commercial, industrial, and residential uses, rental units had been allowed by absentee landlords to degenerate. Black families displaced by Project One had begun moving into this section, but because it was separate from the other residential blocks, there was none of the violence or strong community reaction that had occurred in Brambleton or Coronado. In short, Atlantic City had "integrated without any difficulty . . . without any fanfare, any publicity, or Klan activity."[53] Moreover, the fact that blacks were now moving into these units meant that they could command higher rents, and the landlords were thus more willing to make the investments necessary to bring the dwellings up to code.

For this reason, the sudden announcement of the demolition of the entire area caught both the residents and the Health Department by surprise. The code-enforcement project had just been completed, and nearly every dwelling had been brought up to the city's new minimum housing code, some at considerable cost to the property owners. According to Monola, the Health Department had been meeting regularly with the N.R.H.A. executive staff, and demolition of the neighborhood was not mentioned until it was announced in the press. The fact that the N.R.H.A. had used the Health Department surveys as justification for the demolition helped to deepen the rift between the two agencies. Although there were a "surprisingly large number of owner-occupied dwellings" in the area and most of the buildings were well worth saving, especially now that they had been rehabilitated, the N.R.H.A. persisted in its effort, against the advice of the Health Department, to push for demolition of the entire area. Although a building might meet all the requirements of the city's minimum housing code and still have major defects, the Health Department felt that the N.R.H.A. had gone overboard in its rush to expand the project beyond the fairly restricted area of blight. Block after block where only a few defects were listed were also included, but because these were lumped together with the worst houses, the entire area was able to meet the minimum requirement of five defects per dwelling to qualify for federal funding.

Thus, in an ironical twist, the Atlantic City housing units that had been rehabilitated as a result of N.R.H.A. Project One, were then torn down in Norfolk's second phase of redevelopment. Residents were furious with the Health Department, especially when they learned that the appraisal of their property from the N.R.H.A. was less than the amount they had just spent to bring their dwellings up to the minimum housing code. The Health Department's code enforcement effort suffered as a result of the uproar, and disagreements over the size and scope of the Atlantic City project eventually led to a split between the two agencies; no longer would the Health Department help in the housing rehabilitation efforts of the N.R.H.A.,[34] and even in 1992 the City still operates two separate housing agencies with overlapping authority, mission, and purpose.

Obviously, after eight years of rumored destruction, and the general state of despair and disrepair that follows such rumors, portions of the Atlantic City neighborhood were in danger of becoming a slum. The Norfolk Redevelopment and Housing Authority pointed to the Health Department surveys as proof that it had higher incidence of tuberculosis, venereal disease, juvenile delinquency, dilapidated housing, racial unrest, crimes, fires, and rat infestation than other neighborhoods in the city,[55] but the residents complained that all of these had come to the area since the talk of redevelopment:

> It seems that considerable time and effort has gone into preparing reports by various functions of the city government to show that Atlantic City has been a detriment to the rest of the city. If it was such a blight . . . and its effects so far

reaching . . . wouldn't this fact have been so outstanding that it would speak for itself without having to be figured to prove it?[56]

Few citizens and even fewer organizations were willing to take up these cries and oppose the project. Only those most affected by demolition—the owners of homes, apartment buildings, or commercial properties in the area—showed any inclination to fight. The most vigorous opposition came not from the residents, but rather from yachting enthusiasts and environmentalists who opposed the Brambleton Avenue bridge that would close the Smith Creek Marina.[57] Replacing the old two-lane drawbridge with a broad fixed span was, however, one of the few necessary proposals in the project: Norfolk desperately needed another thoroughfare connecting the downtown area with Hampton Boulevard, and the Brambleton Avenue route offered the best alternative.[58] Moreover, almost all of the deteriorated dwellings in the project area could have been demolished by careful placement of this one highway alone. The rest not only could have been spared, they were truly worth saving.[59]

Other aspects of the Atlantic City Project were either too vague for thorough assessment, too long-term in their design, too haphazard in their application, or else so incompatible with the other developments as to be strikingly ill-conceived. The project area itself was a strange configuration that zigged and zagged its way from Claremont Avenue in West Ghent to Monticello Avenue in downtown Norfolk, never stretching more than just a few blocks in width (see Figure 3, page 87). The lines were purposely drawn to exclude certain blocks, specific commercial and industrial structures, and even single residences from demolition, while the area around them was completely leveled. The 700 block of Yarmouth Street, for instance, was spared by an odd gerrymandering of the district, while the neighboring 700 blocks of Botetourt, Dunmore, and Duke Streets were slated for removal. All the waterfront property along the southern edge of Smith Creek was slated for demolition while the rotting wharves, sagging warehouses, and crumbling storage facilities on the Elizabeth River a block away were spared.

Outside of the close to 40 acres that would be used for hospital, public health, highway, and tunnel facilities, there was little reason for including the rest of the area at this time. Plans for their use were as yet unspecified, but the N.R.H.A. felt that the remaining 95 acres would provide a basis for industrial sites, semiluxury apartments, and improvements along the Hague (Smith Creek) waterfront,[60] yet none of these uses was fully compatible with the realities of the site: The proposed path of Brambleton Avenue swung too close to the southern border of the Hague to render anything but a corner on each edge of the remaining waterfront property suitable for these purposes. If the area was ever to have a real future as a high-rise or luxury housing development, the sites along the Elizabeth River should have been cleared. Similarly, the 56 acres that were set aside for light industry had little hope of attracting prospective customers when realistically compared to the 468 acres of prime industrial land being opened up in Broad Creek. In addition to major rail and highway connections, Broad Creek Industrial Park was close to both the central business district and the population center of the entire region; its sheer size meant that a number of related manufacturing, assemblage, and storage facilities could all be located in close proximity. The Atlantic City Project offered instead a number of smaller, oddly-shaped parcels which carried the higher taxation rate and building restrictions inherent in a downtown location.

In sharp contrast to earlier endeavors of the People's administration, planning of the public expenditure portion of the project was more than just vague, it was counterproductive. Only the proposals for highway facilities and tunnel access ramps were fully conceived before demolition began. It was true that Norfolk's hospital and public health needs would grow in coming years, but the Atlantic City Project proposed to clear in 1957 land for expansion of the medical center complex that would not be occupied for at least twenty years in the future. At the other end of the project, the N.R.H.A. was condemning the land around the Norfolk Museum upon which the People's planners had once hoped to build the Cultural Center extension of the downtown business district. Because of the city's extensive involvement with the Downtown Redevelopment Project—more than 200 acres in the heart of the city's commercial district were swept bare and "only a dozen buildings were left standing, giving the downtown the appearance of having been ravaged by a massive air raid"[61]—the library, monument park, civic center, and other public expenditures were needed instead to help fill in the hole left by demolitions farther downtown. The land where the People's

Figure 3 – Atlantic City Redevelopment Project

Included in the Project
A   Patrick Henry Elementary (white)
B   Mixed-race areas housing 13 plaintiffs in the school desegregation suit
C   Norfolk General Hospital/Medical School complex

Excluded from the Project
1   Fort Norfolk and waterfront industrial area
2   Proposed Norfolk Cultural Center (never built)
3   Norfolk (now Chrysler) Museum
4   Center Theatre/Municipal Auditorium complex

planners once hoped to attract a convention hotel, consulates' row, charity headquarters, outdoor cafés, and specialty shops was given over instead to long-term parking lots, open fields, and misplaced convenience stores. Hopes for a Cultural Center and other orderly expansions of the central business district were decimated by the sudden oversupply of vacant land that now ringed the downtown.

Clearly, there was no immediate need for all the vacant land that had suddenly been made available through the enormous scope of this new redevelopment activity. Although each of the four projects had a noble purpose at its heart—expansion of industrial, highway, tunnel, education, or medical facilities—none evidenced any of the signs of precision and clarity of purpose that had so completely characterized the endeavors of the People's administration. When one considers the tremendous destructive force unleashed upon the city in these four new enterprises, the more than 800 acres scheduled for clearance, the 20,000 individuals uprooted, the demolition of whole communities, the heavy financial burden that would be carried even far into the future, and the tremendous urgency with which the whole affair was undertaken, it becomes obvious that some underlying ulterior motive knit these projects together into a unified plan, and that, whatever the objective, immediate demolition of properties that had somehow become offensive was a far higher priority than rebuilding. Duckworth had proven himself to be too skillful at administration during the "Building Phase" to so lose control during the "Bulldozer Era;" he had shown too great a mastery of power politics not to be brokering some sort of deal with these developments.

※ ※ ※

The Bulldozer Era

Views of Norfolk's seaside neighborhood of Atlantic City, near downtown, before, during and after redevelopment.
Sargeant Memorial Collection;
Tim Rudzienski

5

✺ ✺ ✺ ✺ ✺

Redevelopment Rationales

THE PROCESS OF PLANNING and redevelopment had come full circle in Norfolk: What had begun under the People's administration as a noble attempt to build the great city of the future had become corrupted by more pressing political and social concerns. Thus Norfolk, because it was the very first city in the nation to attempt redevelopment and among the earliest to initiate urban renewal on any large scale, also became one of the early leaders at manipulating its exemplary purposes to serve a more personal, partisan end. Redevelopment in Norfolk had fallen from its position as part of an overall program of community improvement, and had instead become but one weapon in the arsenal of a powerful political leader, one who was willing to employ this new tool to chastise his enemies, reward his supporters, and otherwise strengthen his grasp on municipal government. Mayor Duckworth was not so much trying to rebuild Norfolk as attempting to redesign it in a more personally acceptable form; in so doing he was guided as much by the vagaries of redevelopment law as he was by more salient considerations.

Although Norfolk's four redevelopment projects proposed massive new public and quasi-governmental facilities—new hospital, public health, educational, highway, tunnel, and municipal structures—all of these, and in fact most of the other elements associated with the renewal plans, could have been achieved without subjecting the city to the tremendous destruction necessitated by redevelopment. Norfolk already had the power under its grant of eminent domain to acquire private land for just such public uses, but the city was attracted by the additional grant of authority offered by redevelopment. Under redevelopment, a city could legally acquire private property, clear it, and then resell it to new and different private owners. This was supposed to correct the misuse of valuable urban land, but instead, it encouraged cities like Norfolk to acquire more land than they could ever use. Redeveloping areas, as opposed to just condemning the land necessary for public facilities, actually rewarded cities for expanding the scope of their public works proposals: First, it allowed them to acquire huge tracts of valuable private property that they could never have otherwise obtained; second, the cities were paid by the federal government in matching funds to clear the land for reuse; finally, redevelopment cost no more than the cities would have spent anyway on smaller scale public works projects. Thus, although it had plans to use less than a third of the acreage in the Downtown and Atlantic City Projects for public facilities, Norfolk, because it could qualify the entire area as redevelopment projects, was able to acquire close to 200 acres of additional land on the edge of the central business district, including some of the most potentially valuable commercial and waterfront sites in the city. In addition, in purchasing, clearing, and redeveloping this land, the city did not have to put up a penny more than it would have had to spend anyway on the necessary public facilities.[1]

Thus redevelopment, because it gave Norfolk these vast tracts of highly valuable land, was a boon to both the business leaders who sought to reuse the properties and the power brokers who controlled their eventual disposition. The Atlantic City and Downtown Projects were an immediate hit with the remnants of Norfolk's Silkstocking establishment for a number of other reasons. Just as in N.R.H.A. Project One, redevelopment destroyed unwanted uses of land, and it was easy to see why the old People's planners would have dreamed of wiping out parts of the two project areas. The Downtown Project contained some of the city's worst slums that, because of their close proximity to the central business district, would forever impede further commercial expansion in the downtown area; in addition, the city's notorious East Main Street "sin strip" and red-light district, Norfolk's most repugnant reminder of the shady days of its wartime past, were likewise targeted for demolition. By contrast, the housing and small commercial establishments in the Atlantic City area were not nearly as deteriorated or as offensive as those downtown, but the Silkstocking crowd had never been happy with having this deteriorating working-class community so close to Ghent, one of Norfolk's most prestigious neighborhoods, and home to most of its Silkstocking establishment. The declining fortunes of Atlantic City were a great concern to homeowners in nearby Ghent, and the N.R.H.A., one of the last bastions of the People's rule, felt that the demolition slated for the area was the only way to save Ghent from similar deterioration.[2] The Old Dominion Project also helped to create a convenient buffer zone between the working-class community of Lambert's Point and the wealthier white subdivisions nearby.

Some of the members of the old People's coalition had undoubtedly been in on planning a portion of Norfolk's new endeavors. Since 1950 the City Planning Commission had been proposing an additional access route to the downtown area by extending Hampton Boulevard; the Elizabeth River Tunnel Commission had been lobbying almost as long for another underwater link to Portsmouth in the area;[3] the city's Health Department, so much a part of the People's cleanup and code enforcement campaigns, had been in desperate need of expanded facilities for some time. For more than a decade a general consensus had prevailed among the business community that the fate of any New Norfolk would be invariably linked to proposals to expand the Norfolk's two-year college and its general hospital into vast urban educational and medical centers. Indeed, the list of those who served on the governing bodies of Norfolk General Hospital and the local division of William and Mary/Virginia Polytechnic Institute during these planning years very nearly matches any comparable listing of Norfolk's power elite during the People's administration. Not even the United Fund, the major civic endeavor of the People's group, could match the drawing power of these two popular institutions: At least five of the seven people who had served as commissioners of the N.R.H.A. had served on the hospital's board. Two city managers, two judges, one state senator, one city councilman, the school superintendent, three N.R.H.A. commissioners, two planning commissioners, two newspaper publishers, and a former governor had served in a similar capacity for the fledgling precursor to today's Old Dominion University.

Redevelopment, and especially these four new endeavors, involved a number of other factors that were immediately attractive to large segments of the business community. Especially when it was attempted on such a grand scale, redevelopment was good for business because it brought an infusion of new jobs, revenues, developmental opportunities, and numerous other spin-off and multiplier effects to the local economy. Some businessmen would obviously profit directly from the initiatives, either because they owned property affected by the projects, or because their own enterprise would participate in some stage of the work. Those firms directly involved in demolition, construction, contracting, building supply, and related activities, including many enterprises owned by the power elite of the People's era, favored these new redevelopment proposals; so did the lawyers who would handle the condemnation proceedings, the realtors who would appraise the properties, and a host of bankers, building and loan executives, real estate brokers, and others who stood to gain by having so many new people suddenly on the move. Others looked forward to unloading failing properties that might otherwise have been difficult to sell: slum housing faced with major renovations under the beefed-up health and housing codes, landlords in the fading red-light district, expanding industries and commercial enterprises that needed to unload outmoded and obsolete facilities, and sagging retail establishments faced with heavy competition from suburban shopping centers. Others saw the massive clearance operation as a way to preserve the value of their investment by placing open-space barriers between their own property and deteriorated areas. Some would gain by new development possibilities already under consideration—the medical center complex, for instance, would enhance the practice of every local physician, attracting many of them to new office facilities within close proximity—while others felt they would gain by participating in planning the use of massive tracts of cleared acreage that were still uncommitted.

The myriad economic benefits of redevelopment were readily apparent to all who had participated in N.R.H.A. Project One, which had provided an unparalleled economic boost to the area, and its well-conceived Tidewater Drive industrial minipark was filled almost before it opened.[4] No one doubted that Norfolk would continue with new redevelopment proposals, and a number of plans were eagerly bandied about in the business community—some of that speculation may have made new projects necessary by hastening the decline of neighborhoods under consideration. There were also, however, some very solid reasons why no individual businessman or corporate entity would want to oppose the projects under consideration, no matter how far-fetched or ill-conceived they might be. Mayor Duckworth had never been an easy man to confront, and now, with the very special powers inherent to redevelopment, any person who openly sought to oppose the mayor, his programs, or his policies would be committing an act tantamount to social and financial suicide. With so much of the downtown and neighboring Atlantic City residential and commercial properties scheduled for clearance—326 acres with more than 500 commercial and 700 residential structures—four powerful new economic weapons fell to those who controlled the city.

Foremost among these was the power to determine the exact boundary lines of the projects, and, by inference, to decide which structures would be exempt. Since few solid commitments for either public or private development existed at the time of demolition, the N.R.H.A. had tremendous leeway in determining which structures would fall and which would be spared. Initial plans showed that only 90 acres in the Atlantic City area would be cleared,[5] but it was quickly expanded,[6] and then enlarged again[7] to include an another 50 acres of commercial properties. The final shape of the project zigged and zagged its way across a wide expanse, purposely avoiding a few commercial structures, such as the newly built Greyhound Bus garage facilities on Colley and Brambleton Avenues, and just as randomly including others for demolition.[8]

Second, the city had considerable leeway in determining the acquisition value of land scheduled for demolition. In most cases a flat fee, without regard for the actual value or condition of the structure, was offered for all buildings in a certain class. Those with buildings equal to or below the value offered were obviously satisfied; those with more valuable properties faced the costly prospect of hiring an attorney and additional appraisers in order to undergo a prolonged legal battle. One local attorney, a member of an old-line family with solid connections in the Silkstocking establishment, was willing to fight condemnation and appraisals of business properties, but in case after case he found local appraisers unwilling to buck the city: They knew that if they attested to the true value of the properties in question they would never get appraisal work from the city again.[9] Corollary to the ability to fix the value of the building was the power to actually drive down the worth of property under consideration, a not uncommon complaint from Broad Creek[10] and Atlantic City residents.[11] Robert A. Caro tells in *The Power Broker* how New York City handled recalcitrant landowners who attempted to appeal low appraisals: Bulldozers moved in to demolish uncontested properties, leaving the holdouts stranded in a vast wasteland of rubble, debris, swirling dust storms, and unguarded excavations. Electric, sewer, gas, and water lines to the remaining homes were cut by city workers. Hordes of scavengers and looters descended upon the area to pick the remaining buildings clean, and each day the holdouts had to fight their way through this tortured course of rubble, muggers, and derelicts. One resident still tried to hold out until an adjoining building with a common wall was torn down: He dropped the appeal and packed up his family before his own home collapsed.[12]

Additionally, redevelopment gave the city considerable leverage with the local banks and lending institutions. The National Bank of Commerce (later Virginia National Bank, Sovran Bank, NationsBank and now Bank of America) was the locus of power for the Silkstocking crowd: Its officers and board of directors included two former People's Ticket councilmen, two N.R.H.A commissioners, three planning commissioners, and numerous other bluebloods of the Silkstocking crowd that had once backed the People's revolution;[13] a year later Mayor Duckworth was added to the board. Not surprisingly the bank kept a sizeable portion of both the City and N.R.H.A. funds, which ran somewhere between four and five million dollars at this time.[14] In 1970, the first year that such reports were made available to the public, the N.R.H.A. kept more than a million dollars in that bank, while most of the other banks had less than a tenth that amount. One establishment lawyer willing to oppose the N.R.H.A. soon found that his business clients were refused bank loans because "they had the wrong lawyer."[15] For most other attorneys, realtors, appraisers, contractors, and building supply houses, the lure of fat fees, healthy commissions, and the purchasing power of the N.R.H.A. and the City was enough to assure support.

Finally, the city had considerable leeway over the disposition of land once it had been cleared. Redevelopment land suitable for business use was considerably cheaper than competitive sites that would still have to be cleared; thus the power to establish a pecking order to decide which business or corporate entity would be rewarded with prime building sites was an important motivator in the effort to drum up support. Whether or not the City and its agencies actually ever used its considerable powers over commercial properties, finances, and land disposition on any grand scale to force compliance and cooperation really makes very little difference; there were those, like the establishment lawyer mentioned earlier, who suffered for their token opposition to the mayor's redevelopment programs, and their example was evident to all other members of the city's commercial and professional establishment. The fact that those powers, containing both awards for cooperation and punishments for opposition, lay in hands that were not above using them to excise whatever was deemed objectionable, was enough of an incentive for at least tacit support in these undertakings. Businessmen, especially those with influence that stretched beyond the realm which the mayor could ordinarily reach, soon found that cooperation with Mayor Duckworth's redevelopment proposals could be a mutually profitable agreement; those who opposed the City or its agencies for whatever reason, faced the prospect of certain defeat anyway and probably considerable needless hardship. So those who might have spoken out to oppose plans so loosely formulated and so obviously capricious needed no other incentive to remain silent.

Thus, when the mayor ran into heavy opposition from Atlantic City residents, he quickly scheduled a second public hearing, which was packed, as one reporter described it, with members of "the leading business and financial interests representing organizations who [sic] foster the overall needs of the city."[16] With the backing of the Silkstocking establishment assured, the project was pushed through over the anguished cries of its residents. Similar support enabled the mayor to crush opposition to both the Downtown[17] and Broad Creek Projects.[18] The earlier warnings of Norfolk's newspapers—"the powers of a housing authority should be zealously guarded and used only in proven cases as a last resort"[19]—the traditional spokesmen of the business community, were now hushed. Neither paper spoke to the vast uncertainties or incongruities in the projects; instead, the

Ledger-Dispatch praised the vision of the proposals:

> This will be a dramatic second stage in a process that is giving much of Norfolk a splendid new look. But the really important factor—and the one which is encompassed in the very phrase slum clearance—is the ugly *old look* which the city is casting off.[20]

Even in its saddest editorial lament, a poignant piece that bemoaned the passing of a portion of Atlantic City that had "a Greenwich Village flavor" and a "Bohemian and cosmopolitan character," the *Virginian-Pilot* added: "Change must come and better things for the whole downtown area will be wrought through the Atlantic City Redevelopment Project.[21]

Nowhere did either paper question why so many acres had to be leveled so quickly, especially when few solid commitments for construction were evident. Perhaps access to information was really limited to the official press releases; maybe the editors were afraid to undertake an *exposé* when so much of the city lay in ruins and so much of the city's future was tied to the success of the projects, or else, as one editor later revealed, a reporter really was measured by what he knew but couldn't write.[22] The sad truth is that a local newspaper would never want to reveal the compelling motivation behind these four new redevelopment endeavors, nor would any scion of the business establishment seek to oppose the urgency of the projects. More was involved than a pressing need for new public service facilities, more than a desire to provide growing room for popular institutions, more than a longing to destroy deteriorated or unwanted properties, and more than just a desire to build a new and exciting city. The actual size and shape of the Downtown and Atlantic City Projects were in part dictated by the requirements of the controlling federal legislation. Title I of the Housing Act of 1949 forbade the taking of land for nonresidential uses, unless the area was: "(a) a slum, deteriorated or deteriorating area, and (b) is predominantly residential in character."[23]

In order to acquire the vast areas of light industries, warehouses, flophouses, commercial properties, and honky-tonks proposed, the project borders were made to wend their way through just enough slum housing to qualify the entire area as both "deteriorating" and "predominantly residential in character." The Broad Creek development, since it was not technically a redevelopment project at all but rather a gift from the Navy, was not bound by the same restrictions. The housing included in the Downtown Project undoubtedly composed one of the worst slums in the city: More than 85 percent was badly deteriorated by census estimates. But Atlantic City was no slum—in spite of massive efforts by the N.R.H.A to prove otherwise. The Atlantic City neighborhood may have been in danger of becoming a slum, and it might thereby legally qualify for clearance under the U.S. Housing Act, but Norfolk still had a number of other *bona fide* slums, like Oakwood, that should have merited first consideration for clearance long before Atlantic City; indeed, that was why the area was the prime contender for a neighborhood rehabilitation and restoration project, and not demolition. Premature talk of redevelopment and overhasty speculation about clearance had produced a dramatic change in the neighborhood—not a shift in the housing or the living conditions, but nevertheless enough of a modification of the character of its residents to vault the neighborhood to the top of the list of priorities for clearance under the political conditions of the era. This same change in the character of population, not so much the need for space or the condition of the buildings, was what doomed Broad Creek Village and the Lambert's Point neighborhood in the Old Dominion Project as well. In spite of the fact that these three projects meant the almost simultaneous uprooting of more than 4,000 families and the destruction of a large percent of the city's lower- and middle-income housing stock, the simple truth is that the city's political leaders had no interest in preserving these neighborhoods in their existing character, regardless of the condition of the structures—in fact, they were in a hurry to demolish the homes as quickly as possible.

A similar situation existed with Norfolk's schools (*see* Figure 4). Although the city had at least three schools still in service that were built before the Civil War (i.e., J. C. Smythe, Lott Carey, and John B. Goode), these buildings would see almost two more decades of service. Instead, Norfolk was proposing to tear down Broad Creek[24] and Benmoreell[25] elementary schools, both barely more than a dozen years old; close the even newer Pine Ridge Elementary[26] for a few years; and convert Patrick Henry Elementary for use as administrative offices.[27] Although Benmoreell and Broad Creek were

Figure 4 – Norfolk's Dual School System, *circa* 1954

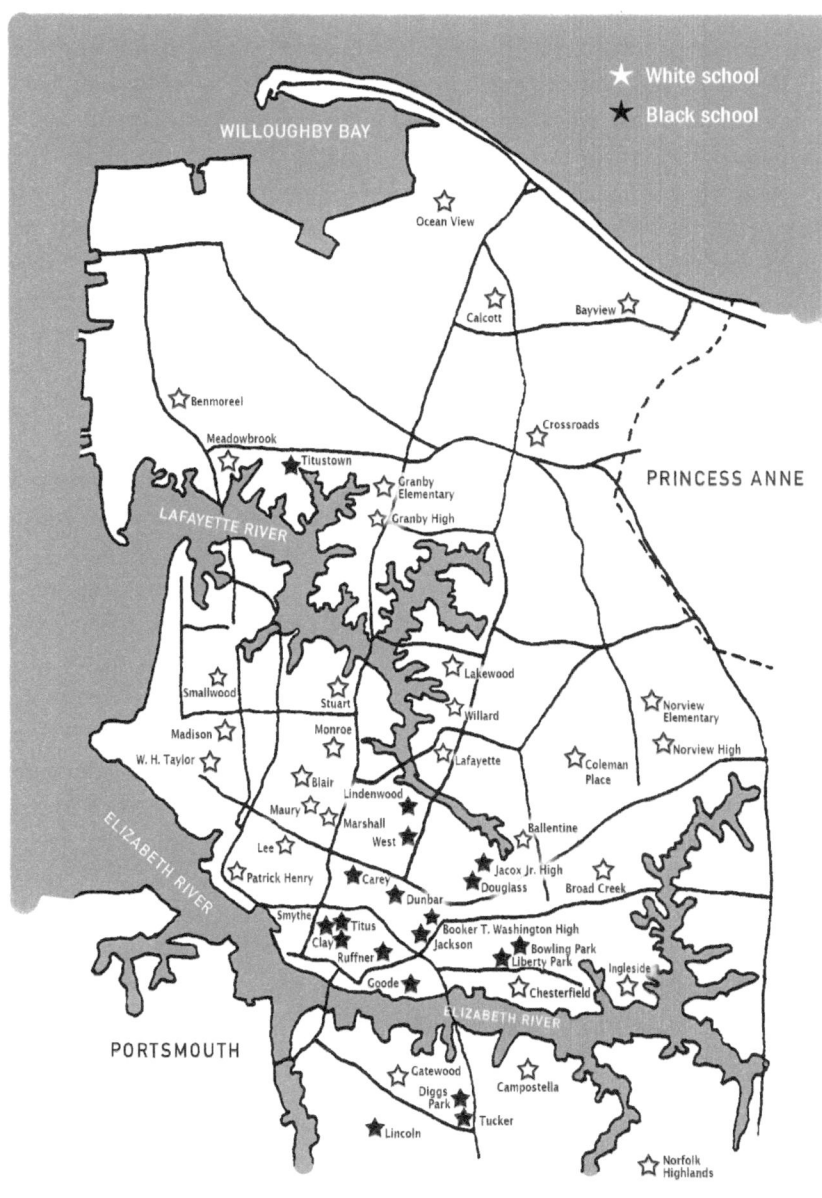

Source: *Norfolk Ledger-Dispatch*, May 18, 1954

wood frame buildings that were erected as "temporary" structures during World War II, they were still serviceable, especially if funds were invested in upkeep. Pineridge, a concrete block structure built in 1947 on a ten-acre site at Sewells Point and Progress Roads, was one of the newest elementary schools. Moreover, both Broad Creek and Pineridge were in the rapidly expanding Tanner's Creek district just annexed from Norfolk County, where the school board had just been told it needed to add four new schools a year for the next ten years.[28] Patrick Henry, built in 1892 and expanded in 1920,[29] was being converted to office use even though the school administration had been saying for years that it wanted to move out of the downtown area to a site closer to the center of the city.[30] Why would it now acquiesce to such a drastic plan of school closings, demolition, and altered use?

The reason may best be seen in the Atlantic City neighborhood: The 1950 census revealed that it was the only predominantly white area in the city where black families comprised more than ten percent of the population;[31] since that time the newspapers reported "the changing character of the neighborhood from white to Negro." Premature talk of redevelopment had helped to break down the already tenuous color barrier, and landlords who were reluctant to make major improvements to properties threatened by demolition found they could still charge higher rent to black families because of the housing crisis in the black community. One contemporary news account described the situation this way:

> The talk in Atlantic City is that property owners are realizing higher rentals from Negros [sic] than they had in the past from whites. "A lot of them are partitioning the interiors (into additional units) to get a lot more money," one resident says.

The fact that Atlantic City was a transition neighborhood going through a change in its racial makeup was underscored in a caption to a newspaper photograph: "I've no idea where I would go . . . but I won't live with Negroes all around me."[32]

Similarly, Lambert's Point, a predominantly white neighborhood, showed, even in 1950, a small concentration of blacks in the vicinity of the college;[33] by 1957, this small black community had expanded, due in part to the squeeze put on the housing market by redevelopment, the city's population explosion, and the lack of homes built especially for the black community. Broad Creek Village, on the other hand, had begun its existence in 1943 as a navy housing project for whites only, but when the armed forces were integrated after World War II, a number of black families began to appear. As uncertainty about the project's future increased in the 1950s, so also did the small percentage of black population, isolated at first in one corner of the community.[34] A similar situation existed in the Benmoreell Navy Housing Complex just outside the base: Although only a few blacks lived there in 1950,[35] their numbers had grown as whites gained other housing opportunities in the increasing number of private whites-only developments which ringed the base. Blacks had cracked the previous racial barriers in the Berkley area, and the school board noted with dismay "the pronounced tendency for whites to leave Berkley, and for Negroes to move in."[36] The Downtown Project areas, which had been predominantly black for several decades, still housed at least 19 white families.[37]

Thus, one of the major reasons for Mayor Duckworth's sudden and massive reliance upon the powers inherent in redevelopment was to accomplish the one thing that neither the courts nor the legislature, nor any political leader, local or national, could promise: Mayor Duckworth was attempting to replace *de jure* segregation (i.e., mandated by "Jim Crow" laws) with *de facto* (i.e., the separation resulting from one's choice of residence in a predominantly black or white neighborhood) segregation. The Duckworth Plan proposed to do more than just control urban blight: It aimed to wipe out all of the city's transition neighborhoods where indistinct color lines had failed to produce two distinct neighborhood school communities, one black and the other white (*see* Figure 5, page 102). The concept of geographic proximity and neighborhood schools is essential to understanding the mastery of the mayor's approach. The U.S. Supreme Court had been carefully led to its finding that separate schools were inherently unequal by meticulous documentation of unequal treatment: The *Brown* case involved the child of a black minister who was living in an otherwise all-white neighborhood. Because Linda Brown was forced by state law to go to an all-black school farther from her home than the all-white school attended by her neighbors, the Court ruled that this separate treatment of black

Figure 5 Norfolk's Racial Patterns and Redevelopment Areas, *circa* 1958

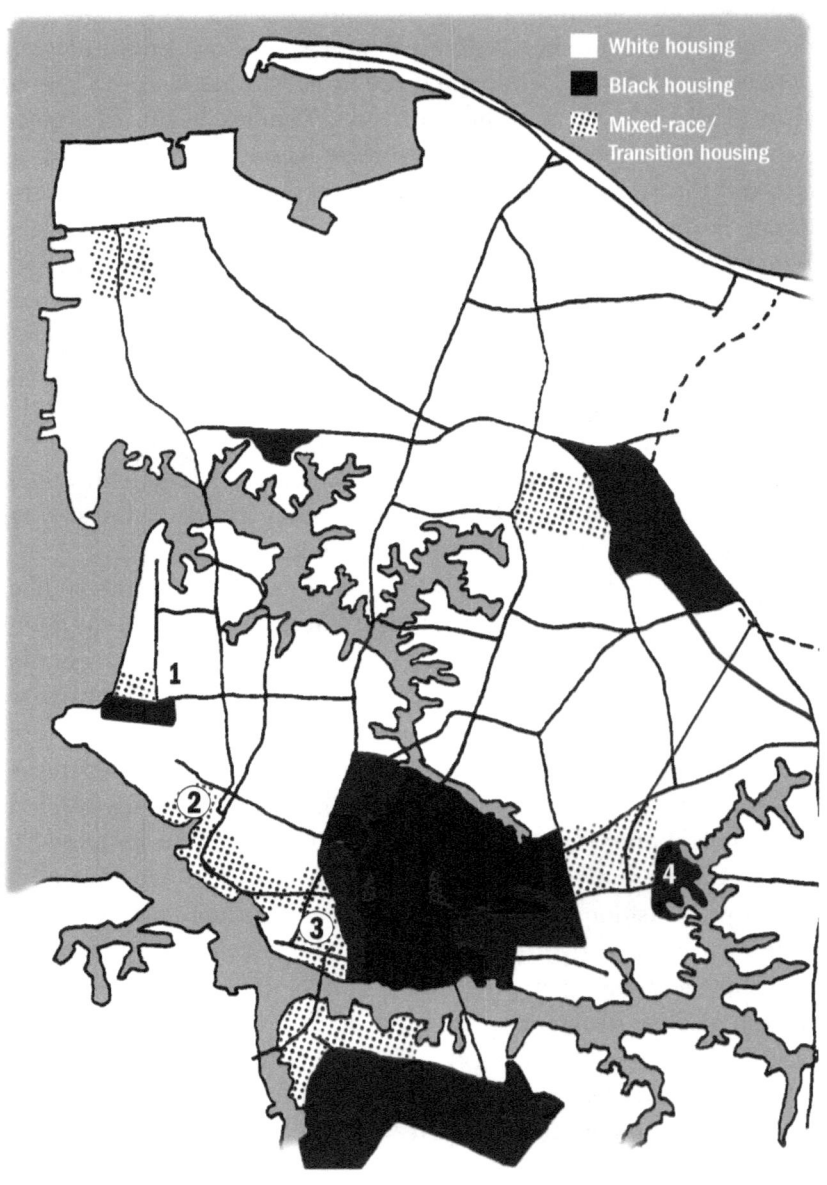

1 Old Dominion Project
2 Atlantic City Project
3 Downtown Redevelopment Project
4 Broad Creek Park Project

students living in white neighborhoods was unequal, and therefore unconstitutional. Other companion cases involved school systems where there was no comparable school for blacks or where lawyers could show by a preponderance of statistical evidence—differences in teacher salaries, per-pupil expenditures, quality of textbooks, age of physical plant, lack of support facilities, and the like—that proved that the black schools were clearly inferior to those operated for whites only. In such instances, the Court ruled, where separate schools are demonstrably unequal, then the laws requiring such separation are unconstitutional.[38] Thus, a careful reading of the legal situation at the time revealed that segregation was safe from attack as long as all of the city's black residents could be served by a black school closer than a white institution; if blacks lived closer to a white school, then either the school would have to be closed or torn down or the neighborhood demolished.

Norfolk was no longer worried that its black schools would be found inherently inferior to its white: The city had made great strides at improving and upgrading its black schools, even to the point where black teachers were better paid, better educated, and more experienced than whites.[39] Indeed, writing in February 1957, District Court Judge Walter Hoffman commented on Norfolk's success in achieving a "separate but equal" dual system of education:

> The sum and substance of the School Superintendent's evidence is that the City of Norfolk has substantially complied with the "separate but equal" doctrine, which was applicable prior to the decision in *Brown v. Board of Education*. The City of Norfolk is to be commended for its rapid strides in bringing about an equalization in physical equipment, curriculum, teacher load, and teachers' salaries. If the "separate but equal" doctrine were now in existence, there would be no grounds for relief to be afforded these [black] plaintiffs.[40]

Mayor Duckworth was worried, however, that a close scrutiny of the city's neighborhoods would reveal several areas where color lines were indistinct or where black students actually lived closer to the all-white school than the black school they were attending. His plan aimed at stamping out any potential variance to the *de facto* segregated school concept still tentatively approved by the U.S. Supreme Court because it was based upon geographic proximity, rather than state law. Top priority among those schools that would have been forced to integrate on the basis of neighborhood proximity was Patrick Henry Elementary in Atlantic City. The *Virginian-Pilot* underscored this concern:

> The increase of Negro population in Atlantic City in recent years is reflected in Patrick Henry School, which would feel the highest proportionate integration of the thirteen Norfolk white schools in "fringe" districts. Recent figures indicated that there would be 50 Negro pupils to 300 white pupils at Patrick Henry in the event of desegregation.[41]

Thirteen of the plaintiffs in the school integration suit filed by the N.A.A.C.P. lived closer to Patrick Henry Elementary than to the black institution they were attending when the suit was filed in May of 1956.[42] When the Atlantic City Project was first announced, the case had just finished its discovery phase, and Judge Hoffman was about to order the integration of Patrick Henry Elementary, which had previously served just the white students in the area. Judge Hoffman apparently realized that the N.R.H.A. was rushing to reduce the impact of his decision: "As to the Patrick Henry School, there is a redevelopment and housing plan now in its early stages which, if carried through to its completion, will substantially reduce the number of colored children who would ordinarily be assigned to [the] Patrick Henry School."[43] Not even Judge Hoffman realized the speed with which the N.R.H.A. would undertake demolition of the project area. Although the project was not announced until December, 1956, its boundaries were not set until late May, 1957; even so, by the start of the 1957-1958 school year, demolition had been extensive enough to close more than two-thirds of the Patrick Henry classrooms.[44] By the start of the crucial 1958-1959 school year, the school had closed entirely.[45]

Five other plaintiffs in the suit lived closer to the all-white Gatewood School in the Berkley section of the city than to one of the black schools there; by the time the 1958-1959 school year was about to begin, the Gatewood School, the other school that Judge Hoffman had indicated would experience extensive integration, had been shifted to the black system, thereby relieving that threat as well. The political powers that governed Norfolk at the time were well aware, as was the *Virginian-Pilot*, that such actions weakened the force of the N.A.A.C.P.'s argument:

> The significance of a plaintiff's proximity to a school has been pointed up repeatedly in other places where desegregation was ordered.... Two elementary schools that formerly faced the prospect of desegregation apparently don't any longer. Gatewood School, now white, will become a Negro school next fall. For five plaintiffs, it was the closest school. Patrick Henry School is nearest for thirteen plaintiffs, but this school will be converted to administrative uses.[46]

The other nine plaintiffs in the suit lived closer to a black school than a white one,[47] thereby giving the school board "legitimate" reasons for denying their transfer applications. The N.A.A.C.P. had filed the action in May 1956, and only the city's headlong rush into redevelopment in Atlantic City had averted the immediate threat; bulldozer diplomacy achieved the desired result in less than two years' time from conception to completion.

The mayor and his advisors knew that under current state law, if even one of Norfolk's 46 elementary schools were forced to open with mixed classes, then state funds, which then accounted for one-fourth of the local school budget, would be cut off to all 46 schools.[48] Although their precipitate actions in the case of Patrick Henry and Gatewood elementary schools had temporarily "saved" the elementary school system, they were not disposed to take any chances: For this reason Pineridge Elementary in the Broad Creek section was closed,[49] and Henry Clay Elementary in the downtown area[50] and the Broad Creek Village School[51] were torn down as a result of the other redevelopment projects. The school board, whose earlier $15 million school building program had been rejected because of past differences with the city council, was now sent scurrying back to the drawing boards for a quick, and less costly, revision. An amended $5.5-million proposal included an immediate go-ahead on the combined elementary, junior, and senior high school for blacks in the Oakwood-Rosemont area and a cutback of

40 percent of the improvements earlier proposed for existing black schools.[52] The Oakwood-Rosemont combination school was designed to alleviate the triple threat of integration to Norview Elementary, Junior, and Senior High schools in the newly annexed area. The mayor was anxious to dispense with the preliminaries and break ground as rapidly as possible. A *Virginian-Pilot* reporter quoted his rationale: "This is the school that the school board promised the court it would build by this fall. Let's go ahead with it as rapidly as we can."[53]

The only other area that might possibly be affected immediately by court-ordered integration lay in the Lambert's Point section of the city. Although six of the plaintiffs in the N.A.A.C.P.'s suit attended the Smallwood Elementary School (black), all lived closer to that school than to nearby Madison or Larchmont (both white) elementary schools.[54] Nevertheless, the Old Dominion Redevelopment Project (N.R.H.A. Project Two) would bulldoze 40 acres in the area, wipe out the transition neighborhoods, and reestablish readily identifiable color lines in that community. Thus, of the more than 500 blacks who were determined to "threaten" the sanctity of the white segregated school system in the winter of 1956,[55] fast action towards redevelopment and school construction had alleviated the legal standing based upon geographic proximity of all but about 40 of the potential plaintiffs, and none of these as yet posed any immediate threat in current litigation.

The mayor's plan to make *de facto* segregation a permanent substitute for *de jure* segregation appeared to be a masterful success: Only black students in the tiny Bollingbrook community (near Suburban Park Elementary School) in the Granby district and secondary students in the Titustown and Benmoreell areas remained as yet unaffected by changes already instituted. Of the fifteen schools potentially threatened by a court order to integrate upon the doctrine of geographic proximity, two (Patrick Henry and Broad Creek Village) were in the path of the redevelopment bulldozer, another (Benmoreell) was to be torn down for a park, two (Gatewood and John Marshall) had been transferred from the white to the black school system, one (Pineridge Elementary) had been closed, three others (Norview Elementary, Junior, and Senior High) had been spared by the Rosemont combination school then under construction, and four others (Taylor Elementary, Blair Junior High, Maury High

School, and Madison Elementary) had been rescued from much of their potential threat by the aggressive redevelopment program (*see* Figures 6 and 7, pages 108, 109).

Mayor Duckworth's plan to achieve total *de facto* segregation was in full keeping with the political realities that then existed in Virginia. The school board, the city council, the city's legislative delegation, and other astute political leaders knew that if Norfolk took any steps to comply with the impending desegregation litigation, then such action would "provoke" the rest of the state into a "Stop Norfolk" movement that could have dire consequences for the city.[56] They knew that the city's best hope lay in delaying the eventuality of such a decision long enough so that a number of other areas would be forced into the "same boat" as Norfolk, and thereby form the impetus for a more realistic approach by the rest of the state. A crisis hitting several localities simultaneously, most political leaders felt, would increase the pressure on the governor to convene a special session of the legislature to enact some "reasonable" plan for gradual desegregation. Thus the city's best hope in the winter of 1956-1957 was to hold out long enough for cases already pending against Newport News, Arlington, Charlottesville, Prince Edward County, and, hopefully, other localities to achieve a simultaneous decision.[57]

The Norfolk case, which was decided by Judge Hoffman on February 12, 1957,[58] was by then wending its way through the appeals process to the Supreme Court, but local legal experts privately doubted that legal maneuvering could stall desegregation for the one more year it would take the cases in other cities to catch up.[59] The emergency state laws that established the state pupil placement board had already been declared unconstitutional in the Norfolk case, and that decision had been upheld by the U.S. Supreme Court.[60] In the winter of 1956-1957 there seemed little the City could do to forestall desegregation of its white public schools in the fall of 1957—at least a full year before any other locality would be faced with a similar crisis—except sit back and accept the calumny of the rest of the state.

Thus, the Duckworth Plan, although no such proposal was ever publicized, was introduced within this atmosphere of political panic; there was no announcement of any concerted program to achieve anything other than the publicly espoused goals of the redevelopment and school building projects, nor was there any widespread understanding of just why the City was taking these particular steps;

Figure 6 – From *De Jure* to *De Facto:* School Resegregation in Norfolk, 1956-1958

SCHOOL	BLACK STUDENTS	ACTION	DISPOSITION	DATE
Benmoreell Elementary	Navy Housing	Closed	Torn Down	5/7/56
Marshall Elementary	Extensive	Transferred to Black	Transferred	3/21/57
Broad Creek Elementary	Navy Housing	Broad Creek Project	Torn Down	5/7/57
Patrick Henry Elementary	50	Atlantic City Project	Closed	7/10/57
Madison Elementary	25-30	Old Dominion Project	Rezoned	7/10/57
W.H. Taylor Elementary	1-3	Atlantic City Project	Rezoned	7/10/57
Maury High	Some	Atlantic City Project	Rezoned	7/10/57
Blair Jr. High	Some	Atlantic City Project	Rezoned	7/10/57
Pine Ridge Elementary	Navy Housing	Broad Creek Project	Closed	12/20/57
Norview Elementary	35	Build Rosemont/Coronado	Rezoned	3/27/58
Norview Jr. High	200-225	Build Rosemont/Coronado	Rezoned	3/27/58
Norview Sr. High	75	Build Rosemont/Coronado	Rezoned	3/27/58
Gatewood Elementary	50-60	Transferred to Black	Transferred	5/20/58
Monroe Elementary	1-3	N/A	N/A	N/A
Granby Jr. High	Some	N/A	N/A	N/A

Norfolk Virginian-Pilot 2/13/57

nevertheless, a certain calm prevailed among the citizenry that "something" either would be or was being done to avert the crisis, regardless of the cost of such a diversion. The immediate action—the time between the first public hearing to the first demolition was less than six months—on the Atlantic City Project, and the transfer of the Gatewood Elementary School to the black system solved the crises at hand by frustrating the 14 litigants who would probably have been assigned to white schools during the 1957-1958 school term. With the state pupil-placement legislation declared unconstitutional, a local-board policy of denying transfer, regardless of the race of the applicant, to a school at a greater geographic proximity was just enough of a legal loophole to delay speedy enactment of Judge Hoffman's order. It was a brilliant ploy, and one that won an additional one-year reprieve for the school system.[61] That extra year gave the city time to plan for additional delays by using the powers of redevelopment and the policy of school construction to forestall additional transfer requests based upon geographic proximity; until this was achieved, the school board was apparently instructed to deny all requests for transfer from a black to a white school, even if it was faced with court order to do so.[62]

Figure 7 – Impact of *De Facto* Segregation on School Locations in Norfolk, 1958-1959

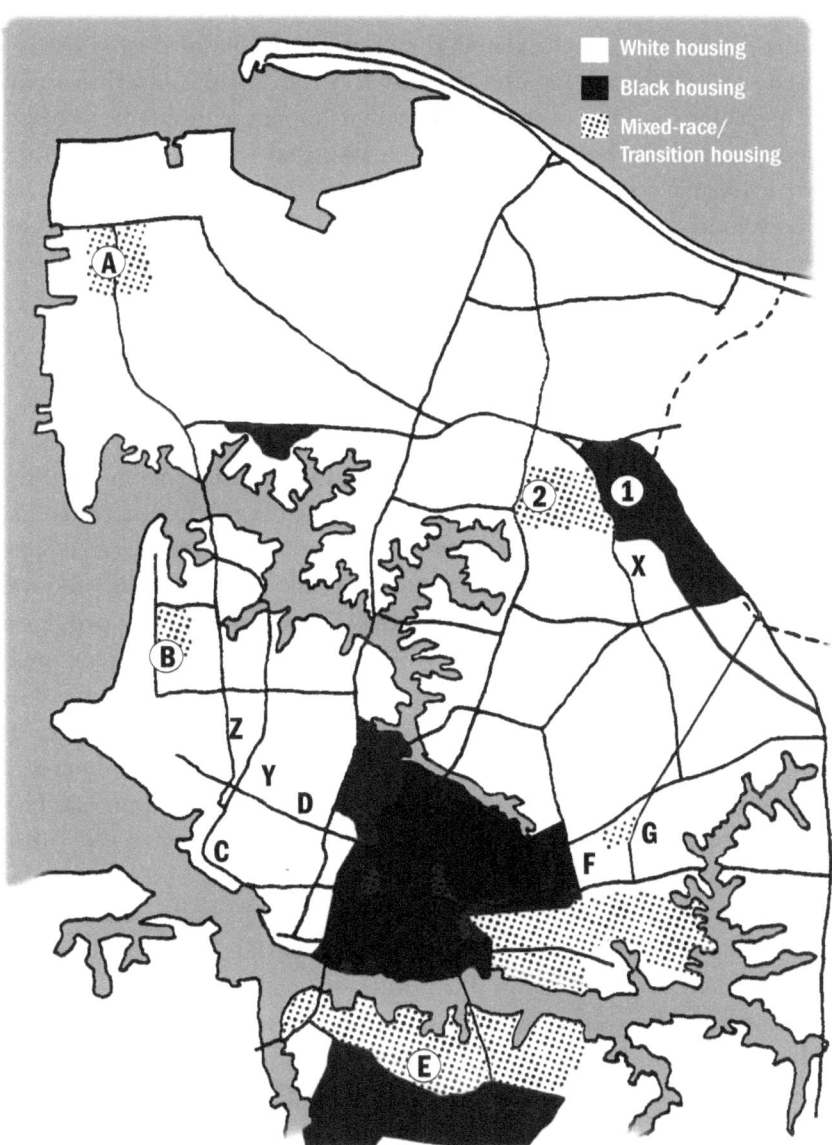

A Benmoreell Elementary	F Broad Creek Elementary	Y Maury Sr. High
B Madison Elementary	G Pine Ridge Elementary	Z Blair Jr. High
C Patrick Henry Elementary	X Norview Elementary and	1 Rosemont Elementary
D Marshall Elementary	Jr. and Sr. High	and Jr. High
E Gatewood Elementary		2 Coronado Elementary

At its very least, Mayor Duckworth's program of concerted redevelopment and school construction helped to buy time before the city had to face the eventuality of school desegregation; at its very best, the plan lessened the impact of school desegregation upon specific areas targeted by the N.A.A.C.P. suit, and thus made it possible for the court to diffuse that impact as much as possible among all the schools in the city—a step that was crucial in leading to eventual compliance and acceptance of desegregation. In all likelihood, the city's white voters, given the political climate and emotional conditions of the day, would probably have concurred with his program had they been given a chance.

The important thing from the point of view of history, however, is that the public was never given an opportunity to approve or disapprove the overall program; neither were the people given a chance to understand either its ramifications or political consequences. Mayor Duckworth's Plan had been carefully handmade in a political vacuum of his own construction, one that maximized his personal powers and control of the decision-making process. Redevelopment projects, especially, had to fulfill federal requirements that the affected individuals had been provided a full opportunity to be involved in the planning, design, and implementation of the program. Norfolk, however, was extremely remiss in this regard, and its officials preferred to run the city as much like a company as they could—as if they were the board of directors, major decisions could be made in secrecy, and no one else mattered much.[63] The people, however, seemed to care very little one way or another about the decisions that faced the city; so long as they were spared the gory details of complicated policy, they would approve by inertia whatever actions, no matter how drastic, were undertaken to preserve the status quo.

As for the business community, its consent was assured from the outset. Redevelopment was too good for business in general, and too important an economic boost for the Tidewater area as a whole, to be opposed. The mayor was simply enacting their most far-fetched dreams, although with a speed, scope, and urgency they may not have understood. Surely there were those among the business community who fathomed the true motivation behind the redevelopment proposals, but these same leaders knew how disastrous a school confrontation would be for the city. The state had backed the city against the wall on desegregation: The federal courts would not allow it to continue public education as before, and yet the state would not let it retreat towards token integration. Credit is due Mayor Duckworth because he at least found a way to break out of that corner. Probably no one, not even the mayor, expected redevelopment to provide a permanent solution to the problem, but it did supply the city with a grant of additional powers that might help him negotiate some sort of settlement short of desegregation with the black community. At the very least, the Duckworth Plan answered the court directives, bought additional time for the city to work out a more permanent solution, and gave the mayor flexibility to deal with both the crisis at hand and the rebuilding of the city. No one in the city's business or political leadership really expected that black children would ever attend white schools in Norfolk,[64] and so nobody suspected how much the city had traded for what would turn out to be a temporary fix. Ironically, by advancing such a far-reaching program under these less-than-honorable motivations, Mayor Duckworth had finally achieved the promise of his 1950 Harmony Ticket: The city's business establishment and its political organization were at last joined together in a consensus on municipal directions, more united than they had been at any time since Duckworth had assumed control of its destiny.

6

✼ ✼ ✼ ✼ ✼

Prelude to Confrontation

NORFOLK, AND ESPECIALLY its established business and political leaders, began to harden into a stronghold of Massive Resistance for a number of reasons—in spite of the apparent success of the mayor's redevelopment program in preventing school desegregation. For several years since the *Brown* decision, the local chapter of the statewide Massive Resistance support group—the Defenders of State Sovereignty and Individual Liberties—had labored to establish a respected political force that could be counted on to endorse the Byrd Organization when it advanced ardent segregationists, but also to oppose it when it backed more moderate local-option resisters. In spite of its penchant for lost causes, such as support for the Separatist Party candidate for President in 1956, the local Defenders had carved for themselves a minor following among the city's small businessmen, the major component of their statewide effort. In the past it had been pushed dangerously close to the fringe of accepted political behavior, but it had always fought its way back to the core of this small constituency.

The logic of the Defenders' argument was powerfully convincing for most of Norfolk's white citizens: They felt that the Supreme Court had made an "unconstitutional" decision in the *Brown* case, and, because it substituted its own "judicial legislation" for the more legal process of constitutional amendment, the decision posed a grave threat to the powers of the states, the time-honored tradition of state control of public education, and the rule of the majority. Since most of the people in the country seemed to favor a continuation of segregated schools, they argued, the *Brown* decision really worked to undermine rule by the majority in favor of the interests of a few. The Defenders backed their claim of an "unconstitutional" court decision with a supporting document signed by three-fourths of the nation's state supreme court justices. Most of Norfolk's white voters apparently agreed with the Defenders' unconstitutional-court-order sentiment; it was the second part of their logic they resisted: The Defenders felt that closing public schools in defiance of court orders to integrate was the only way to show opposition against such dangerously political decisions.[1]

Partly to test the depth of Massive Resistance feeling in Norfolk, the Defenders fielded a three-man slate in the June, 1957 Democratic Primary to challenge the local Byrd Organization and its more moderate legislative delegation. The race provided a classic confrontation between the progressivism of the incumbents and the more extreme approach of the Defenders. In spite of the considerable strength of the Organization and the backing of the business community, the Defenders' Ticket of Colonel J. Addison Hagan (U.S.M.C., Retired), jeweler Frank R. Ford, and attorney Harvey E. White, Jr. waged such a vigorous campaign that the outcome hinged on late returns from a few critical voting precincts; Colonel Hagan later claimed that Billy Prieur stole the election by stuffing the ballot boxes to ensure victory.[2]

The attitude of Norfolk's voters was hardening against moderation, and a position of defiance that included the sacrifice of closed schools was gaining in popularity. When the issue emerged five months later in the gubernatorial race, it pitted Democrat J. Lindsay Almond, widely seen as the legal brains behind Massive Resistance, against the more moderate Republican challenge of Ted Dalton. Although four years earlier Dalton had come within just a few percentage points of winning, Almond swept to easy victory by calling for hardline defiance all the way to the school house door. In spite of his appeal, Dalton was swamped by events beyond his control: When federal troops were sent to Little Rock, Arkansas, to enforce court-ordered desegregation, all hope of a Dalton victory faded forever. Although no one in Virginia really wanted to close schools, Almond's promise of Massive Resistance provided a way to prevent integration without having to face a similar threat of armed troops in Virginia.³

The intervention of federal troops in Little Rock had a profound effect upon local residents as well. Whereas only a few months earlier most citizens seemed prepared to accept a minimum of desegregation in order to keep the schools open, now a majority appeared to prefer closing the schools to accepting even token integration. The sight of rifles, bayonets, and uniforms had seemed to underscore the resisters' argument that the South was at war with the federal courts, and that any tactic which bypassed or postponed a similar confrontation in Norfolk was acceptable. The shift became most evident when the local legislators began to back away from their own earlier position of moderation in favor of Almond's hardline posture.⁴ They were obviously aware that not even ballot box finagling could have saved them if Little Rock had occurred just before their own primary race against the Defenders' slate. As a result of the strength of the Defenders' challenge, the events in Little Rock, Almond's impressive showing in the city, and an emerging sense of defiance on the part of the citizenry, Norfolk's legislators now found themselves supporting a Massive Resistance stance that every one of them would have found repugnant only a year earlier. Events were moving rapidly to a showdown. No wonder that, in this context of defiance, the mayor's plan of immediate and selective redevelopment was accepted by all those in a position to guess its true intent.

One other factor contributed to the shift shown by the local legislators: the unrelenting legal pressure still being applied by the N.A.A.C.P.'s attorneys.⁵ Any thought of congratulatory action on the mayor's part for avoiding a Little Rock in Norfolk in 1957 quickly faded; the N.A.A.C.P. refused to back down. Mayor Duckworth's plan and his willingness to employ the myriad powers of redevelopment against the homes of black litigants had bought time, but had not intimidated the N.A.A.C.P. into withdrawing its case. Instead, they forced a rethinking of the strategy, and the N.A.A.C.P. went ahead with plans to enlist new plaintiffs in order to continue the challenge. If the N.A.A.C.P. had erred it was because it had followed the *Brown* precedent too closely, and sought elementary students who lived in similar mixed-race areas as plaintiffs. The mayor had won the first round because he was willing to demolish both the threatened areas and their neighborhood schools.

The N.A.A.C.P. was determined to win this next round, and decided to aim its second legal assault at Norfolk's white junior and senior high schools. This tactic seemed appropriate for a number of reasons. First, the assault seemed to block the mayor's use of the redevelopment weapon: each secondary institution served too many students and too wide a geographic area to make it a target for either closing or urban renewal. Second, the attack on secondary schools meant that there were potentially hundreds of litigants for whom the argument of geographic proximity could be made. Third, the new approach would involve older students who could more easily be prepared physically and mentally for the personal hardships, isolation, and even dangers inherent in integration. Finally, the N.A.A.C.P. hoped that the white community might be more sympathetic to breaking down the doors of segregated secondary institutions rather than an assault on the city's primary schools: Older students might be more open to new ideas, their parents less protective, and the bastion of the neighborhood school, so important to both the black and white communities, would be protected by expanding the concept to include racial as well as geographic neighbors. There was only one high school and two junior highs in the black system, and to many, the most insidious form of racial discrimination was evident in the lines of black youths forced to queue up at an early hour for long bus rides across town to these institutions.[6]

The shift in strategy was a brilliant legal maneuver, and one which the N.A.A.C.P. sensed would ultimately prove successful. Duckworth, however, was not disposed to give up so easily; he could foresee doom if the N.A.A.C.P. won, and so, with the powers of redevelopment useless against this new threat, he began to seek other means to intimidate the black community into withdrawing its litigation. By late spring of 1958, the pressure upon him had become so intense that he became embroiled in a prolonged name-calling battle with the black community. The opening shots in the verbal battle were fired by the mayor when a group of traditional black leaders approached the city council with a request to establish a biracial advisory commission to address the deterioration in race relations that had taken place. It was a simple request, and one with which the old People's administration would have complied forthrightly. Dr. Lyman Brooks, the president of Norfolk's black state college, and a figure of gentility highly regarded by both the black and white communities, rose to present the request.⁷ Before Dr. Brooks could get through reading the first lines of the entreaty, however, the mayor felt prompted to utter a prolonged racial slur which included the comment that there were "too d—n many blacks behind bars and not enough at the tax counters." The mayor's off-color remark at the usually staid and highly predictable city council session caught the press and spectators off guard. Most, including the news reporters present, pretended not to hear the invective, and Dr. Brooks, much to his credit, did not argue the point, but the affront came in for some mild criticism at the hands of the editorial writers as "an unwelcome and irrelevant note that is not a politically sound one."⁸

If Mayor Duckworth had hoped to provoke an outburst from the black leadership, and so turn public reaction against them, he was sadly mistaken. Instead, his off-color invective only served to strengthen their resolve to air their grievances before a broader representation of the white citizenry. Newspaper reporters who sought a response from Dr. Brooks, found only this staid assessment:

> There really are no relations between the races in Norfolk. . . . Richmond is considered to be a more conservative city, yet Negroes are on all the important commissions in Richmond. . . . Norfolk has no police officer above the rank of patrolman, and there are no Negroes on any policy-making commission under city government.⁹

Dr. Brooks, a powerful force in arranging conciliation between the races, was attempting to point the way towards several symbolic shifts that would help to placate the black community and resolve the current impasse. Indirectly, by pointing the finger at City hiring and appointment practices, he was laying the blame for nonexistent racial communications at the feet of the mayor and his political organization. P. B. Young, who had served on a number of advisory boards and biracial special commissions during the People's reign, indicated that:

> The deterioration in race relations—in business, government, welfare agencies, the Community Fund, school

administration—has been noticeable since the Supreme Court decisions began banning segregation in public schools and public parks.

He also listed several other reasons why the city's blacks were agitated:

> The current housing shortage, difficulties in obtaining credit for [black] construction, and the activities of the Defenders of State Sovereignty and Individual Liberties.[10]

The uproar caused by the mayor's prejudicial remark only served to unite the black leadership more closely than ever before behind the goal of attaining desegregated public schools. In the absence of other symbolic goals befitting their rank and standing in the community, the desegregation of Norfolk's all-white schools in direct defiance of the wishes of the mayor and the Prieur Organization that had fought so hard against them, took on new meaning for the city's black leaders. A group of prominent black ministers responded to Duckworth's retort by opposing his desire to have blacks "waive their civil rights" as a condition to restoring racial harmony; other black leaders joined them in repudiating the mayor's attempts at "biracial bargaining."[11] The N.A.A.C.P. declined comment in the white press, and, instead, redoubled its efforts to attain black plaintiffs for its litigation. Before the mayor's remarks, 44 black students had requested a transfer;[12] after the imbroglio, more than 100 new plaintiffs joined the effort,[13] in spite of the fact that the school board was releasing their names for publication[14]—an action that subjected them to the dangers of verbal abuse, intimidation, and the possibility of physical assault.

By the summer of 1958, the black and white communities were thus locked in a head-to-head struggle over school desegregation from which there could be no retreat. The effects of racial intimidation, both official and unofficial, had failed to force the N.A.A.C.P. into withdrawing its suit from the courts. As a final attempt at intimidation, the school board delayed the reappointment of the black teachers,[15] but this action also failed to produce the desired panic. The black community rallied around the N.A.A.C.P. and its efforts to desegregate the city's secondary schools; the harshness of the mayor's attitude and the viciousness of these tactics precluded any hope of an out-of-court appeasement with symbolic gestures—something that might have worked earlier. Far from discouraging new litigants, however, these actions produced 151 plaintiffs, only one of which lived closer to the white secondary school to which he had applied than the black school he currently attended.[16]

Now that the integration of at least some of Norfolk's secondary schools seemed assured, public opinion began to coalesce around three separate philosophical responses. The Defenders firmly believed that closing the public schools in defiance of a court order to integrate was necessary to show united opposition to the Supreme Court's political decisions. If the South held solid in its efforts to resist the Court's encroachment upon state's rights and individual liberties, then, they argued, the federal government would be forced to back down. There were not enough troops, the Defenders argued, to force integration in every Southern community; they did not want trouble here in Virginia, and that was why the state's political leaders had endorsed their idea to close the threatened public schools rather than invite the type of conflict that had occurred in Little Rock. As one of the first communities in the South to be faced with of court-ordered integration, Norfolk stood at the brink of a historic moment. If Massive Resistance worked here, the Defenders argued, every other Southern city would be heartened. In light of the prominence of the city's position, the closing of the school house doors was a "small sacrifice" to pay for the freedoms of the majority.

> Maybe the schools will be closed for a time, maybe for a whole year. But it's a mighty small sacrifice to pay to prevent integration and discourage the federal courts from further encroachments on state's rights. We can teach them [the white students] just as well in private schools; maybe better, because we'll have a little more control over what they're going to learn. . . . When we close the schools in September, I say to mothers, don't start squawking.[17]

In order to provide a "temporary" substitute for the public schools that might be forced to close in September, the Defenders had formed the Tidewater Education Foundation (T.E.F.) to operate segregated alternative schools for students locked out of public classrooms. To help defray the cost, the state was willing to provide substantial "tuition grants" to pupils who chose private or parochial schools over integration.[18] Thus, the T.E.F. offered parents a way to have segregated schools with public support, without sacrificing the schooling of their children. In addition, the T.E.F. would be able to make its pitch free from the political connotation of the Defenders' name. If the "small sacrifice" the public was expected to bear grew into more than a year's duration, as most Defenders believed it would, the T.E.F. was ready to buy the closed buildings for a nominal fee and reopen them as segregated private schools.

The great majority of Norfolk citizens, however, did not yet seem ready to accept the separate system of private schools proposed by the Defenders and the T.E.F. The epitome of the city's moderate opinion even as late as the summer of 1958 was expressed by School Board Chairman Paul Schweitzer, who, when he contemplated the possibility of closing all of Norfolk's white public schools, proclaimed: "I just can't imagine 36,000 children out on the streets. . . . Let's don't lose our faith yet."[19] There were two scenarios of how a school lockout could be prevented: The first was the rather Pollyanna belief that "it couldn't happen here"—that either some event or, as before, some means would be found to further delay or defer the imminence of the legal challenge. Nothing as dramatic as the plan of selective redevelopment was envisioned in this scenario, but the full appeals process had not yet been exhausted, the court order was not yet absolute, and some legal gimmickry was still possible. Others believed, as did Joseph Leslie, editor of the *Norfolk Ledger-Dispatch*, that the public schools would have to be closed, but only for a brief period of time.[20] These individuals held that the decision to close public schools in defiance of court orders to desegregate was a powerful political weapon that, once wielded with resolve, would force both the courts and the black community to withdraw and accept some other symbolic victory short of desegregation. This was the essence of the Massive Resistance theory: Once the white community stood solidly against integration, even going so far as to accept private school alternatives, the crisis could not continue, and Congress, the courts, the President or the state authorities would seek a settlement. Local Byrd Organization chieftain Billy Prieur, the bulk of the state's political leaders, and the majority of Norfolk's business community apparently held this belief.[21]

There were others who felt that a school crisis was both more imminent and more long lasting than most suspected, and could not be as easily resolved as the Organization promised. Foremost among them was Lenoir Chambers and his editorial staff at the *Virginian-Pilot*. Once schools were closed, they argued, Norfolk faced a more difficult confrontation than it might otherwise have experienced: The black community would not back down, the courts would not relent, and the city would be forced to submit to an even greater federal authority over its public schools once they reopened. The greatest effect of closing the schools, they argued, would be the calumny Norfolk would face as the scapegoat for 300 years of Southern culture:

> If our schools are closed, not only our children suffer, but the entire city will be severely damaged economically. Norfolk's black eye on the national scene as a result of closed schools would be one of the most disastrous effects. Norfolk is in the market for industry . . . but industry would not likely come to a city with a closed school reputation. . . . The closing of any schools, and the disorganization of the school program might have a disastrous effect on the Community Chest . . . naval facilities . . . efforts to attract industry . . . and every aspect of the economic well-being of our city.[22]

The only hope that the anti-resistance forces could offer was that the public schools could survive a minimum of integration: Accepting a few black students would neither dilute nor destroy the education program of the white majority. Only in this way, they argued, could the city take its school system out from under the authority of the federal courts and continue economic growth undeterred. The most important action the people could take, the anti-resisters argued, would be an outpouring of public support for the school system regardless of its racial purity.[23] The school board had labored for almost four years to achieve this end, but as yet had been unable to build much of a constituency for keeping the schools open in the face of desegregation. In spite of the fact that they owed their advancement to a political organization advocating Massive Resistance, the board members were each deeply committed to continuing quality public education, part of the rationale for their appointment. Board members were quickly becoming aware that at least some of the N.A.A.C.P.'s 151 litigants would slip through whatever screening criteria they could legally impose, thereby closing all the (white) schools at that level.[24] Chairman Paul Schweitzer summed up the situation the board faced that summer: "It is obvious that this irresistible force of [a] court order is about to collide with this immovable object, the state.[25]

If differences between the school board and the more conservative city council existed, they were not made public, and, in general, the school program progressed with the solid backing of the Council. In July, Chairman Paul Schweitzer was cordially reappointed without any indication of differences with the mayor or the Prieur Organization;[26] the city council apparently felt that the board's willingness to close threatened schools, transfer facilities, redraw district lines, and carefully target its construction plans were all supportive of Massive Resistance, even if their intent was "to minimize the effect of integration by using a plan for gradual desegregation."[27] Even the board's earlier posture of moderate compliance seemed to have been forgiven as the work of the Silkstocking holdovers then on the board; since that time a majority of the board had been replaced with Duckworth appointees. Subsequent statements by the school board had been issued jointly with the Council and the city's legislative delegation, both of whom had at one time similarly vowed to keep Norfolk's schools open at all cost.[28] Up until then, the board had cooperated in every way with the Council and its efforts to delay, avert, and even sabotage the eventuality of school desegregation. Its actions that summer (1958) were no different: The board waited until mid-August to render its decision on the N.A.A.C.P.'s transfer applicants, and even then, it resisted the pressure from the court to make a determination. Finally, the board rejected all 151, using both rational logic and subterfuge to do so: Sixty-two applicants were denied because they had failed to submit to follow-up interviews or the testing program required to support their transfer request; another 60 were found unsuited for transfer because of low test scores, poor grades, or a record of "too frequent transfers;" 34 applicants who applied to schools in the Norview area were denied because of the district's past history of racial disturbance. Four other applicants were denied admission to Maury High, Granby High, or Blair Junior High schools because:

"The isolation which would be caused by such an assignment would be detrimental to educational progress and may well cause emotional instability and even detriment to health."[29] Only one of the potential transfers was rejected because it came from a black living closer to a black school than a white one.[30]

The board's denial did not, however, last very long; in less than two weeks Judge Walter Hoffman rejected the rationale of "potential racial tension" and "probable isolation," and the folders of the 38 applicants in these two categories were returned to the school board for appropriate assignment. A slight modification in the district lines for the projected Rosemont School, the black combination elementary and junior high school (earlier it was referred to it as a combination elementary, junior and senior high) that was part of the mayor's *de facto* segregation plan, brought most of the 38 applicants within the school's boundaries. Although School Superintendent Brewbaker admitted that the district lines for Rosemont were hastily redrawn only "after he had learned the addresses of the applicants involved [in the litigation]," Judge Hoffman allowed the board to deny the transfer requests of these petitioners. The school board was also able to manipulate district lines to accommodate all the remaining litigants challenging the city's elementary schools, but when every possible readjustment had been made, 17 black secondary students still retained an unquestionable right to legally transfer to the white school which was closer to their homes than the black school they presently attended.

Ironically, the most important decision ever made by the Norfolk School Board took place not in a public meeting, but rather in a private home. Because Boardmember Francis Crenshaw had just undergone an emergency appendectomy, the rest of the board gathered around the bedside of his West Ghent home to discuss their options. Meeting without legal counsel, except for Crenshaw, who specialized in maritime and redevelopment law, the board faced the grim prospect that they might have to go to federal prison if they defied Judge Hoffman's orders. Slowly they came to the conclusion that, in the long run, integration would be easier to accept if the assignment of black pupils to white schools came from fellow Virginians and not an officer of the federal court.[31] Finally, acting "against the board's better judgement, but pursuant to the law as interpreted by the court,"[32] the school board, under threat of legal duress, was forced to accept these final 17 applicants just days before the 1958-1959 school year was scheduled to begin. By dragging the decision out over as long a period as possible, the board was hoping to delay even further the implementation of the assignments. It immediately filed a motion asking for a postponement on the grounds that it was "wholly unprepared at this time for immediate compliance," and that the board needed additional time to arrange for the security of the transferees and otherwise "prepare" school officials, patrons, teachers and students for "the sudden shift" in the traditional pattern of Southern education.[33] Their plea was based on the hope that the violence and uproar that followed similar court action in Little Rock would be reason enough to dissuade the local court from imposing its will upon a community still not ready to accept integration. Even though Judge Hoffman would not accept the argument at this late date, the board postponed the opening for two more weeks while the Supreme Court pondered their appeal for further delay.[34]

When seen against this backdrop of legal stall, foot-dragging, and delay, the statewide vilification of the school board is hard to comprehend. Only after every conceivable legal maneuver had been exhausted and its members seriously threatened with criminal contempt citations, had the Norfolk School Board voted to assign black students to a white Virginia school. Even so, the state's political leaders rushed to heap abuse on the board for making the assignment "voluntarily"; their objection was that the board, itself—a group of Virginia citizens empowered by state and local laws—had accepted the transfers, rather than leaving the task to the court, which they viewed as an illegal usurper of the state's authority. This was a crucial distinction in Virginia's interposition argument: Governor Almond, the Byrd Organization's calmest and most reasoned spokesman, stated that the courts had the "power" to make such assignments, but lacked the "constitutional authority" to do so. Local school boards, he continued, were restrained by the state's Massive Resistance statutes from making such assignments.[35] In Almond's scenario, the Organization had every right to curse the board because, when given the chance to obey one governmental authority and defy the other, Norfolk school authorities had chosen to follow the dictates of the federal court, and ignored the sovereignty of the state. More than that, the board's action threatened to undo the tenuous interposition logic of Massive Resistance.

It seems improbable that the board had made this very deliberate decision without some degree of calculation on the part of its best-informed members. There was one major difference between the Norfolk School Board and the posture of the Byrd Organization, both the statewide leadership and its local affiliate: The appointed members of the board were willing to operate the city's schools even if integrated, and the elected politicians were adamantly opposed to such a course. To the board, the assignment of 17 black students to six previously all-white junior and senior high schools was the type of "minimum of integration" that both the city council and the city's legislative delegation had once said they could abide. The political climate had changed drastically since the Council had assented to such moderation, and the Council was now committed to closing the schools in defiance of the court's authority; the board, however, felt that this course would be highly destructive, both to public education and to the Southern culture in general. For this reason, the board purposely acted to undermine the state's intention to interpose its authority in a show of Massive Resistance. The Norfolk School Board was composed entirely of individuals who personally preferred segregation; they had made every effort to resist assigning blacks to previously all-white public schools until forced to do so by the courts, but once having done so, they were determined to abide by that ruling in order to preserve the public educational system they held more important than segregation. This was the basis for the underlying disagreement that existed from this point onward between the individual members on the school board and the city council.

The Norfolk School Board represented an unlikely pairing of individuals destined for such heroics, and considering the climate of casual malaise that then characterized the majority of the population, their action in defense of public education could well be termed "heroic." It was not a blueblood Silkstocking group, although most of its members bordered on the periphery of the city's business and financial establishment. There were no First Citizens, bank presidents, major industrialists or corporate entrepreneurs on the board; only one had achieved any renown for charity work, and only one was even active in the Chamber of Commerce. Just like the other independent boards and commissions, the appointees of the People's era had long ago been replaced by respectable, but politically unknown, small business leaders and professional people who owed their advance entirely to Duckworth and the Prieur Organization. An examination of its membership revealed a group of prosperous individuals striving for respectability in a city which, in spite of its size, still carried much of the atmosphere of a small town: Chairman Paul Schweitzer ran an industrial pump manufacturing firm; Benjamin Willis managed the plush carpet and salon furniture establishment started by his father; W. Farley Powers was an executive with one of Tidewater's few large industrial concerns; Francis N. Crenshaw practiced maritime and redevelopment law; William P. Ballard managed the family seafood business; and Mildred J. Dallas, although retired, had started her own private kindergarten in the prestigious Loch Haven neighborhood.[36] They were just the sort of small-business and professional leaders who had the most to lose by provoking an open confrontation with the dominant political forces of the state and city government: They depended too heavily upon government contracts, professional fees, inspections, and favorable regulation to lightly defy such authority. On the integration question in particular, they had the most to lose if they or their businesses became the target for boycott or vigilante activity. In short, they were not the sort of individuals who ordinarily defy such authority, especially when it is backed by strong, effective leaders and a highly passionate cheering section.

The school board's singular act of courage set in motion a variety of forces which now vied for public acceptance; at the same time, because it held out the hope of yet one more reprieve from the courts, its action made it difficult for any other coherent plan of action to win that endorsement. For the mayor, the two-week delay in the scheduled opening of the schools provided one more opportunity to pressure Norfolk's black leadership into withdrawing the final 17 litigants. Both publicly and privately, the city council used every resource at its disposal to force some sort of compromise from the black community,[37] but racial antipathies had progressed too far in the last few months for the city's black leadership to accept any sort of token remuneration now that victory appeared so close at hand. Although this time many Norfolk newspapers, fearing reprisals against the individuals involved, declined to print the names and addresses of the 17 approved transferees. The *Journal and Guide* suffered no such qualms: All 17 were featured in a photo-essay that praised their courage and pioneering spirit, even though it recognized that, under Virginia's school-closing laws, they "may not gain their goal immediately."[38]

In the weeks leading up to the school board's defiant action, the organizers of a fledgling pro-school lobby, the Norfolk Committee for Public Schools, had begun to move into a more public posture. Earlier that summer a small group had approached the mayor about the need for such a support group. Duckworth was not opposed to the idea; he even thought it might be helpful if the schools actually closed.[39] Quietly the group had begun the task of contacting the city's respected and conservative citizens—the cream of the city's business and civic elite—asking them to join, or even form themselves, a pressure group that would work to keep the schools open in the face of court-ordered integration. The Committee organizers were convinced that the Governor would have a hard time closing the schools in any community where he felt strong opposition from the conservative business establishment, and this thought gave new impetus to their push for membership. Although most of those approached were sympathetic to the cause, they were nevertheless unwilling to come forward publicly at this time. Typical was the reaction of one well-known civic leader: "I'm with you one hundred percent; however, you know my position. If I place myself in the forefront of your movement, it might harm my organization. Come back when you get your first hundred business leaders, and I'll be glad to join."[40]

Other community stalwarts found similar reasons for refusing to join the Committee: Businessmen were worried about possible economic reprisals; executives did not want to face loss of position or prestige; municipal and state employees feared pressure from the Byrd Organization; doctors, lawyers, realtors, and other professionals worried about losing clients; ministers did not want to face divided congregations; civic workers wanted to avoid pressure from their governing boards; naval officers were concerned about the effect upon their careers; federal workers were specifically instructed by Washington authorities that this was a "local affair," and that they should not play a public role;[41] and everybody was concerned about the subtle social pressures and ostracism that might be applied against anyone who deviated from the silent norm and took a vocal stand one way or the other. Many of the community leaders approached by the Committee urged the group to wait longer before making any public move; they might help once the schools were actually closed and the hardships were real, but the time was not yet right, they felt, for going public with such an organization.[42]

The Committee, however, was in a hurry to publicly launch a legitimate pressure group before the schools were actually closed. They saw that, in spite of the atmosphere of acquiescent hesitancy that blocked their movement, the Defender-backed Tidewater Education Foundation could boast a membership that had passed the 2,500 mark, including several attorneys and prominent small business leaders. The organizers of the Norfolk Committee for Public Schools surveyed this roster and decided that the public had to be offered a calm and rational choice that stood in opposition to closed schools and Defender-sponsored private education. Most of those business and civic leaders who had earlier indicated support for such a group were invited to attend an organizational meeting at the residence of Professor Robert L. Stern, a native New Yorker who embodied the predicament faced by the organizers of a group that was too Northern, too liberal, and too Jewish to compel much community support. The meeting was a dismal failure to all those who had worked to establish the group: The few citizens who had any claim to the city's social and financial elite stood on the front porch of the residence, showing their private sympathy for the cause, but also indicating their reluctance to join the proceedings inside. There were no bank directors, attorneys, corporate executives, leading merchants, elected officials, naval officers, government officials, or major religious leaders present; only a handful of Parent Teacher Association (P.T.A.) activists, interested professionals, and small businessmen were in attendance. Even so, the Committee felt that the issue was so great and the demands so pressing that they must push ahead and expose themselves to the risks involved in taking a stance of public advocacy.[43] Since the Norfolk Committee for Public Schools lacked any ties to the city's business and financial leaders, the Committee announced instead its intent to form a parents' lobby in support of public education, and to finance legal efforts to block the closing of the schools. The organizers chose as their leader Reverend James Brewer, pastor of the Norfolk Unitarian Church, hoping that having a minister at the head would lend credence to their appeal, even if the Unitarian Church was held in less esteem than the Baptist, Methodist, Episcopalian, Presbyterian, and Lutheran congregations that dominated the city. Other officers included Irving F. "Buddy" Truitt, the head of a small real estate and insurance firm, P.T.A. activist Mary Kidd, civic leader Mary Thrasher, pediatrician Dr. Forrest P. White, real estate broker Ellis James, Professor Robert L. Stern, high school government teacher Margaret White, and "another member who requested that his name not be disclosed."[44] It was not a prestigious assemblage—reporter Luther Carter once referred to the organization as "mostly a grouping of little people,"[45] an assessment that was true even by the Committee's own standards. The unnamed board member, gynecologist Mason C. Andrews, the only person with any real standing in the Silkstocking community that had backed the People's revolution, felt that he could best serve the Committee in attracting people of equal prominence if his name was not released to the press. The group was so desperate for such a link that it grudgingly accepted this unusual arrangement, even though others on the board were not told that Dr. Andrews had removed his name before publication.[46]

The Norfolk Committee for Public Schools, just like the school board and the editors of the *Virginian-Pilot*, had overestimated the public's capacity to either comprehend the gravity of the situation or to resist the scapegoat fate to which Norfolk had been condemned by the state's political leaders. Events proceeded at such a rapid pace that these desperate pleas for support were rendered moot. The final legal hurdles were quickly overcome, the last-ditch appeals for one more delay denied, and on September 22, 1958, in accordance with Virginia's Massive Resistance laws, the doors of the city's six previously all-white junior and senior high schools remained locked, while those of its segregated elementary schools opened for the fall semester. There were no closings in the city's parallel black school system, where all twelve grades opened as usual. Thus, nearly 10,000 students were locked out of their classrooms, and neither the Governor nor the President could offer much hope for an early resumption of classes.[47] Even with the school doors actually padlocked, however, few citizens were willing to discuss the implications or project the consequences of such drastic measures; even fewer seemed willing to gather to talk about what should be done. The majority of the city's leaders apparently still dismissed the idea of a prolonged school closing as "scare talk," and promptly banished these thoughts from polite conversation. Most appeared to cling to the belief that the Byrd Organization had outsmarted the federal authorities by daring to close the schools, and that soon either the courts or the black community—they did not really care which—would back down.[48] The realities of the confrontation that had taken place the year before in Little Rock, or the relative success of school integration in cities such as Charlotte, St. Louis, Nashville, and Washington, remained far from their thoughts. "The best of the Southern leadership" and "the majority of Southerners" that the *Virginian-Pilot* had earlier predicted would rise up to abide by the authority of the courts[49] were nowhere in evidence. The cream of the city's civic and business elite, at one time so vocal in determining the course of the Norfolk's direction, remained completely silent, abandoning the stage to the mayor, the Organization, and others who shouted encouragement from the periphery. Instead, prejudice—the unreasonable adherence to the conventions, traditions, and mores of the past—reigned supreme, replacing civic pride and boosterism as the underlying force behind every phase of municipal policy.

The Norfolk 17: The "threat" that kept 10,000 white students out of classes for five months. Getty Images

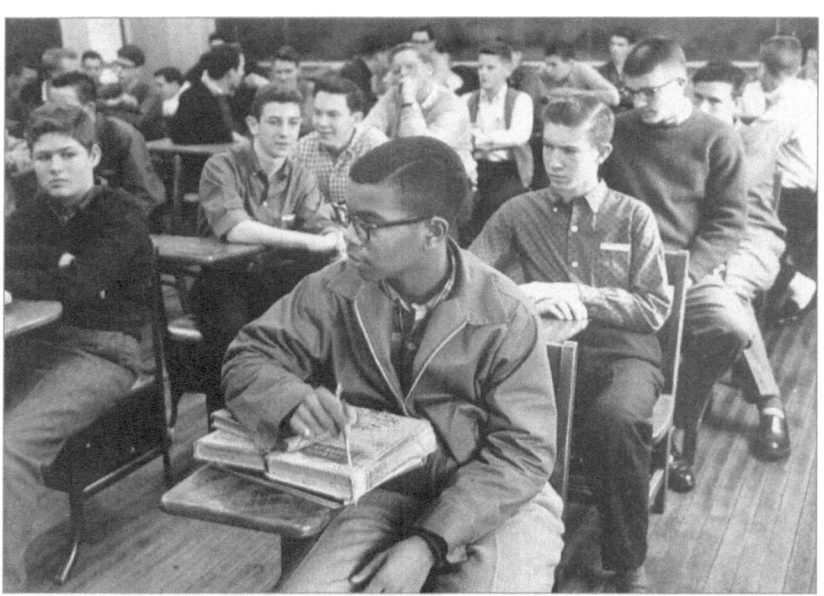

Lewis Cousins, one of the brave "17," eventually integrated Maury High School. Getty Images

7

✵ ✵ ✵ ✵ ✵

In Pursuit of a Mandate

NORFOLK'S WAS NOT the only educational system affected by Virginia's school closing laws: Schools in County, Charlottesville, and, to a lesser extent, Arlington and Front Royal were closed as well. But Norfolk was by far the largest scale test of the state's Massive Resistance plan to replace integrated public institutions with a system of private, segregated academies, financed in part by public funds.[1] There was never any question that Prince Edward County, the birthplace of the Defenders of State Sovereignty and Individual Liberties, would prove how well Massive Resistance could work on a small scale. There the Defenders were a well organized and respectable segment of the community; when blacks moved to desegregate the only public high school in the county, Prince Edward Academy opened its doors to most of the county's white secondary students. Even when the public school was finally reopened after years of litigation (the Prince Edward suit had been a part of the *Brown* v. *Board of Education* decision), most of the county's white students continued on at the Academy.

Of all Virginia's small cities, Charlottesville was perhaps the poorest choice from a political perspective for the Organization showdown over school integration: Because of the strong influence of the University of Virginia, education was too highly prized and its citizens too independent for Massive Resistance to succeed there.

Under ordinary circumstances, Norfolk, with all its liberalizing influences, would have been an equally poor choice for a Massive Resistance showdown. Richmond, with its close ties to the Southside and its capital-of-the-Confederacy heritage, would have provided a more malleable citizenry. The leadership dynamics in Norfolk, however, gave Massive Resistance a far greater opportunity for success than most would have thought possible: In spite of its size, the city had a generally small and inbred leadership that was usually united in its aversion to outside authority—a fact that had made Norfolk unpopular with both the Organization and the State Legislature. W. Fred Duckworth, one of the few outsiders to be truly accepted by all levels of Norfolk's society, had come to occupy a unique place of leadership in the city. In the years since he had come to power, Duckworth had employed his consummate political, financial, and managerial powers with such success that he had become not just the leader, but the true focal point of the community. In short, Norfolk was far from typical for cities its size: Few other municipalities were so completely dominated by a single personality or had dissent so thoroughly silenced by his restraints.

Public education in Virginia was under attack in the Norfolk crisis at its weakest link—the secondary school. Historically, since little more than basic skills was all that was necessary for comfortable survival in the agrarian economy of the Old Dominion, Virginia was among the last states in the nation to support universal public education, and certainly among the most reluctant to fund any more than a program of minimum competency. Alongside its impoverished system of public education, however, was a highly structured system of private preparatory schools and semipublic universities, such as the College of William and Mary and the University of Virginia, to which the average graduate of the state's public schools could hardly aspire. These public institutions helped to reinforce a sort of social caste system that allowed the state's leading citizens to follow this parallel education tract, in part underwritten by scarce public funds, and often at the expense of the more universal, public school system. The growth of secondary schools in the state can be traced back to the appearance of an urban middle class just before the turn of the century, but even as late as 1958, several rural counties still lacked their own public high school and others did not go beyond the eleventh grade—major reasons why Virginia consistently ranked near the bottom of any measurement of education quality in the country. Even in urban areas, secondary education was not universal, and was still the property of the middle class. Mandatory school attendance laws did not apply beyond the age of 14, and because wartime and Depression era dropout levels had run unusually high, even a significant percentage of the middle class had been forced to forego secondary schooling. The median education level for adults in Norfolk, with one of the finest school systems in the South, was still less than tenth grade, and more than one-fifth of the teenage population over fourteen had already dropped out of school.[2]

It is against this backdrop of closed leadership, one-man politics, and spotty support for public education in general and secondary schools in particular that the concept of Massive Resistance faced its most important test in Norfolk. In one sense the Defenders' plea had a great deal of validity: If Massive Resistance could be made to work here, it might be successful all across the South. Norfolk was not just their first large scale test—the time, the circumstances, and the leadership dynamics of the city offered the Byrd Organization a reasonable chance to score a major victory for their cause. Since public schools were still open for elementary students, only a small percentage of the city's white pupils would actually be locked out of public classrooms. Of these, perhaps as many as one-fifth would drop out of high school anyway. Another group could successfully make the shift to one of the city's private preparatory schools, all of which were then undergoing an unprecedented building boom, prompted in part by the school desegregation crisis.[3] The navy was concerned enough about the permanency of the crisis that it, too, was drawing up plans to expand to a series of off-base institutions for military dependents.[4] Another group of secondary students, perhaps as many as 500, could be expected to transfer to segregated public schools in nearby communities[5] or leave the area to live with friends or relatives in other parts of the country.

Thus, although almost ten thousand students would actually be locked out of public classrooms, the maximum load to be carried by the Tidewater Educational Foundation and its substitute system of private schooling would actually be less than 5,000 pupils. The T.E.F. hoped that the enhanced status of private schooling and the chance to strike a blow at outside intervention would provide a strong incentive to prospective patrons. For the first time many of the city's middle-class residents would be able to afford the luxury of private schooling for their children now that the state provided tuition grants to students in communities with integrated public schools—one of the hallmarks of Massive Resistance. The group's major effort, however, focused upon a day school operated at Bayview Baptist Church, and the T.E.F. began to make ambitious plans to use other buildings if the need for more facilities arose. In addition, the T.E.F. arranged to rent the public schools in nearby South Norfolk for less than three dollars a month per student. It found a powerful ally in William J. Story, Jr., Superintendent of Schools in South Norfolk and a member of the State Board of Education, who agreed to start his city's schools one hour earlier so that the buildings could be cleared by 2 p.m. for the T.E.F.[6] In spite of its optimism, the T.E.F. faced enormous logistical problems in its effort to provide private replacements for even half of the city's closed secondary schools. Norfolk employed a whole staff of administrators, supervisors, principals, and teachers to struggle with the sort of textbook, personnel, curriculum, transportation, guidance, accounting, and maintenance problems that awaited the handful of staff members and volunteers at the T.E.F. Lenoir Chambers and the editorial staff of the *Virginian-Pilot* hammered away at this shortcoming:

> Substitute private schools are by their very nature "inferior education." [They would] be hurriedly makeshift, even if adequate teachers, adequate facilities, or accreditation could be found. Providing public education is the duty of the American government.[7]

Mayor Duckworth, however, was not willing to risk the entire fate of Massive Resistance on the T.E.F.'s plans alone, and a few days after the schools were closed, he proposed to Governor Almond an elaborate scheme to close only those grades actually under court orders to integrate; students in the grades unaffected by desegregation could then be reassigned to other public schools in the city. Because Norfolk was then operating on a split-year system, with graduations in both January and May, Duckworth felt that the city could open the second semester (the "H" sections) of the eighth, ninth, tenth, and eleventh grades. Since blacks had not been assigned to the twelfth grade, schools could have opened for seniors and the "H" sections—roughly 40 percent of the white students locked out of classes. Governor Almond and the state superintendent of schools quickly lined up the schools in South Norfolk, Norfolk County, Portsmouth, and Princess Anne County to accommodate the remaining students in the "L" sections of each grade.[8] Although it is unclear whether their opposition was based upon operational considerations, conscientious objections, or, as one newspaper report indicated, legal grounds,[9] the Norfolk School Board apparently refused to participate, and the plan died without implementation. Regardless of its reason, the board's rejection helped to increase the level of conflict with the mayor and city council.

Even if the public had been willing to overlook the administrative shortcomings of the T.E.F., its ambitious plan to replace the closed, integrated public schools with a private system of segregated academies was crushed by forces that had been up to now only incidental to the struggle. Many of the churches that could have provided a power base and alternative source of educational facilities instead refused to support the T.E.F.'s schools. The Catholic Church was among the first to speak out at the national level in urging compliance with the *Brown* decision; locally, Norfolk Catholic High and its feeder parochial elementary schools had been successfully integrated since 1955. Although the historically strong Jewish belief in the importance of education was a sustaining force behind the Committee for Public Schools and other efforts to oppose Massive Resistance,[10] the Jewish community was so intimidated by the possibility of reprisals that it never took a united action to support public education. The big break in the battle against Massive Resistance came when the Protestant denominations began openly to align their forces against the T.E.F. Even before the schools were closed, the Norfolk Presbytery voted nearly unanimously to support the dictates of the federal courts, and cautioned member churches against allowing their facilities to be used as alternative private schools.[11] Lutherans and Episcopalians soon followed with similar instructions for their congregations. Methodist and Baptist churches had a more difficult time following this lead: Bayview Baptist and a number of other Southern Baptist facilities already figured strongly in the T.E.F.'s plan of resistance. The Norfolk Ministerial Association, however, a Protestant organization largely in the control of Methodist and Baptist clergymen, took a united stand when they requested that Duckworth and the city council reopen the schools on a local-option integrated basis.[12]

The ministers soon found themselves aligned with an even more vocal professional group in their effort to reopen the public schools. Although several teachers were active in the formation of the Committee for Public Schools, as a group Norfolk educators resisted efforts to take a stand early in the crisis; once the schools closed, the Norfolk Education Association voted overwhelmingly to petition the city council to reopen the closed schools under local authority (i.e., without state funding) on an integrated basis.[13] Individual teachers then joined with the more active of the city's ministers to establish tutoring groups for almost 3,500 students in a number of private homes, storefronts, and in 23 churches across the city,[14] not as substitutes for public schools, but rather to prepare pupils to resume classes once the schools reopened. School authorities and Education Association officials soon became concerned that these "parlor schools" were degenerating into replacements for public schools, and were thus accomplishing the same end as the T.E.F. Also, they feared that support for public school teachers, who were still receiving full pay at state expense,[15] would wane if educators were discovered making money as a result of the school crisis. The N.E.A. thus adopted a resolution that recommended a salary of only $50 a month, about what teachers were spending out of their own pocket for books and supplies.[16] In addition, the N.E.A., in an effort to put pressure on the city's elected officials, voted to withdraw from the stopgap schools at the end of the semester, even if the public schools were not yet open; it feared that its members' efforts to continue teaching might make parents complacent and less prone to push for quick reopening of schools.[17]

Individually the teachers struck an even more direct blow at the forces of Massive Resistance. Efforts by the Tidewater Education Foundation to informally recruit public school teachers for its private facilities were continually rebuffed by the school board, the school administration, and the teachers themselves. Out of desperation, T.E.F. President James G. Martin IV, went to the mayor for assistance. Duckworth intervened, and assured the T.E.F. an audience with the teachers.[18] Even though they could still draw full state pay while teaching private school classes,[19] the out-of-work educators listened quietly while Martin made his pitch. Then, one by one, they got up and left the auditorium; not a single one of the city's professional educators was willing to support an effort that might undermine public schools.[20] The teachers' unanimous rejection of the T.E.F. was a bitter defeat for the Defenders, the mayor,[21] and all the state politicians who favored Massive Resistance.

In spite of this setback, the T.E.F. hoped to go forward with its plans anyhow, resolving to start small but pick up teacher support as the crisis continued. A handful of retired school teachers, fundamentalist ministers, and housewives were recruited to serve as their temporary educational staff, and late in October (1958) the T.E.F. finally opened Tidewater Academy with only six instructors and fewer than 60 students; plans for expansion of its facilities at Bayview Baptist Church were contingent only upon its ability to find additional qualified teachers.[22] Thus, Norfolk's teachers, by unanimously rejecting the financial rewards that would accompany a defection to the T.E.F., had almost single-handedly destroyed any chance that the Defenders, Mayor Duckworth, or the Byrd Organization had to make Massive Resistance work in the city.[23]

Even though they had unanimously rejected the T.E.F.'s offer, Norfolk's teachers, by setting up their own private tutoring groups, were accomplishing what the Defenders had sought to establish: a segregated alternative to integrated public schools. The tutoring groups that had sprung up in private homes, church buildings, and empty store fronts were actually contributing in a large part to the apathy of the parents and the students themselves. The public tended to overlook the crowded quarters and the lack of textbooks, library, laboratory, and support facilities, and saw instead the makings of an even finer education for their children: classrooms with only a small number of motivated students, dedicated teachers, and a high degree of individual attention. Although these were educational commodities that could be found only among the most expensive and exclusive private preparatory schools, they were now almost universally available for less than $50 a month. Parents began to see how much their children were learning in spite of the makeshift quality of the tutoring groups, and a danger existed that they would eventually shift their support to private schools after all. Leaders of parent and student groups who wished to rally support for public education found that they could not be heard as long as the tutoring groups remained in operation; their best efforts to create a pro-school sentiment produced only hollow resolutions that lacked the backing of their full membership—the individuals with the greatest stake in continuing universal public education.

In Norfolk, no one had as yet been forced to pay the price for closing public schools. The *Virginian-Pilot* continued to hammer away editorially at the long-term economic disaster that awaited the city—naval ship reassignments and loss of industry, ship-repair contracts, business prospects, and the like—but these were intangible expenses that had not yet hit home for the average citizen. The *Pilot* went on to estimate that the cost of operating a public school system in the city without state funding and control would mean at least a one-third rise in real estate taxes and a concomitant drop in federal impact aid funds,[24] which were still channeled through the state. While tutoring groups continued, however, with their primary form of subsidy coming from the state's obligation to honor the teaching contracts of the instructors in the closed schools, the more direct costs of rising taxes and increased local support seemed distant and unreal. As long as no one had to pay directly for Massive Resistance, the great majority of citizens remained silent and aloof from the struggle, preferring instead to allow others to incur the risks of active participation.

In this atmosphere of public malaise, the Norfolk Committee for Public Schools saw little hope for success if it operated as just another local pressure group; after more than a month of frantic activity, it could only boast 6,000 members,[25] large enough to rival the Defenders, but still too small to dodge the "integrationist" label that destroyed its political effectiveness. Instead, the Committee vowed to seek other means to reopen the schools, and turned its attention toward convincing state and national leaders. A delegation from the Committee talked with Governor Almond, and urged him to return the closed schools to local control. The Governor's response that only the courts could reopen the closed schools,[26] strengthened the Committee's resolve to add class action litigation to its rapidly diminishing arsenal. On October 27, 1958, a class action suit was filed in federal court on behalf of the Committee for Public Schools; the suit named Governor Almond, the school board, and others as defendants, and was filed on behalf of 33 white parents and their children.

Although 89 individuals were listed as plaintiffs,[27] realtor Ellis James took the biggest risk by lending his name to the proceedings. The state was already testing the legality of the school closing in *Harrison* v. *Day*, a "friendly" suit filed in the Virginia Supreme Court,[28] but *James* v. *Almond*, the Committee suit, went far beyond this rather limited action. *James* v. *Almond* claimed that the closing of Norfolk's six previously all-white secondary schools had deprived their students of equal protection of the laws guaranteed under the Fourteenth Amendment.[29]

The sudden shift of the Norfolk Committee for Public Schools into the field of litigation caught the N.A.A.C.P. off guard; it was, however, quick to realize the historic significance of the action: *James* v. *Almond* was the first lawsuit of its kind filed by white litigants in the South. When its own suit was filed a few days later, the N.A.A.C.P. took a secondary position, and entered it only as companion litigation to the Committee's action.[30] The N.A.A.C.P. was unwilling, however, to back away in its quest to enlist new transfer applicants for the next (1959-1960) school year, thereby signaling both its intention to keep up the long-term legal pressure to desegregate schools and its refusal to negotiate the issue. Even so, Duckworth and the city council redoubled their own efforts to force the black community to withdraw the 17 pending transfer applicants. At one Council session Duckworth turned to a group seeking to reopen the schools and stated, "If you gentlemen want to help, you could talk to the families of the seventeen Negro children and get them to withdraw. . . . Then we could open these schools tomorrow."[31] Councilman Abbott repeated the Organization's position, "We've got seventeen Negro children who are keeping 10,000 white children out of school." Mayor Duckworth followed by laying most of the blame on the N.A.A.C.P., saying that they

> . . . did not truly represent Norfolk's colored population. The city has demonstrated what Norfolk's colored people mean to it by spending millions on slum clearance and schools, yet Negroes here pay less than five per cent of the taxes and make up seventy-five per cent of the jail population.[32]

His unfortunate repetition of these inflammatory sentiments—an earlier remark had rallied the black community behind its more extreme leadership in the N.A.A.C.P.—reveals a lot about both his famed intemperance and the helplessness he felt in the crisis. It also demonstrates a fatal flaw in the mayor's thinking that tended to reduce complex issues to simplistic terms, especially casting the people behind those issues in roles as either supporters or detractors. For Duckworth there was no middle ground—no way to be both independent on principal, but supportive on the issues—and this made it difficult for the school board and others to take a stand before the mayor had publicly committed himself. Duckworth, although an excellent leader, was a poor coalition builder, and the fact that he had achieved a broad base of support in the white community was more a result of forcefulness than any diplomatic bent.

For their own part, the black community refused to be goaded by his remarks; the city's black leadership did not want to challenge the mayor in a name-calling contest that might make them a target for the frustrations of whites faced with school closings. The mayor probably would have been delighted to have had such sharply defined antagonists, but except for the N.A.A.C.P.'s new litigation, the city's black leadership seemed perfectly content to pull back from the struggle in the white community and let the Committee for Public Schools take the lead. One of their most promising behind-the-scenes efforts was an attempt to prepare the 17 black transfer students for the hardships they would face in integrated classrooms. Black leaders started a separate tutoring group for these "pioneers," and coached them in both the academic subjects and the fine points of dress, poise, and etiquette, as well as to provide them with the psychological preparation and self-defense skills they would need to make integration work. Mrs. W. T. Mason, chairwoman of the project, told the students, "When you sought entrance to white schools, you left your childhood behind."[33]

Mayor Duckworth was too pragmatic to think that those 17 black students would somehow taint the education of the ten thousand whites locked out of their classes, but he was also too astute to attempt to oppose the Organization on its best issue in decades. The mayor was faced, however, with the first real conflict within his Harmony coalition since its formation eight years earlier. The majority of the city's business community was not yet ready to abandon public education, and the school board and the editorial writers of the *Virginian-Pilot* in all likelihood represented the still-private concerns of the Silkstocking crowd, more than even Duckworth would have cared to admit. Although he had shown a great deal of racial intolerance in his remarks and policies, Duckworth was above all else a sharp politician, and the Organization had always found that race-baiting was good politics. He had not so far overtly committed himself to promoting Massive Resistance, only to giving the Defenders a fair hearing before Norfolk's teachers; to do otherwise, in light of the Defender's powerful electoral appeal, would have been bad politics.

The public was probably unaware of the ramifications of Duckworth's involvement up to this point, but they were knowledgeable enough to know that the mayor was the key to any resolution of the current crisis: Both the school board and the Massive Resisters needed his support to prevail. Duckworth was not the type of leader who could sit by while such a momentous crisis ran its course; with the prospect of Massive Resistance failing, he needed a quick and dramatic political maneuver that would shore up his constituency and give new impetus to the drive to retain segregated schools. The school board's request that the Council join it in petitioning the Governor to return the schools to local control—the one loophole in the state's Massive Resistance plan whereby a closed public school could reopen, albeit on an integrated basis—brought this behind-the-scenes conflict into the open. Local control meant opening the schools, but it also meant integration; rejecting the board's request would prolong the school closing and promote Massive Resistance. The political risks of joining the board in its petition were enormous: It meant bowing to the N.A.A.C.P., the federal courts, and the Committee for Public Schools—all enemies in the mayor's eyes. Moreover, it meant forfeiting forever the support of both the Defenders and the Old Guard of the Byrd/ Prieur Organization, Duckworth's natural supporters. If the appeal was successful and schools were reopened without state funding, the mayor would be personally responsible for an increase in local taxes; and finally, such an act would place the mayor far beyond any course of action that the public had as yet indicated it would approve. Denying the board's request, however, would risk provoking the ire of the school board, school patrons, editors of the *Virginian-Pilot*, and probably the Silkstocking element of the business community, still a powerful, yet strangely silent, force in the community. Seen in this context, the mayor's attempt to avoid the question by calling upon the Governor to reopen the closed schools on a segregated basis—something he could not legally do—comes as no surprise. The controversy would not go away; the school board and the editors of the *Virginian-Pilot* continued to press for petitioning the Governor, firm in their resolve to use every opportunity to witness for public education. The issue, however, was not as clear-cut as the board made it appear: Once the Council asked the Governor to return the schools to local control, nothing guaranteed that the Governor would then honor their request. State law was just vague enough on the point that the Governor was under no obligation to make any response at all. If this were so, then the school board was urging a course that might potentially isolate the mayor from his supporters, divide the community, and then make him appear ineffective for attempting such a futile gesture. The simplest solution to the dilemma would be for the Governor to indicate ahead of time how he would respond to a request for local control, but when a Norfolk delegation sought a preliminary indication of his stance, the Governor "just grinned:"[34] Almond was too good a politician to commit himself and risk alienating his own supporters.

Duckworth, however, had discovered another solution, and one that would not only legitimately stall the issue for another month, it would also take him permanently off the hook: He would let the people decide the question in an informational referendum. The mayor, in announcing the Council's intent to delay action until after the referendum, explained his rationale: "Governor Almond was elected by an overwhelming majority to do exactly what he has done. I think the only way to impress the Governor is to let the same voters show him what they want done now."[35] His emphasis on "the same voters" was part of the brilliance of this tactical ploy: Since this was an off year for elections, the referendum would come at a time when less than a fourth of the city's voters had paid their poll taxes; nor was there any time either to register new voters or to allow delinquent accounts to be brought up to date. The question was thus to be put to the same conservative and established electorate that had given a two-to-one mandate to Governor Almond and Massive Resistance the year before. Second, since the referendum "was purely informational in nature," the vote would not decide anything;

the city council would be free at any time to disregard the outcome if it felt so inclined.[36]

The Organization was the clear beneficiary of the mayor's decision: Their constituency would be the ones who would decide the issue; less than a sixth of the voters would be black;[37] navy personnel and others new to the area would be disenfranchised by the poll tax and preregistration requirements, and the shortened time frame would not allow the pro-school forces an opportunity to mount much of a campaign of opposition. Further, it put the school board, the Committee for Public Schools, the editors of the *Virginian-Pilot*, and school patrons in the unenviable position of having to oppose both the mayor and the concept of popular democracy. In an editorial titled "In Principle, Wrong; In Practice, Confusing," the *Pilot* castigated the mayor for his lack of leadership, courage, and statesmanship. The editorial warned that: "It runs directly counter to the views and formal recommendations of the Norfolk School Board, [and] thereby digs a deep and ominous chasm between these two bodies."[38]

The vote and the closed electorate were only part of the overall plan: Duckworth wanted to make sure that the voters—his constituency—would have to face the same tough decision that the school board demanded. Just to underscore this point, the actual question was weighted with code words and catch phrases that would make a clear-cut decision difficult: "Shall the Council of the City of Norfolk, pursuant to State Law, petition the Governor to return to the City control of schools, now closed, to be opened by the City on an Integrated Basis as required by the Federal Court?" Voters were to check "For" or "Against Petitioning the Governor." Another section, labeled "For Information Only, Not To Be Voted On," made the decision even harder:

> In the event the closed schools are returned to the City of Norfolk, and are reopened Integrated by the City, it will be necessary, because of the loss of State Funds, for every family having a child or children in Public Schools... to pay the City a substantial Tuition."[39]

The pro-school advocates who had hoped to rally voter support in favor of opening the schools now found that task impossible: There was not enough time to mount an effective campaign; the electorate was too closely allied with the Byrd/Prieur Organization; and the question was both too confusing and too emotionally charged for voters to make a meaningful choice. The loaded ballot meant that the pro-school forces would first have to undertake a highly organized and well financed effort to reeducate the populace before they could tackle the issue in the referendum. The teachers, the ministers, the Committee for Public Schools, the school board, and even the editorial staff of the *Virginian-Pilot* were incapable of such a monumental undertaking. The Committee for Public Schools saw how hopeless its task had become, and turned its efforts instead to legal actions to block the referendum. Two suits were filed—one challenged the legality of an informational action where no binding decision would be rendered; the other hoped to strike the "For Information Only" portion off the ballot on the grounds that charging tuition fees for public schools was contrary to state law—but both efforts were quickly struck down by the local and state supreme court justices.[40]

The school board, realizing that it had been outflanked by the maneuver, attempted to pull back from a clash over the referendum, and instead chose only to complain about the additional delay; later its members apparently considered campaigning in favor of petitioning the Governor. Mayor Duckworth got word of the board's intent, and publicly lectured them on the virtues of neutrality on the issue: "The Council is maintaining a 'hands off policy' on the referendum. We don't have any idea of politicking one way or the other. I would like to suggest that the school board do the same."[41] School Board Chairman Paul Schweitzer tried to respond that "politics has never entered into the board's decisions," but both of the city's newspapers picked up the tone of the exchange as an attempt to rebuke the board and get them back into line.[42] Even though it backed down on this score, the board still chose a course that was independent from the mayor: Instead, it put itself on record as opposed to charging any form of tuition. Public schools are an essential community service, members reasoned, the cost of which must necessarily be borne by the entire public, and not just those who benefit directly. To the mayor's charge that he was "politicking" even with this stance, Board Chairman Schweitzer answered, "I don't intend to be involved in politics. I intend to inform the public of the facts and let them make up their minds."[43] Ben Willis, a Duckworth appointee and the most conservative member, was even more contemptuous of the attempt to silence the board; "I'll wear no man's muzzle. . . . It is the school board's duty to inject itself into the controversy."[44]

The referendum issue had left the members of the board more isolated than ever before: They were not quite at war with the Council and the city's political leaders, but they were certainly further out on the limb of opposition than any other group of successful businessmen had been in almost a decade. They were cut off as well from the rest of the business community: Not a single civic or financial leader of any note had been willing to join them, the teachers, the Ministerial Association, or the Committee for Public Schools in any action which might threaten the Organization's Massive Resistance program. Norfolk under Duckworth had always prided itself on the unanimity of its business and political leaders, and now the school board threatened to disrupt that hard fought harmony in the middle of the most intense crisis the coalition had ever faced. The pressure on its members to remain quiet was intense,[45] but unanimously they rejected this course as a matter of conscience. They knew that the referendum would be a disaster for the closed schools; not because the concept of public education would be rejected, but rather because the election would only further delay the inevitable decision to comply. In the meantime the forces of Massive Resistance would have a chance to claim some sort of mandate—a unanimity of popular defiance that the Council hoped would impress the federal court and force it to retreat. Instead the board saw it as a futile gesture: The lesson of Little Rock was that the federal government had no intention of withdrawing. Still, the board hoped that by opposing only the references to tuition payments, they had chosen a moderate position somewhere between the two competing demands: they were not instructing the voters to vote "For" integrated schools; neither were they advocating a decision "Against" public education. In reality they were attempting to be moderates on an issue in which there could be no moderation, and each step brought them closer to a choice between further confrontation or compliance. Boardmember Ben Willis thought that they should resign and abandon this collision course—"I feel the school board has served its usefulness," he said— but Chairman Schweitzer was more philosophic: "You follow the detour, take the bumps, and hope that you'll soon be back on the good road again."⁴⁶

At any rate, the six individual members of the Norfolk School Board seemed willing to risk both their political futures and their business ventures over what each must have felt was a matter of conscience. Each had personal reasons for choosing this independent course, but all six were obviously sustained by a common and overriding belief in the merits of public education, and in a way each provided a powerful, living testimony to that ideal. Paul Schweitzer, the chairman and most visible spokesman for the board, had grown up on a ranch in Arizona, where he had experienced an "integrated" education: "My sister and I were the only gringos in that little one-room schoolhouse ... it was a lonely experience."⁴⁷ Francis Crenshaw, the son of a Navy captain, had lived all over the country, and had also attended integrated schools in New England.⁴⁸ Board member W. Farley Powers was born and raised in a log house in the impoverished coal mining counties of Virginia's Southwest; hard work and a solid devotion to learning had been his only escape from the deprivation that surrounded him.⁴⁹ William Ballard had grown up in the equally poor Eastern Shore region, where he was employed by his family fish and oyster packinghouse. After working his way through high school and then college, he returned to raise the family seafood business into one of the area's leading employers.⁵⁰ Although heir to his father's posh furniture salon, an upbringing that was more typical of the rest of the business elite, Ben Willis owed his fortitude to something his father had taught him: "There are two things you cannot compromise—principle and equality."⁵¹ Mildred Dallas, the only woman on any of the city's major boards and commissions, brought a minority prospective of her own.

Thus, although on paper they were similar to many of the city's civic and business leaders, the members of the school board had a profound commitment to the concepts of equality and public education—a conviction strong enough to endure the sense of helplessness and isolation they now faced. Although publicly in favor of petitioning the Governor and privately opposed to even putting the decision to a vote, the school board still backed away from openly campaigning on the issue—Mayor Duckworth's scolding had produced at least that much compliance—instead abandoning that cause to the Committee for Public Schools and the other zealots of the pro-school movement. In spite of the fact that the odds were heavily stacked against them, the Committee still nursed vague hopes that Duckworth and the Organization had blundered by putting the issue to a vote. It was a remote possibility, but the Committee nevertheless prepared guide ballots, handbills, and a massive newspaper advertising campaign to promote a vote "for" public schools. The Defenders of State Sovereignty and Individual Liberties led the forces that urged a vote "against" the resolution—the Council remained true to its pledge to stay out of the contest once it had drawn up the ballot.[52] In one sense it was a classic struggle between the liberal Committee and the ultra-conservative Defenders, but the odds were too heavily stacked against the resolution to make it a fair fight. The wording on the ballot, the nature of the electorate, the short duration of the contest, and the tacit opposition of the Organization all doomed the Committee's efforts to failure before they had even begun. The only surprise in the results was the paucity of the turnout: Only 21,000 people—less than half of those eligible, and only a tenth of the city's adult population—showed up to cast a ballot in the most important election in a decade. The referendum to petition the Governor to reopen the closed schools lost by a healthy three-to-two margin, the same figure by which Senator Harry Byrd and Governor Almond had defeated their recent opponents. Only 3,600 black voters—still less than half of those eligible—turned out to help the pro-school forces; their presence, however, helped to dilute the harshness of the two-and-a-half-to-1 rout that the Committee suffered in the white precincts.[53] Even so, the vote was much closer in the Silkstocking precincts on the West Side than in the largely blue-collar neighborhoods in the northern, eastern, and central portions of the city.[54]

❋ ❋ ❋

8

✻ ✻ ✻ ✻ ✻

A Very Massive Resister

THE PEOPLE HAD SPOKEN, or so it seemed; the message of their mandate was, however, indistinct. On the one hand, they appeared to endorse a continuation of the school-closing strategy to avoid court-ordered integration; on the other hand, they gave no indication of just how long they would support this tactic. The message was clouded by the fact that as yet no one had really suffered greatly from the closings: Tutoring groups and the heightened sense of shared emergency had helped to mask the fact that the burden of Massive Resistance had fallen disproportionately upon the young, poor, and transient populations not represented in the established electorate. The people had not, as spokesmen for the Defenders claimed, endorsed Massive Resistance: The tutoring groups and the dismal patronage drawn to the Tidewater Education Foundation's segregated private academies gave substantial testimony to the fact that Norfolk parents wanted the education of their children to continue in the public realm. If there was any significance at all to the election, and any meaning to the events that fall that preceded the contest, it was that most citizens were still waiting for some sort of dramatic action that would resolve the crisis—the scenarios proposed by the T.E.F. and the Committee for Public Schools were both unacceptable—and most were hoping for a return to segregated public schools—the one option not available. Thus, the people were not ready, as the Governor surmised, to reject racially mixed schools;[1]

they were just not prepared to accept them yet.

The one man who bore the heaviest responsibility for reading these auguries was Mayor Duckworth, but both time and events were conspiring in such a way as to cloud his judgment of the referendum's relative importance with other, largely political, considerations. Far from lessening the pressures upon him to act, however, the referendum had served instead to focus new attention upon his response. The referendum and rebuke of the pro-schools advocates had won him newfound respect among the state's conservatives:

> A gleam has replaced the old suspicious look when you mention Norfolk in the politically potent domain called the Virginia Southside. It's because of a new feeling that Norfolk is not going to bow easily to school integration. And that gleam shows when the name of Norfolk's frank-talking mayor comes up. The word most often heard in describing his actions is that he has "guts."[2]

Increasingly, the eyes of the state's political leaders began to turn away from the staid and passive elegance of the Governor to the energy and dynamism of Norfolk's mayor; there was no question that they liked what they saw. Almond had won office by portraying himself as the brains behind Massive Resistance, but now it was Duckworth who was seen as the guts, and his blunt, outspoken "go-getter" image proved a sharp contrast to the rolling rhetorical rodomontade that characterized Almond's style. Almond appeared to be the consummate silver-haired patrician, the type Virginians had always sought for higher office. Thus, it was ironic that now, in crisis, they should turn instead to Duckworth, the epitome in appearance of the urban political boss with his stocky, even pudgy, five-foot, ten-and-a-half-inch frame, and jowly visage. Even his trademark, the ever-present cigar and cigar holder, was more a big-city stogie than the plantation Havana of the genteel; he smoked three a day, but unlit, all three did double duty as the maestro's baton of his furious pace of action. "He thinks fast and calls the shots quickly—sometimes with a suddenness that is startling" is how one reporter described him, going on to add that he "can snap with a voice which is some where [sic] between a bark and a bite." It was this very openness—"he's no diplomat, but he lays his cards on the table face up"³—that was attracting the attention of the most ardent segregationists; they sensed a steely harshness in his opposition to federal authorities that seemed lacking in Almond's calm demeanor. In short, Duckworth, not Almond, appeared to be the emerging hero of Massive Resistance, and already his name was being bandied about by political insiders across the state as a gubernatorial contender.⁴ Local Byrd Organization chieftain Billy Prieur had begun to take him to Skyland, Harry Byrd's mountain retreat, for regular sessions with the Senator, both to underscore the importance of continued resistance and to explore the possibilities of advancing the mayor's political career. For the first time, Duckworth was entertaining ambitions that stretched beyond municipal service, and he was eager to parlay this new statewide following into the Organization's nod for governor.⁵

All of this political speculation—as yet only the talk of insiders who thrive on such badinage—led Duckworth to misinterpret the results of the referendum as both a personal endorsement of his policies and a call to arms for further resistance. For the time being, however, the vote seemed to both solve all his present problems and to promote new opportunities: First, it relieved the city council of having to make any decision on the Norfolk School Board's appeal for action from the Governor; second, it seemed to mend a potential rift in his business/Organization constituency by allowing the people, not the politicians, to rebuke the school board for entertaining thoughts of surrender; it had bought him time to establish that cool and rational citizen response to the crisis was possible; and finally, and most important, it had convinced the rest of the state of the solidarity of Norfolk's resistance to school integration, relieved the pressure from the Southside to overreact, and bought time in which to affect a purely local decision. Unfortunately personal ambitions and political pressures blinded the mayor to the beneficial escape-valve qualities of the referendum, and led him instead to overreact in favor of Massive Resistance. Duckworth possessed a marvelously analytical mind that was well suited to the rough-and-tumble realm of urban politics; he now sized up the situation in terms of potential obstacles, options, and sources of opposition, and then proceeded one by one to clear the obstacles and opposition from the path that blocked his choice of options.

Chief among those obstacles was the threat still posed by actions before the courts. It was not the *Harrison* v. *Day* "friendly" suit brought to test the legality of the state's Massive Resistance laws, nor even a continuation of the N.A.A.C.P.'s integration litigation, that most observers feared; instead, the Committee For Public Schools' *James* v. *Almond* action was the challenge upon which the fate of Massive Resistance hinged; this entreaty, wholly unexpected by both Duckworth and the Organization, had Governor Almond and the legal experts concerned. Almond knew that the state could not continue to offer public secondary schools for black students, but not to whites, and that this challenge by white parents would ultimately sink the interposition logic of Massive Resistance. Duckworth, however, was not inclined to accept defeat so easily, and instead began to lay the groundwork for a plan that would undermine the Committee's action. At the first city council meeting after the referendum Duckworth proposed a "cut-off of funds" clause in the school board budget slated to begin on January 1, 1959, thereby reserving for the city council the right to "change or cancel the unexpended portion" of school funds at any time during the year, even prohibiting specific expenditures if it wished. There were several reasons for such a ploy: First, it brought the more moderate school board more directly under his control by giving the city council the power of month-to-month approval of every facet of the board's budget[6]—a potent check on the independence of the board. Second, the measure was partly designed to retaliate against the errant teachers who had undermined the Organization's Massive Resistance strategy. According to reports, the mayor had personally intervened to set up the meeting, and was still smarting from the teachers' rejection of the T.E.F.'s offer. When Superintendent J. J. Brewbaker expressed his concern, "I hope we don't do anything to encourage teachers to look for other jobs—we have good teachers," Mayor Duckworth snapped, "With what some of them have done . . . I would have to disagree with you."[7]

These two retaliatory aspects of the funds cut-off measure were, however, only secondary to other more pressing considerations. With the added power, city council now directly controlled a potential solution to its legal dilemmas. In the event that the ruling in the Committee For Public Schools' *James* v. *Almond* suit went against the city, the Council could close the remaining white junior high as well as the City's black junior and senior high schools, a move that would put Norfolk's case in uncharted legal waters. No court had yet ruled that a municipality was required to offer secondary education to its citizens; in fact, Virginia Attorney General Albertis S. Harrison had already indicated that the U.S. Supreme Court's *Brown* decision had struck down the entire state constitutional mandate to provide public schools at all, because the establishment of a public educational system in Virginia was entirely conditional upon the schools being segregated.[8] The legal arguments in the *James* v. *Almond* case turned upon the fact that Norfolk was providing public secondary schools for some and not all its patrons; if the remaining secondary institutions were closed, the ploy would at the very least tie up the legal efforts to integrate the schools for several more years, perhaps giving the Organization enough time to permanently salvage its Massive Resistance plan to substitute private, segregated academies for integrated public schools. In fact, a similar maneuver in Prince Edward County was not definitively broken by the courts until 1963.[9]

Closing the city's black junior and senior high schools was at this time, at least, a last resort and only an ancillary aspect of the proposal. The major purpose of the clause was not to serve as a legal dodge, but rather to stand as the most formidable in a series of power plays to pressure the black community into finally withdrawing their integration efforts. Up to now the school board had been able to serve as a buffer between the mayor and the black community, insulating the black educational system from political reprisals. Now that the school board had been short-circuited out of direct control of any portion of its funding, the entire black educational system was dangerously exposed to reprisals. Councilman Lewis Layton renewed the mayor's call for a black withdrawal from integration efforts, and dangled the potent threat of the funds cut-off as the cutting edge of that demand. Duckworth, too, wanted the black community to know that this time he meant business: "The only way schools can reopen now is by getting the cooperation of the colored citizens."[10] The black community knew that the mayor's threat was no idle bluff: He had both the inclination and the capacity to carry it out. "We could do nothing less in the light of the school referendum,"[11] was the mayor's carefully worded counter to those who challenged the cutoff. The threat was real enough: Unless the N.A.A.C.P. withdrew its efforts to integrate the city's schools, the black community would be faced with at best a prolonged shutdown and, at worst, a permanent closing of its secondary school system and additional retaliatory encroachments upon its elementary schools. The enormous progress in black education that had taken place in the twelve years since the People's group first took over the city government would now come to an abrupt halt, and was even in danger of retrogressing. Was the black community willing to trade the future of an entire generation of its young people for the expanded educational opportunities of seventeen youths? The mayor was betting that they would not.

The mayor's funds-cutoff proposal was a direct result of the lopsided referendum victory, a growing awareness of his aspirations for higher office, and an increase in the hostile attitudes of a few of the state's most powerful and most ardent segregationists. The referendum had helped to quiet much of the rabid rhetoric coming from Virginia's Southside counties, but some highly visible step to preserve the legal façade of Massive Resistance still seemed necessary to appease former Governor Bill Tuck and others who had been roused by the *Virginian-Pilot*'s editorial policy and its continued coverage of the pro-school advocates. Mayor Duckworth had come under increasing pressure, in spite of his own growing personal popularity with these resisters, to prove that Norfolk was not a "hotbed of integrationists" as Tuck and his cohorts were charging. The funds-cutoff measure was designed in part to appease these sympathies, as well as to buy the city enough time to negotiate some sort of out-of-court settlement of the issue. Tuck and the rest of the Southside's Massive Resisters represented a powerful political force in the Organization—one with which even a mayor lacking in ambition for advancement would have to deal in order to secure continued state funding for the highways, bridges, tunnels, institutions, and other projects that were so crucial to Duckworth's development desires—and they were not above threatening to cut off state funds earmarked for any political jurisdiction which bowed to court-ordered school integration: "If Norfolk won't stand with us, I say let them stand alone" was Tuck's philosophy.[12]

Duckworth's quick action on the funds-cutoff measure—so soon after the referendum— earned him accolades of praise from the Byrd Organization hierarchy and the Southside cheering section. Even so, no immediate end to the crisis was possible until January, when the Council assumed control of the school board's funding, the court cases were slated for resolution, the black community would have to respond, the tutoring groups were scheduled to cease,[13] and the school board threatened to resign if the mayor's funds-cutoff proposal went into effect.[14] Norfolk was thus stuck in a holding pattern: The flurry of activity that followed the first weeks of closed schools had all but died away; the doors had now been locked for more than three months; and the federal government showed no signs of quick surrender. Onlookers could not agree whether the citizens were "complacent" or just "frustrated" by their inability to influence the crisis;[15] even so, Norfolk was remarkably quiet for a city with 10,000 students out on the streets, and the future of both its public educational system and continued racial harmony at stake.

In the air of official calm that prevailed, Norfolk's rumor mills worked overtime, helping to shift the focus of attention away from the political arena. Increasingly the attention of parents and civic leaders began to turn away from the student leaders towards a different type of pupil—not the ones who attended the tutoring groups, lead protests, or were active in school clubs and organizations. More and more there was concern that the effect of the closings would be tallied as well in the sudden upsurge of teenage unemployment, hostility, delinquency, crime, pregnancy, forced marriages, dropouts, and the like—the kind of effects that have a lasting impact upon the future of the community. Lenoir Chambers and the editorial staff of the *Virginian-Pilot* hammered away at this theme as well as the long-term economic ruin that lay ahead. Washington continued to sound ominous notes about the crisis' potential impact upon naval contracts, ship assignments, and billeting arrangements—the navy was reluctant to make assignments to a community that lacked public schools—but these warnings seemed to go unheeded. Rumors spread about officers who had requested transfers, ships that had been reassigned, new business prospects frightened away, and the likelihood of congressional retaliation.[16]

In spite of these dire warnings that the underpinnings of Norfolk's economy were severely threatened, the full impact of the crisis had not yet hit the business community. Local business leaders and economic trends were still pointing as late as January, 1959, to a bright outlook and a rapid recovery from the national slump that occurred in the last years of the Eisenhower administration.[17]

Even so, elements within the business community never gave up their attempt to attract the remnants of the People's group to the pro-school camp. To no avail, School Board Chairman Schweitzer, businessman Sam Barfield, psychiatrist William F. Blair, Committee for Public Schools' lawyer Archie Boswell, and Lewis W. Webb, Jr., provost of the junior college that was the precursor to Old Dominion University, pleaded with the Chamber of Commerce to take a stand in defense of reopening the closed schools.[18] Over and over again Lenoir Chambers and the editorial pages of the *Virginian-Pilot* echoed the theme that the business leaders must put a stop to the school crisis, and that the city's future as a major naval base was threatened;[19] in spite of this, not a single leader of the old People's group, not one major corporate executive or civic leader, dared to take up the challenge. The only corporate voices that were heard came from outside the city, although some, like John Fishwick, the president of the Norfolk and Western Railroad, former governor Colgate Darden, brother of Norfolk's former mayor and now president of the University of Virginia, political leader Francis Pickens Miller, and other statewide industrialists,[20] had a special relationship with the city. Only Frank Batten, publisher of the *Virginian-Pilot* and *Ledger-Dispatch* newspapers, was willing to join with three dozen business leaders from across the state who were urging Governor Almond to reopen the closed schools.[21] Most of the rest of Norfolk's business and civic establishment remained quiet on the issue, giving Duckworth a free hand to negotiate with the black community.

The black community refused to back down from their efforts, in spite of the fact that almost every element of the white populace stood poised against them—or at least seemed prepared to silently assent to the closing of their schools, too, in retaliation. Norfolk's blacks gave every indication that they were prepared to choose closed schools rather than give up on integration.[22] Their defiance led Duckworth to announce on January 13, 1959, the intention of the Council to close down after February 1, all grades above the sixth— an additional 1,914 white pupils and 5,259 black students would be locked out. A small band of pro-school advocates made an emotional plea at the session for Council to "think it over" before taking this drastic step, and once more appealed to the business community to end the crisis.[23]

Ironically, the first crack in the mayor's coalition came not from any of these sources, but rather from within the Council itself. For the first time in the history of the crisis, a single councilman split from the pack and voted "No" to a Duckworth proposal. Councilman Roy B. Martin, Jr., a Duckworth appointee, caused a ripple of surprise and then applause from the pro-school advocates. Martin listed the reasons for his opposition:

> I sincerely feel we are headed for a definite backward step economically if we do not straighten out our school situation, not further impair it. My strong apprehension about the economic future of Norfolk impels me to vote "No."[24]

Years later, Martin would indicate that it was the punitive nature of the measure, as much as the economic considerations, that made it objectionable: "It was stupid to enlarge the problem by closing more schools."[25]

Instead of serving as the rallying point for business opposition to the mayor's retaliatory tack, Martin was left to stand alone in moderation; the Silkstocking crowd remained as silent as before, failing even in this eleventh hour opportunity to back one of its own in an act of raw political courage. Roy Martin's vote, although a seemingly useless act of defiance, was not as suicidal as it may have first appeared. Thirty-seven years old and the youngest member of the Council, Martin was fast emerging as the one member of the Duckworth coalition closest to both the people and the business community. The editors of the *Virginian-Pilot* were determined that his action not seem an isolated incident, and therefore promoted the split with unprecedented news and editorial coverage for a single council vote. The pro-school advocates—the teachers, ministers, Committee For Public Schools, P.T.A.s and their sympathizers—who up to that point had carried the banner of opposition to Massive Resistance alone, took heart. If Roy Martin was willing to risk his political career on a single vote, they figured, he must have sensed some new surge of sentiment stirring. For this reason, they planned a flurry of activity, unmatched since the first week of closings, to probe this new development. The *Virginian-Pilot* sensed the change in the city:

At present Norfolk may be likened to a bus coming down a narrow mountain road in the command of drivers who have misread the road map, neglected to read the warning signs, and who are cheered on by a group of front-seat passengers who don't know what they are doing. . . . Norfolk's task would be difficult under any leadership . . . but the difficult task is horribly compounded when the leadership acts on vain and dangerous assumptions. There will be hope only when a lot of silent, unhappy people screw their courage to the sticking point and speak and act.[26]

The first shots in the new barrage were fired at a meeting of the Granby High School P.T.A. Granby had been closed four months, but suddenly 450 people jammed a standing-room-only meeting to demand a more vocal opposition to the school closing plan. The most telling fusillade in the new barrage came not from the closed secondary schools, but rather from the Bay View Elementary P.T.A., long a stronghold of Defender sentiment. Even though only 26 Bay View seventh-graders would be effected by the cutoff, a crowd of angry parents at a packed meeting of the P.T.A. shouted down the objections of William I. McKendree, president of both the T.E.F. and the Bay View P.T.A., and voted unanimously to pass a resolution opposing the closing of any more schools.[27] The editors of the *Virginian-Pilot* were shocked: "In these dark days, the action of the Bay View P.T.A. lights a candle of hope." Five more P.T.A.s followed their lead, and the *Virginian-Pilot* took these actions as a cue to ask, "Has the Counter-Revolution Begun?"[28]

The next salvo was fired by the school board, a group that had been relatively silent since it had been stripped so unceremoniously of its financial power. In an action of silent defiance, board members served as the star witnesses for the Committee for Public Schools in its *James v. Almond* suit. Even though the school board had been named as a codefendant along with the mayor, it supported each of the Committee's claims of economic and educational hardship. Moreover, the school board now took two remarkable actions that brought it dangerously close to direct confrontation with the Council. First, Chairman Paul Schweitzer issued a carefully worded statement that skirted the edge of defiance by indicating the board's displeasure with the new closings tactic.[29] Next, the board gave every indication that it would like to lose this new suit, and when City Attorney Leonard Davis joined them in withdrawing from the case, the Council was left alone to face the court.[30]

A new harshness in the mayor's attitude had brought about the situation where the school board, his city attorney, and one of his Council members were willing to risk open disagreement; for the first time they understood just how far Duckworth was willing to go to make Massive Resistance work, and the prospect frightened them. At the very time most Norfolk residents were beginning to entertain thoughts of reopening the schools, Duckworth was calling selected members of the school board and the city council to a secret strategy session at his home. There, Mayor Duckworth, Vice-Mayor George Abbott, and Organization head Billy Prieur—Martin was not invited—indicated both their willingness and their intention to close every school in the city, if necessary, in order to prevent integration.[31] Since they knew that this was no idle threat, the prospect of even more closed schools and a continuation of hardline resistance frightened the board members present almost as much as Duckworth's next announcement: The Council was considering an offer by the T.E.F. to buy up the closed schools and operate them on a private, segregated basis.[32] This was the final step in the total abandonment of public education: With the schools closed, buildings sold, teacher salaries cut off, and low-cost tutoring groups phased out, the teachers and students would be forced to accept Massive Resistance, and the schools would be reopened on a private, segregated basis with the help of the state's generous tuition grants. Mayor Duckworth and the Organization had at last the machinery that would make Massive Resistance work, and the fact that they were willing to use it, was enough to make both the school board and Councilman Martin revolt in spite of the risks of defying the mayor.

Events began to proceed at such a rapid pace that they quickly outstripped these hopeful signs of protest. On the same day that the school board was announcing its opposition to the funds-cutoff plan, the entire legal structure of the school-closing maneuver was being struck down in both the state's "friendly" *Harrison v. Day* action before the Virginia Supreme Court and the Committee For Public Schools' *James v. Almond* suit in federal court.[33] The court decisions, however, spoke only to the issues presented in the fall, and failed to address the new obstacles presented by the mayor's funds-cutoff plan. Although they could prevent any scheme to keep the desegregated schools closed, the courts could not stop further closings, thus leaving Duckworth free to enact the next phase of Massive Resistance.[34]

The fact that both the federal court and the Virginia Supreme Court handed down their decision on exactly the same day was no accident. In early December, 1958, when U.S. District Judge Walter Hoffman ran across Chief Justice Eggleston of the Virginia Supreme Court on a golf outing, Eggleston drew Hoffman aside and inquired as to whether the three-judge federal court had reached a decision in the *James* v. *Almond* case. Hoffman replied that it had, and that he was writing the opinion for release on December 22, 1958. Eggleston indicated that the Virginia Supreme Court had reached a conclusion in *Harrison* v. *Day*, but the dissenters would not be ready with their opinion until January 19, 1959. Hoffman took the hint, and signaled that he would delay his opinion until then. Judge Eggleston nodded, and departed with a smile.

> We both knew it was better for Virginians to hear it [the death of the state's Massive Resistance plan] from their own court. Judge Eggleston never said which way his court had decided, but I knew what he wanted, and which way the [state] court was leaning when he said he was writing the majority opinion.[35]

Now that the courts had finally acted, the issue of more school closings came in for a new round of response. In a fiery speech to a statewide radio and television audience, Governor Almond referred in lurid terms to the:

> . . . livid stench of sadism, sex immorality, and juvenile pregnancy infesting mixed schools. . . . Let me make it abundantly clear for the record now and hereafter, I will not yield to that which I know to be wrong . . . we have just begun to fight![36]

Congratulations poured in from Senator Byrd, legislative leaders, and hard-core resisters all across the Commonwealth, all expressing their desire to lead Norfolk into another round of school closings, legal obfuscation, and delay.

Public reaction in Norfolk to the fast-breaking chain of events was loud and angry, even if its message was unclear. At a stormy session of the Council following the courts' pronouncements, Mayor Duckworth found for the first time that he was unable to conduct the city's business. In a city inured to years of meaningless Council sessions that only reinforced the actions of private presessions, a strange event took place: An angry crowd, three-fourths of whom were women, was determined to prevent the Council from enacting its usual show of empty democratic pageantry. The entire meeting was repeatedly interrupted by clapping, catcalls, boos, and laughter from a rowdy crowd of onlookers; finally, after thirty-five minutes of this verbal assault, Duckworth adjourned the meeting in disgust.[37]

The Norfolk school crisis had long been the focus of national media attention—Governor Almond's picture adorned the cover of *Time* magazine on September 22, 1958, in an issue that featured the Norfolk crisis as its lead story—but now an event took place on prime-time national television that helped to crystallize both local attitudes and national opinion. At the height of the turmoil and just two days after the court rulings, CBS television ran an Edward R. Morrow/Ed Friendly production titled "The Lost Class of '59: The Norfolk Story" at 8 p.m. Wednesday, January 21. The production was remarkably objective,[38] and sought to portray opinions from both sides of the issue. It also featured a segment that brought the viewers up to date on the recent legal developments, including a telling interview with a resolute Governor Almond. In spite of the factual documentary presentation of the hour-long program, the chief impact for local residents was emotional. Parts of the program that focused poignantly on the hardships of the locked-out students—how the closing had fragmented the goals and dreams of the best and the brightest and doomed their less achievement-oriented classmates to the dismal prospects of teenage unemployment and listlessness—were instrumental in shaping half-formed local opinions: For the first time Norfolk really saw the crisis as it was viewed by the rest of the world.[39] For businessmen who had up to now been relatively unconcerned about the city's loss of national reputation, the prime time exposure, the documentary objectivity, the emotional impact, and Edward R. Murrow's reputation for honesty helped to project an urgency to the crisis that was not present before: Slowly the realization dawned that the Organization had brought the city to the brink of a municipal disaster unlike any it had faced since the postwar People's revolt, and that if the gimmickry of closed schools continued, a decade of municipal reform, national leadership, social concern, and vital fence-building with the navy would be destroyed, along with the city's reputation and its hopes for a secure future.

Events had moved so rapidly that week of January 19-23, 1959—first, the advancement of the funds-cutoff measure; next, the two simultaneous court orders striking down the legal framework of Massive Resistance; followed by the sight of both the Governor and the mayor vowing further resistance; and finally, the prime-time appeal of the Murrow/Friendly production—that the state's political leaders, including Mayor Duckworth, apparently lost touch with the changing mood of the people. The politicians were still preparing to take their cue from the November referendum and a quiet December of public acquiescence—they assumed that the people still wanted to fight integration to the bitter end, even if it meant more school closings along the way. Something, however, had happened to the public mood, and more and more individuals were apparently now ready to quit the fight. No one is really sure which event, or even which combination of events, triggered the shift, but for the first time a massive change was evident. To many of the city's business leaders it was the finality of the state supreme court—a Virginia, and not a federal court—decision. "My own court had spoken—I had divorced myself from the U. S. Supreme Court and I had given up any allegiance I had to it—that's when I was willing to lay down the fight."[40] For others, it was the spectacle of the Governor in full red-faced harangue in spite of the personal tragedies portrayed by "The Lost Class of '59" that finally brought home the realization of how Norfolk must appear to the rest of the nation.[41]

Even though a surface tranquility had descended upon the city that weekend, a strange hubbub of activity was taking place in a number of subterranean circles. Mayor Duckworth was plugged into a statewide hookup of frantic political leaders scurrying to help plot the Organization's next step. A bloc of Southside legislators headed by Mills Godwin (later Governor) was attempting to devise a series of desperation measures that would block the reopening of the desegregated schools. Among the plans under consideration was a ten-day school holiday, a proposition to close every school in the state until each could be selectively recertified by a safety inspector, a statute that would make it a felony for courts to assign pupils to any school without the backing of the state's pupil placement board, a repeal of the state's compulsory attendance laws, and an amendment to the Virginia Constitution that would allow local jurisdictions to close down their own schools. There was even a proposal that paralleled Duckworth's funds-cutoff plan, only reaching out to a statewide application.[42] It was just this sort of frantic activity—the high-level phone calls, the hurried conferences, the official entreaties, and the speculative nature of the schemes being advanced—that deafened Duckworth and the Byrd Organization leadership to more subtle murmurs in the rest of the community. Another factor seemed to influence the mayor in his deliberations: Duckworth reported receiving between 50 and 100 phone calls that weekend threatening to "blow up the schools" if they reopened integrated. Whether the calls were local or part of some Southside effort to stiffen his resistance makes very little difference: By the close of the weekend, Duckworth was committed to another round of closings, intimidation, and legal obfuscation. The specter of violence and the fear of reduced state funding if Norfolk bowed to integration were the reasons he publicly cited for that commitment.[43]

The rumor mills worked overtime that weekend with reports of political intrigue, speculative legislation, and a buzz of excitement that something big was going on in the business community. The grapevine had it that a downtown meeting had been held between the navy's top brass and some gilt-edged Norfolkians, the remnants of the Silkstocking crowd; in it, supposedly, the navy issued an ultimatum: Either open the schools or lose the fleet. Other rumors had it that two local financial leaders were called to an urgent conference in Richmond with representatives of the state's largest banking and mortgage interests; they were reportedly told that the school situation had to be cleared up before serious economic repercussions were felt.[44] Regardless of the veracity of these rumors, they express some very real fears that were circulating among the city's civic and financial elite: Now that the courts had finally spoken, business leaders were afraid that the navy and the federal government might take some retaliatory action if the city continued its posture of defiance; others could see that efforts to attract new industry were already falling apart; and financial experts had their eye on the collapse of local bond issues in the northern mortgage markets. The substance of these realizations lent credence to the rumors, and may well have formed the basis for what followed.

The Tuesday editions of the *Virginian-Pilot* and *Ledger-Dispatch* carried the most dramatic evidence of the shift in public opinion that had taken place that weekend: a full-page advertisement, really an appeal to reopen the schools now and avoid further resistance, that by itself was the most important single event in the 141 days of the Norfolk school crisis. The advertisement carried the following message signed by one hundred of the city's most prominent business, financial, civic, and industrial leaders:

> While we would strongly prefer to have segregated schools, it is evident from the recent court decisions that our public schools must either be integrated to the extent fully required or must be abandoned. The abandonment of our public schools system is, in our opinion, unthinkable, as it would mean the denial of an adequate education to a majority of our children. Moreover, the consequences would be most damaging to our community. We, therefore, urge the Norfolk City Council to do everything within its power to open all public schools as promptly as possible.

A front-page banner headline and the accompanying story proclaimed the appeal to be "the first time a large segment of the Norfolk business community has taken a public stand in the city's school crisis." The editors hailed it as "a new clear voice . . . a striking and welcome change . . . a striking new development."[45]

In spite of disclaimers to the contrary, the public viewed the document as a personal affront to Mayor Duckworth, his power, and the course of action he had chosen. This was the first time in Duckworth's eight-and-a-half-year tenure of office that any concerted group of businessmen had ever publicly tried to influence a city council decision, much less move so forcefully and so openly to oppose its authority. As a further sign of the intended insult, the signers had handed over the petition to attorneys for the Norfolk Committee For Public Schools so that it could be introduced that day as evidence in the Committee's new *James* v. *Duckworth* effort to block the mayor's plan to implement further closings.[46] Even so, former People's Mayor Pretlow Darden and a representative group of the signers had gone to see Mayor Duckworth on Monday to soften the blow before the appeal was made public. Mr. Darden's recollection of the conversation only underscores the mayor's anger at having been double-crossed:

> Darden: We're doing something good for the city and good for you . . . it gets you off the hook because these schools have got to be opened.
>
> Duckworth: You've stabbed me in the back!
>
> Darden: Well, you can always say . . . that a bunch of these—whatever you want to call us—got this thing up without your knowledge. Would you like to see it?
>
> Duckworth: Hell, no! I don't want to see it if I can't do anything about it!

Although the signers referred to themselves innocuously as the Committee of One Hundred, the appeal marked the re-emergence of the People's group, long since buried in the onslaught of Massive Resistance and Organization politics. The petition had all the markings of a People's production: The inspiration for it came from former mayor Pretlow Darden in collaboration with Frank Batten, president of the parent company that owned Norfolk's two daily newspapers and its major radio and television stations. Darden and Batten had hand-picked the group of eligible signers, and then personally carried it to the chosen, going first to their old allies from the Silkstocking days. Former People's campaign chief Charles Kaufman, now chairman of the Norfolk Redevelopment and Housing Authority, polished the wording of the final draft, just as he had done for every major campaign announcement a dozen years before. Besides Darden and Kaufman, the list was spotted with names of those activists and appointees who had helped to lend credence to the People's crusade: John Alfriend, Charles Burroughs, Richard Cooke, C. W. Grandy, George Foote, Henry Clay Hofheimer, John Jenkins, Clarence Robertson, Dan Thornton, Thomas Wilcox, and Rives Worsham.[47] More than anything else, the Committee of One Hundred was the purest representation of the city's financial elite that had surfaced in a decade—a veritable roster of the banking and business fraternity, highlighted by the realization that at least ten of the signers no longer lived in Norfolk.

The statement by the Committee of One Hundred was both an opinion-maker and the most important milestone in marking how far public sentiment had shifted in the past week. Once the city's major business and financial leaders had so openly crossed the power and authority of the mayor, it was both safe and fashionable for others who had been long silent to express their own pro-school sentiments. Typical of the community's gratitude at the eleventh-hour conversion of its former Silkstocking leadership was the action of one downtown florist who sent a red rose to each of the signers. Also symbolic was the appeal of Harvey Lindsay, Jr., and 35 young business and civic leaders—too young to have been a part of the People's regime—who ran their own advertisement so that their voice could be counted.[48]

One example helps to underscore both how committed the mayor was to continued resistance, and just how opposed he was to the surrender sentiments of the Silkstocking crowd. The same day that Pretlow Darden and others approached him with their appeal, but well before the existence of their effort was made public, Mayor Duckworth had the perfect opportunity to turn the statements to his own personal and political advantage. The Committee For Public Schools had brought suit against the mayor and the city council, seeking to enjoin them in its *James* v. *Duckworth* litigation from cutting off the school board's funds and closing more schools. Armed with the still-secret knowledge of the Committee of One Hundred, Duckworth could have appeared as the initiator of the appeal by withdrawing the city's defense in the suit, thereby conceding the issue and effectively dropping the school closing plan. Instead, he argued all the more forcefully for the funds-cutoff plan, specifically detailing his fears about potential racial violence if the schools were allowed to reopen.[49]

The mayor had badly miscalculated if he had hoped that the usual plodding pace of litigation before the federal courts would give him time to reconsolidate his political power and position. With unprecedented speed, Federal Judge Walter Hoffman—a Norfolk native with strong ties to the Silkstocking establishment—ruled against the Council the very next day, the same morning that Norfolk citizens were reading in their papers about the Committee of One

Hundred. The very existence of the Silkstocking appeal, and the fact that it had been sent to the Committee For Public Schools to strengthen their legal position, was important in negating, as far as Judge Hoffman was concerned, the mayor's fears of racial violence;[50] in any event, the evidence that a substantial portion of the community now favored reopening the schools enabled Hoffman to enjoin the city council from engaging in any action which might withhold funds or otherwise interfere with the school board's plans to reopen the closed institutions.[51]

The speed and impact of this new ruling was a shocking reversal for the mayor, doubly so because it increased the perception that the Silkstocking crowd had fought him and won. Even so, the mayor was not entirely defeated: He still had two courses of action open, either of which would preserve his status as the hero of Massive Resistance and advance his standing within the statewide Byrd Organization. The Defenders were urging him to declare the closed school buildings as surplus and quickly sell them to the T.E.F before they could be reopened by the court.[52] The Byrd Organization was apparently urging him to defy Judge Hoffman, continue to withhold the school funds, and appeal the ruling. Either course would risk a contempt of court citation and possible imprisonment, but this was a prospect that the Organization actually relished, and was even then urging upon Governor Almond as well.[53] The sight of a political leader behind bars to preserve the freedom of choice rights of the majority was just what the Organization needed to promote its Massive Resistance plan as a *cause célèbre*: If Duckworth or Almond would but risk personal martyrdom, they would be treated to national media attention, public prayer vigils, certain canonization in the Organization's ranks, and an endless stream of little old ladies, housewives, and mothers bearing baked goods and other wares for their jailed hero.[54] On the other hand, there was no guarantee that the mayor could get a majority vote on the council if he chose either route: Roy Martin's opposition a week before had been the purest political gamble—a bet that had paid off already in the flurry of following events—and there was every reason to expect additional resistance in the changed political atmosphere that was emerging after the Committee of One Hundred's statement. Finally, his options were limited by the fact that the school board was ready to open the schools anyway, even if the city council continued to withhold funds in defiance of the courts: The board apparently had enough surplus funds, coal, and other supplies remaining to open for a few days even without Council's support.[55]

It was these latter considerations—Mayor Duckworth could not risk losing a bitterly split vote on the Council for a point that would be rendered useless anyway by the school board—that probably weighed heavily in his decision to abandon the struggle. In spite of the dire warnings of Senator Byrd that his Organization would be "wiped out" if Virginia gave in to integration,[56] Massive Resistance was over, at least in Norfolk. The mayor bitterly refused to discuss the matter further, flatly telling all comers to a historic Council session that marked the end of his own resistance: "We [the Council] have been taken out of the school business [by the court]. Anyone who came here to talk about schools can go to the school board."[57] Thus, there was no obstacle to the schools reopening on Monday, February 2, 1959, as the board had promised the Court. Duckworth, in admitting defeat, was doing his best to retain whatever was left of his old Harmony coalition in spite of the setback.

If Mayor Duckworth's fall from the heights of municipal and political power was dizzying, it was no less dramatic than Governor Almond's sudden about-face on Massive Resistance. The Governor, who usually possessed a calm and rational demeanor, punctuated by both a thorough knowledge and deep appreciation of the law, was also on occasion given to stentorian bombast.[58] These two facets of his personality—his keen legal sense and his equally cutting rhetorical style—had collided. Although Almond had been the studious legal brains behind legislative efforts to block integration, he must have known that this house of cards would one day tumble down. The Governor's fiery bombast following the double court orders to reopen the schools—"We have just begun to fight"—may have also been partly responsible for Mayor Duckworth's overly repressive reaction. Almond explained in later years that he was tired, distraught, and just not thinking clearly when he made "that damn speech" in defiance of the court orders. He had meant to assure Virginians that he would do everything possible to preserve segregation, even though he knew a few schools would have to integrate, but the rumble of his rhetoric got the best of him, and by the time he got to the conclusion, he had falsely led many to think that he was still saving one more legal gambit to preserve Massive

Resistance.[59] It was a much quieter and rational Almond who now stood before a special session of the Virginia General Assembly—only eight days after his rabble-rousing speech, and just two days after Judge Hoffman canceled Duckworth's funds-cutoff plan—to inform them that he could not prevent integration in Virginia:[60] The best he could do was to minimize the racial mixing that would occur. The Massive Resisters were thunderstruck, and a few even referred to him as "Benedict" Almond,[61] especially after he threatened to veto the last-ditch efforts of Mills Godwin and the Southside legislators.[62] Instead of legal obfuscation, Almond pressed for a more moderate program to modify tuition grants, repeal compulsory attendance laws, strengthen prohibitions against violence, and establish a commission to recommend additional proposals.[63]

With both the mayor's and the governor's surrender, Massive Resistance in Virginia was finally dead. The only stumbling block lay not in the politicians, but in those other individuals who had resisted so massively, and who even now were not prepared to drop the cause. The mayor's fears of possible racial violence were very real; even in Norfolk there still existed an element of rabble that would stop at nothing to prevent or disrupt school integration. They were, however, unable to rally much support: local newspaper, radio, and television news reporters remained faithful to a private understanding not to publish stories of or lend credence to rumors of racial violence or intimidation that would lead to "another Little Rock." Even a cross-burning across from Norview High and within sight of the black homes in Coronado went unreported.[64] Behind the scenes there was at least one other hopeful force moving to assure a peaceful resumption of classes: The Silkstocking crowd, relishing their recent reemergence, were not now content to sit back and rest on the laurels of their newspaper advertisement. Besides lending their collective voice quietly to those who were calling for an orderly resumption of classes, Norfolk's business and civic leaders sought a more active role by promoting a "Back to School, Keep It Cool" movement. They turned their efforts to their youthful counterparts in the hierarchy of the school's social and service clubs. The Key Clubs (Kiwanis-sponsored) of the closed high schools purchased billboards and bought newspaper advertisements that pleaded, as their Silkstocking elders had petitioned, with youth and adults alike "that the orderly reopening be completed as smoothly and as quickly as possible so that we may proceed with our immediate objective—to obtain an education."[65]

Monday morning, February 2, 1959, would prove to be a crucial test of Silkstocking diplomacy when schools reopened integrated after months of Massive Resistance hysteria. There was a widespread fear among the city's leadership that in spite of all their preliminary precautions, more was still required to signal once and for all the end of Massive Resistance. As the representatives of the nation's leading newspapers, magazines, radio, and television networks poured into Norfolk that final weekend in January, the Silkstocking business establishment began to realize just how much would be at stake Monday morning. One single, isolated racial incident, or worse, one random act of violence, once it had been flashed around the world in newspaper headlines and television broadcasts, could erase more than a decade of concentrated effort to restore the city's once-fallen reputation. Not since the lusty wartime days of booze, racketeering, prostitution, and the sleazy honky-tonks of East Main Street—already undergoing demolition—would so many eyes be on the city; not since the Staylor Raid of 1948 was it so completely at the mercy of its hoodlum elements.

So much was riding upon peaceful resumption of classes that the city's leadership dared to approach Norfolk's most effective proponent of Massive Resistance for a final symbol of defeat and racial reconciliation. Behind the scenes that weekend there was one final effort to arrange instead a visual image that would ensure both domestic tranquility and Norfolk's good name. Friends, business associates, civic leaders, relatives, and even minor political kingpins descended upon the mayor, urging him to make the most difficult decision of his political career: He must walk, they argued, with the handful of black students that were to enroll in the previously all-white schools in Norview.[66] If there was to be violence or racial incidents, the media were betting that they would occur at Norview High School, and indeed the crush of cameramen, reporters, photographers, and correspondents that would surround Norview on Monday could well encourage potential neighborhood troublemakers—identified in the local vernacular as "suedes" because of their reputed addiction to suede shoes[67]—to show off. There was more than just the reputation of the local toughs, however, that had earmarked Norview as the focal point of Monday morning's news coverage: The area had been one of the most fruitful bastions of Massive Resistance sentiment, evidenced by the recent cross-burning incidents there; the rhetoric of Norview whites was still salted with vague references to the bombings and racial strife that had taken place four years earlier in nearby Coronado; as a newly annexed territory, Norview was one of the few areas that did not owe any allegiance to the calm, deliberative progress of the Silkstocking reign; and finally, in these largely blue-collar neighborhoods, the official pronouncements of the business and civic elite probably counted for less than elsewhere in the city.

The course now urged upon the mayor by the delegations that descended upon his private residence was painted in the most pleasing colors possible: One quiet, dignified walk up the school house steps—in sharp contrast to the tirades of Arkansas' Governor Faubus in Little Rock—once it had been carefully immortalized by the electronic eye of the nation's media, would do more to promote the city, the mayor, and even the Byrd Organization than any other step he could take. Business leaders argued that it was the one action that would help to focus positive national attention upon the city's cosmopolitan image, the integrity of its leadership, its spirit of rejuvenation, and its efforts to attract new industry. Political leaders argued that both the mayor and the Organization had the most to lose at the hands of the local voters if violence marred the resumption of classes. Further, they implored, that with such a visual event, the mayor could upstage Governor Almond's split with Senator Byrd, and cut short efforts to unify opponents of Massive Resistance into a threat to the Organization. Finally, they urged, this was a ready-made opportunity for both the mayor and the city to escape the onus of school closings—a chance for him to prove his political resilience, reestablish his rapport with the rapidly shifting mood of the people, and solidify his base of support in the business community. Unless he took some such action to insure the tranquility of the reopening ceremonies, the mantle of political leadership would pass from him to the school board, Roy Martin, and other "moderates" who personally supported segregation, but who also had the courage to oppose the final stages of racial retribution associated with Massive Resistance.

No one really knows how close Mayor Duckworth came that weekend to accepting this unusual reversal: On its surface the offer was attractive enough, but, it also involved a good deal of betrayal of principle and admission of guilt. The decision, however, was his and his alone; no other political, civic, or governmental leader could substitute for him and have such impact. Mayor Duckworth, however, would have no part of such a gesture, and no one will ever know whether personal pride, prejudicial animosities, devotion to principle, or more mundane political considerations figured most prominently in his decision. An increase in uniformed police, the heightened visibility of school personnel, and the welcoming gestures of the principal would have to suffice; when school opened on Monday morning, the mayor was nowhere near the waiting cameras at Norview High.

9

✼ ✼ ✼ ✼ ✼

A Second School Crisis

ALL WAS CALM as Norfolk's closed junior and senior high schools reopened. In spite of the presence of almost one hundred journalists and television cameras, most of them massed outside of Norview High School, there was nothing unusual to report: Stories noted that there were "a few instances of name calling," but that the "windy 26-degree weather discouraged parents from lingering." The *Virginian-Pilot* praised the "display of sanity, poise, and dignity that made a difficult day a notable one." President Eisenhower, who received hourly reports of the progress through a special telephone connection in the federal court house,[1] telegraphed his congratulations to the 63 students who led the "Back to School, Keep It Cool," campaign;[2] the *New York Times* viewed the scene as a "turning point for integration;"[3] and the televised footage of orderly students reporting to class stood in sharp contrast to events in Little Rock, Mobile, and other points across the South. Norfolk's calm reopening was praised across the nation, and at least a portion of its ugly wartime image had been erased. The *New York Times* ironically, credited "redevelopment and public housing" as factors in preserving "comparatively good race relations." The paper went on to report that "a number of handsome new Negro schools have been built [here] in the last decade," and that: "Norfolk is distinctive among Southern cities in that it has a powerful and articulate group of moderates who balance off the Defenders and their followers on the school controversy."⁴

Although the *Times* obviously had the Silkstocking Committee of One Hundred in mind, its appraisal came as something of a shock to the Committee for Public Schools and others who had labored without much success during the five months of closings to provide a counterpoint to the Defenders;⁵ nevertheless the *Times* was only one of many publications to note that Norfolk was unique in that the critical legal action to reopen the closed schools came from white parents, and not black plaintiffs. In reality, the only really "powerful and articulate" opposition to Massive Resistance came from Lenoir Chambers, and the editorial staff of the *Virginian-Pilot*, who richly deserved the Pulitzer Prize he received for his efforts to keep the public schools open.

Other researchers have perpetuated the myth that "a powerful public school movement organized very quickly" in Norfolk to defeat Massive Resistance.⁶ In point of fact, the Committee for Public Schools, the school teachers, and others who hoped to spark a pro-school movement were relatively powerless until after the schools reopened, and the Committee of One Hundred, who had played almost no role during the controversy, only meant to signal that it was time to surrender in Norfolk, not signal any opposition to either Duckworth or the dominant Byrd Organization.⁷ Duckworth, however, misread their intent, and instead helped to promote the ragtag elements of opposition during the school crisis into a full-blown resistance movement a few months later.

Duckworth could have easily retreated with grace and blamed the collapse of Massive Resistance on Governor Almond, as U.S. Senator Harry F. Byrd, Sr. apparently did.⁸ Certainly the mayor personally had done more to keep Massive Resistance alive than even the staunchest Defender could have expected. Even though Pretlow Darden and others in the Silkstocking establishment tried repeatedly to counsel him to adopt such a course,⁹ Duckworth refused to retreat from the battle lines he had drawn. Norfolk, for all its cosmopolitan image, was still a Southern city, and its voters continued to harbor strong segregationist sentiment. Even as late as the week of January 26-31, 1959, after the court decisions but before the schools reopened, a team of researchers from the University of North Carolina found that almost 80 percent of Norfolk's white residents clung to their support for segregated schools: More than a third still denied the legality of the federal courts to order desegregation, and 40 percent thought the city should resist further. However, only one adult in five thought that continuing segregation was a viable option, and there was almost no sentiment for sacrificing public education to preserve segregated schools.[10] It was precisely this last sentiment that Duckworth now misread.

In commenting on the reopening of schools in Norfolk, the *New York Times* indicated that although a major victory for public education had been won, this was a "Gettysburg," a turning point that signaled a retreat, and not an "Appomattox," or final surrender of the Massive Resistance forces.[11] Duckworth and the Byrd Organization seemed bent upon continuing the fight, even though the tide of war had turned against them. Almost before the national press departed the city, Mayor Duckworth fired the first salvo in what was to be a continuing attack against the school board and its efforts to continue public education in the city. At a meeting with the board, the mayor warned that the city council was going to "cut the devil out of the 1960 [school] budget," and as to prospects for any more funds for school construction, "it will take an act of Congress to get it out of us." Duckworth then disclosed a plan to build a number of three-room schoolhouses, each accommodating 90 pupils in grades one through three, in the eastern half of the city. In commenting on the proposal, the *Virginian-Pilot* editorialized that: "While the plan apparently would slow down desegregation of the first, second, and third grades through the creation of smaller school districts, councilmen stressed it was prompted by the need for inexpensive schools."[12] Although the educational drawbacks were evident, the school board found itself giving serious scrutiny to the Council's minischool proposal. Still, it refused to be stampeded into adopting this flawed approach, especially when it held such dire long-term consequences. A biracial task force appointed to study the proposal found instead that buildings with 16 to 20 classrooms were the "ideal" size for a three-grade primary school.[13] The committee nevertheless approved of the idea of using smaller schools "strategically located to relieve crowding" in several areas of the city, and then proceeded to list nine such areas (Lindenwood, West, Clay, Goode, Carey, Titus, Jackson, Bowling Park, and Young Park) already served by small black schools.[14] In the end, however, the school board was forced to bow to the pressures of the Council, and five "vest-pocket" schools were built for whites during the next year: East Ocean View, Easton, Fairlawn, Pretty Lake, and Poplar Halls[15] (*see* Figures 8 and 9, pages 176. 177). The board also included an "emergency ordinance" condemning a 2.5-acre site in the Coronado area, "a predominantly Negro section," for six demountable classroom units. Reporter Luther Carter noted that:

> The opening of the Coronado school will have the effect of reducing, if not entirely eliminating, the number of potentially qualified Negro applicants in Coronado for Norview Elementary. . . . The proximity of the Coronado schools [Oakwood and Coronado] would give the School Board a valid reason to assign Coronado children there even should they meet the academic and other standards for a nearer white school. . . . [The Coronado school] will represent a modification of the City Council's "little red school house" [plan]. [It] . . . would not have a cafeteria, auditorium, playgrounds, and certain other facilities which have been incorporated in larger elementary schools.[16]

Black leaders were understandably upset by the proposal, and complained that the new school would be both "educationally unsound" and an "obvious attempt to circumvent" the courts. The school board attempted to reassure the black leaders that the "same facilities will be lacking at some new white schools now being built." They explained that the board did not want to build a large, expensive school that might be in the path of an interstate highway then under consideration, but a cafeteria, an auditorium, and additional classrooms would be added to the Rosemont combination elementary and junior high school for blacks in the same area.[17] The city's black leaders were not impressed by this defense, and promptly filed suit in federal court seeking to enjoin what they called "makeshift schools . . . constructed for the purpose of pursuing the policy of racially segregated schools."[18]

While it was fighting this battle over what the papers were calling the mayor's "little red schoolhouse" proposal, the school board also had to worry that Duckworth would make good on his promise to "cut the devil" out of the rest of Norfolk's public school program. Since school districts in Virginia are dependent upon their municipal

176   BLACK, WHITE AND *BROWN*

Figure 8 – New School Buildings in Norfolk, 1959

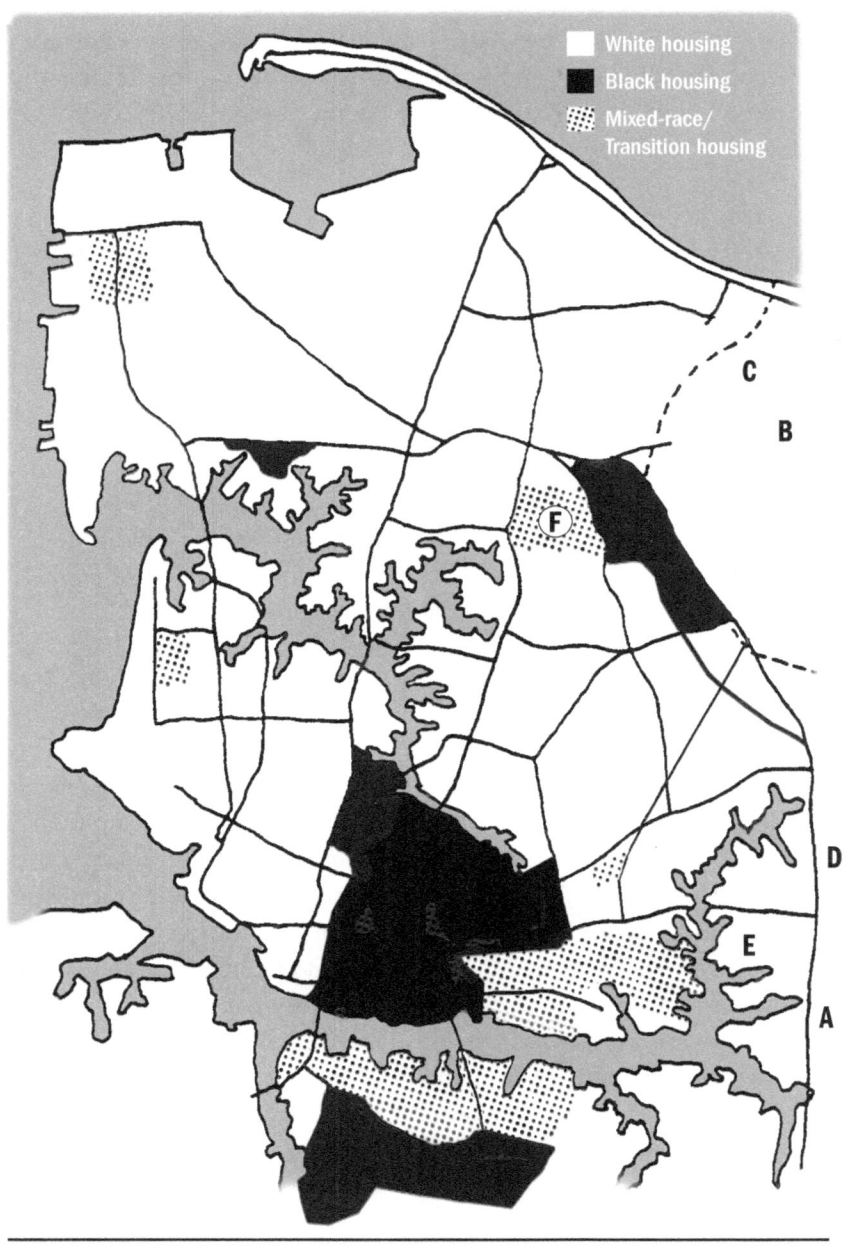

A   Easton Elementary
B   East Ocean View Elementary
C   Pretty Lake Elementary
D   Fairlawn Elementary
E   Poplar Halls Elementary
F   Coronado Elementary

Figure 9 – Norfolk School Construction Statistics, 1952-1959

YEAR	SCHOOL	SQUARE FEET	ACREAGE	RACE
1952	Calcott Elementary	58,254	12.0	White
1952	Lakewood Elementary	58,254	12.0	White
1953	**Bowling Park Elementary**	**58,254**	**12.3**	**Black**
1953	**Lindenwood Elementary**	**40,635**	**9.5**	**Black**
1953	**Diggs Park Elementary**	**44,400**	**10.6**	**Black**
1954	**Young Park Elementary**	**50,540**	**8.0**	**Black**
1955	Suburban Park Elementary	48,919	15.0	White
1956	Northside Jr. High	114,375	14.5	White
1956	Oceanair Elementary	57,242	17.7	White
1957	Lansdale Elementary	53,100	18.7	White
1957	Sherwood Forest Elementary	53,100	13.3	White
1958	**Rosemont Elementary/Jr. High**	**40,000**	**13.0**	**Black**
1959	**Coronado Elementary**	**7,500**	**2.2**	**Black**
1959	East Ocean View Elementary	10,790	1.2	White
1959	Pretty Lake Elementary	10,790	1.2	White
1959	Poplar Halls Elementary	22,000	17.8	White
1959	Easton Elementary	12,000	11.7	White
1959	Fairlawn Elementary	22,000	16.4	White

Estimate of size and area at the time of construction does not reflect later additions and expansions.

---

government for financial support, the school board lacked any taxing or funding power of its own. When the City Manager announced his spending priorities for the upcoming fiscal year, he proposed a reduction of more than five percent in school funds. Even a cut of this magnitude was not enough to satisfy the mayor, and the Council proceeded to remove additional funds.[19] By the time the budget was passed, the school board found that local funding for public schools had dropped by 13.4 percent from the previous year. The *Virginian-Pilot* indicated that the mayor hoped to eliminate any possibility that the board would be able to give raises to the teachers who had helped to sabotage Massive Resistance.[20] Moreover, the effect of this cutback fell disproportionately upon blacks, since most whites could afford to supplement the education of their children or send them to private schools with the support of the state's substantial tuition grants. Thus Duckworth was finding that he could skillfully use his powers of the purse to keep Massive Resistance alive by keeping the white schools small enough to be immune from integration or else so overcrowded and unattractive that blacks would resist further efforts to desegregate.

Not only did the board have to worry about loss of funding support and the pressure to build small, inadequate, but integration-proof (under the court standards of the day) school houses, it also found that the city council was reneging on its promise to build the badly needed secondary schools that had already been promised. Lansdale Junior High, which had been approved by the Council two-and-a-half years earlier, completely designed, and accepted by the state,[21] was never built; Lakewood Junior High suffered a similar fate. Although there were problems with the suitability of the sites at both locations, both schools had been promised for the 1959-1960 school year. The *Virginian-Pilot* intimated that the delay was linked to other, more political concerns: "The State Board of Education approved the plans in the fall of 1957, but the project[s] failed to move forward. . . . Months went by, and nothing happened. It finally became apparent that the council was waiting to see the outcome of the impending desegregation crisis."[22] Additional annexation and the impact of the redevelopment projects closer in town was putting a tremendous burden on the schools in the eastern half of the city.[23] A disastrous annexation decision—Norfolk had sought 33 square miles in the western portion of old Princess Anne County, but instead had ended up with only 13, a large part of which were the airport and water-system lakes which it already owned—was exacerbating the problem. Norfolk was stuck with the students, but none of the schools which served them, and this urgent need was in part responsible for the school board's acceptance of the "vest-pocket" schools being erected.[24] The fact that the school board would be facing the school year with reduced funds, badly overcrowded schools,[25] and nothing but inadequate minischools in the works was prompting a second school crisis, and one in which the board and the pro-school forces were again pitted against the mayor and the city council.

Public schools, or at least the quality of public education in Norfolk, were again under political attack, and it seemed clear that the mayor had not given up the hope of making Massive Resistance work in Norfolk. The council, which had appealed its earlier reverses in federal court, indicated its intention to continue the earlier fight to cut off the funds to both black and white secondary schools.[26] The school board was apparently unwilling to back the council on this and other anti-education measures, because the mayor and the city's Byrd Organization legislators, began to advance a bill that would expand the number of positions on the board from six to seven members, and shorten the terms of service from three to two years. The bill would have allowed the Council to replace all six of the board members[27] who had worked so diligently to save public schools. Boardmember Francis Crenshaw summed up the politics of the situation:

> At the present time, I believe there is a difference of opinion between members of the school board and the council as to [the] proper handling of the integration problem. . . . The legislation pending in Richmond will . . . bring the board more closely under councilmanic control. I know of no other reason for adding a seventh member . . . nor can I otherwise account for a reduction in the term of office from three to two years.[28]

Fortunately this new school crisis found a political outlet before public education was irreparably damaged. It was in response to public opposition to the effort to fire the school board that Mayor Duckworth let his guard slip in public enough to threaten his Massive Resistance coalition. When an officer of the Norfolk Committee for Public Schools (Dorothy Attaway) inquired whether it was the intent of the Council to reappoint the incumbent members of the school board if the bill passed, Mayor Duckworth replied, "I don't think it's any of your business."[29] Although in retrospect the infraction does not seem severe, the pro-school forces immediately seized upon the incident as a new *cause célèbre* of municipal reform. A flurry of letters to the editor, as well as the editors themselves, questioned whether the public had a right to know, and whether such "despotic" behavior was proper for a "public servant." Pro-school advocates launched a massive campaign to isolate the mayor, his spirited temper, and his legendary disregard for public participation,[30] by emblazoning the slogan "None of Your Business" on matchbook covers, key chains, and other tokens. Even so, the pro-school forces probably could not have made the issue stick had not the timing of the outburst coincided perfectly with the upcoming Democratic Primary for the state legislature. Two seats were open because of the retirement of incumbents; the Byrd/Prieur Organization, the pro-school forces, and the Defenders of State Sovereignty and Individual Liberties all had candidates in the race. In addition, incumbent state senator Edward L. Breeden was under attack by a coalition of Defenders and the most conservative elements of the Organization because he had backed away from last-ditch efforts to save Massive Resistance.[31] The election hinged entirely on the Massive Resistance issue, and all sides posed the question of their election based upon their view of public education.[32] On election day, the pro-school group claimed total victory, winning both the disputed house and senate seats;[33] in doing so, they launched the political career of Henry Howell and a force of progressivism that would be a major player in city and state politics for several decades. The force included an alliance with the city's black voters, who up to that point had voted solidly Republican.[34] The Defenders were crushed, and never appeared in Norfolk again as a major political power.

With champions in elected office for the first time, the pro-school forces found that their cause quickly took on a more authoritative air. The antischool policies of the mayor and the city council soon came under attack from this new quarter,[35] and it was not long before the Organization was in full retreat before a growing coalition that was emerging between the "little people" of the pro-school movement, the city's black leaders, and the mainstream of its business community.[36] Shortly thereafter, Prieur Organization stalwart George Abbott, a seventeen-year veteran of the Council, resigned from office and was quickly replaced by School Board Chairman Paul Schweitzer. Observers saw the move as an attempt to create a new "Harmony Ticket" with the business establishment, or at least an effort to "cut the ground from under" the emerging pro-school coalition.[37] In spite of this move, however, the pro-school forces, now under the leadership of Henry Howell,[38] endorsed Schweitzer[39] and advanced two business candidates of its own, both of whom had sought to re-open the schools during the school crisis. Although only the candidacy of Sam Barfield was successful, the victory was seen as a direct rebuff to Duckworth, his "dictatorial rule," the Council's actions in the school crisis, and the secrecy of the process of city planning and governmental decision-making.[40] Fred Duckworth declined to seek reelection in the next race, and the office of Mayor was turned over to Roy Martin, the one councilman who had dared to break with the Organization in order to continue public education in the city.

Norfolk had thus come full circle, and although the process of government became more contentious as decision-making came back into public view, the primacy of councilmanic support for public education was never again at issue; the biracial coalition of pro-school advocates, the Silkstocking business elite, and the city's black leadership that emerged to promote educational issues following the crisis strengthened and matured into the dominant political force for the next three decades. Not even the shift to a ward system of politics in 1992 could shake the grasp of this coalition. The election as mayor of Dr. Mason Andrews, the one member of the Norfolk Committee for Public Schools who remained anonymous so that he could better court the Silkstocking crowd, is proof that the lessons, the alliances, and the commitment to public education advanced during the Norfolk school crisis continued to provide vision, direction, and leadership for the city. Thus the intensity of Norfolk's experience with the forces of prejudice in the 1950s had been the glue that had bound its citizens together in what was an arduous climb back to a point where they could at last look back with pride at the record of their united accomplishment.

10

✳ ✳ ✳ ✳ ✳

Conclusion

ALTHOUGH THE UNITED STATES Supreme Court's decision in the *Brown* v. *Board of Education* cases sent shock waves of protest across most of the South, only the extent of the decree actually came as a surprise those who were charged with the planning and leadership of Southern cities. That some sort of decision from the Court overruling a portion of the South's elaborate system of segregated education was a foregone conclusion among many in leadership roles; clearly the "separate but equal" facilities maintained by communities, particularly those in rural areas, were so far from equivalent that only the most callous court could disregard the distinction. Moreover, desegregation had already begun in the nation's military, transportation, public accommodation, and recreational facilities, either through administrative action or legal intervention, and it was hard to imagine that a nation that had so recently fought repression overseas would allow its own schools to remain as the last bastion of racial subjugation at home. The main thesis of this work is that the individuals charged with the leadership and management of Southern cities had ample time, plenty of opportunity, and strong motivation to plan for the demise of school segregation in their community, that this planning process began well before the *Brown* v. *Board of Education* cases were ever decided, and that it grew increasingly intense as the prospect of court-ordered integration became a reality. Moreover, this research found that these leaders took deliberate steps to use the powers at their disposal, including both the more obvious control over school-plant planning, educational administration, and student attendance, as well as the more subtle power over land-use planning and redevelopment activities, to delay court-ordered school desegregation in their communities. The study focuses on the link between school desegregation and urban renewal activities in one community, Norfolk, Virginia, that most nearly fit the hypothesized variables.

Since 1938, the National Association for the Advancement of Colored People had advanced a withering legal attack upon the peculiar practices that provided the basis for maintaining segregated schools. Although this assault was aimed first at discrimination in graduate education, their intent was to amass an irrefutable body of precedent that would lead the U.S. Supreme Court to a decision striking down once and for all the logic that separate schools could be equal in America. For this reason, knowledgeable Southerners knew that the Supreme Court would have to follow these same precedents if it were faced with similar circumstances in public schools, that is, the absence of a facility for blacks, separate facilities for blacks that were inadequate or inferior, or instances of separate and degrading treatment of black students. Four of the five cases accepted by the Court in its 1952 session were designed to do precisely that. In the title case, *Brown* v. *Board of Education*, the Court was presented with the appeal of a black elementary student who lived in a mixed-race area. Although Topeka had integrated its secondary schools, Linda Brown was forced to ride a bus across town to the black elementary school, while whites in her area walked to school. The N.A.A.C.P. contended that in light of earlier precedents, such separate treatment was degrading, and thus contrary to constitutional guarantees of equal treatment. Although most Southern leaders expected to lose the Prince Edward County, Virginia (no equal facilities), Clarendon, South Carolina (unequal facilities), and Delaware (unequal treatment) cases, where the quantifiable differences between black and white schools could be remedied short of desegregation, the defeat in *Brown* proved to be the most troublesome, since it could only be remediated by school integration. Even if the South were to build literally hundreds of new and largely unneeded schools, it still might have to integrate some buildings in order to comply with the *Brown* dictate that similarly situated students not receive separate treatment merely to maintain racial separation. Nevertheless, the *Brown* precedent, because it focused on the long crosstown bus ride, cut to the core of what many Southerners, both black and white, felt was most unjust about the separate but equal system of education then in use.[1]

The most immediate effect of the *Brown* decision was to strike down the laws requiring segregated schools (i.e., *de jure* segregation) in seventeen states (Texas, Oklahoma, Alabama, Missouri, Arkansas, Louisiana, Mississippi, South Carolina, Georgia, Florida, Tennessee, North Carolina, Kentucky, Virginia, Maryland, West Virginia, and Delaware) and permitting them in four others (Kansas, Arizona, New Mexico, and Wyoming).[2] Although the focus of the decisions was upon state laws requiring segregation, the impact would be felt more directly in the local schools of thousands of communities across the Deep South and border states of the Confederacy. The decision, however, left intact the kind of separate-race schools found in cities of the North, West, and Midwest, where segregation, although not absolute, was due to choice of neighborhood, that is, *de facto* segregation. Thus, substantially equal schools that served separate race neighborhoods were still permitted by the Court; only the particular circumstance presented by Linda Brown, a black student living closer to a white school than a black one, was first found unconstitutional.

For this reason, most communities could comply with the dictates of the Supreme Court with only a minimum of integration, and most schools could continue as essentially single-race schools, except in the few areas of each city where there were mixed-race neighborhoods, transition areas, or where two racially distinct areas would have to be served by the same school. Even then, Southern cities could copy the elaborate system of gerrymandered districts, transfer policies, "schools of choice," in-school segregation by tracking, staggered enrollment, and other quasi-legal devices used elsewhere to avoid large-scale integration and keep whites from attending predominantly black schools.[3] This careful distinction between continued segregation by place of residence and court-ordered integration was one reason that the *Brown* decree was met with only mild reaction in most areas of the border states where there was a relatively small black population, concentrated in a large, central section of the downtown area, and only occasionally found in small settlements in other parts of the city. This distinction meant that the Northern model of *de facto* segregation could be adopted without undue hardship, except in those few Southern cities with large concentrations of black populations, a history of racial strife, or vast social class distinctions between their black and white citizens.[4]

One finding of this research is that local officials responded to the threat of court-ordered desegregation in the same manner as their counterparts in state capitals, and used every means at their disposal to delay, or defuse, the impact of school desegregation in their community. Clearly they were as cognizant of the threat posed by desegregation as their colleagues in the state legislatures— N.A.A.C.P. legal defense team lawyers began filing court challenges all across the nation shortly after *Brown*—and the local electorate was making the same kinds of demands as the statewide constituencies. And certainly local officials were as adept as their brethren in the legislatures in using the powers at their disposal to frustrate and circumvent the dictates of the courts. Even so, however, most of the case studies of local school desegregation controversies in the South do not begin until almost a decade or two later. The record of school desegregation both before the *Brown* decision and between the decree and its implementation is so blank that one major history of school desegregation covers the entire period between 1954 and 1962 in less than a page;[5] another accomplishes it in six.[6] What happened in the intervening years has been largely unknown, although Norfolk appears to be representative of the overall process used by Southern cities to deliberately move the segregated status of their school systems from *de jure* to *de facto*, a pattern which seems to have continued well into the 1960s.

Before the threat of the N.A.A.C.P. challenges became apparent, all planning in the South, and indeed much of the rest of the nation, appears to have been racially based.[7] In fact, it was not until 1956, several years after *Brown*, that courts began to strike down the practice of dividing communities into separate-race housing zones.[8] Before that time, Norfolk and most of the rest of the South appear to have used an elaborate system of computing the percentage of property taxes paid by each race, and then using these figures as determinants of how the public works budgets would be spent. The result was that, except for those few areas where blacks had moved into middle-class housing formerly occupied by whites, there were few, if any, public amenities provided for black neighborhoods: no sidewalks, streetlights, gutters, curbs, parks, playgrounds, or recreation areas.[9] This lack of services may actually have made the push to expand into white housing areas both more attractive and more practical than waiting for the extensive public improvements necessary to bring most black neighborhoods up to similar levels of service.

Because, for the most part, Norfolk's history during the 1950s is so very ordinary, it may be used to typify the forces and concerns that faced other areas in the urban South. Certainly the scale of its development activity and the desperation of its school-closing crisis make it well suited for a case study of the interplay between the two. Although the story of school desegregation and urban renewal in Norfolk may be more compelling than in most communities, it is not thought to be unique. There is good reason to believe that what occurred in Norfolk on such a grand scale could also be found in more subtle forms in hundreds of other cities across the nation. Norfolk's reaction to the threat of school desegregation in the 1950s was not unique, and, in fact, was so typical that it may well serve as a model of what occurred elsewhere.

Neither is it unusual that the powers of urban renewal came to be employed during this era to achieve more political than purely economic ends—that, too, is a pattern that has been well documented elsewhere.[10] Only the scope, and not the direction, of Norfolk's response is larger and more dramatic than elsewhere. Indeed, the very magnitude of this reaction makes the story in Norfolk so exemplary of three distinct stages, all of which occurred well before the traditional starting date of desegregation studies, that are felt to characterize this response:

1. **An Attempt to Make Separate Facilities "Equal," 1950-1955.** Like their counterparts across most of the nation, leaders in Norfolk were aware that the system of "separate but equal" schools for blacks and whites, at least as it existed in many parts of the rural South, could not long endure a withering legal challenge in the postwar era. Partly because of the overwhelming presence of the military, which had been integrated since 1948, they could see that the old barriers of

segregation were falling. As part of a larger mandate to reform every phase of city administration, the People's Movement of 1946 deliberately set about the task to equalize both the facilities and the operation of its dual public school system. Writing in February, 1957, Judge Walter Hoffman commented on the success of this effort:

> The sum and substance of the School Superintendent's evidence is that the City of Norfolk has substantially complied with the "separate but equal" doctrine, which was applicable prior to the decision in *Brown* v. *Board of Education*. The City of Norfolk is to be commended for its rapid strides in bringing about an equalization in physical equipment, curriculum, teacher load, and teachers' salaries. If the "separate but equal" doctrine were now in existence, there would be no grounds for relief to be afforded these plaintiffs.[11]

The progress in Norfolk caught the attention of other Southern leaders: writing in *Look* magazine, U.S. Senator Sam Ervin (D-N.C.), later of Watergate fame, commented that new schools for blacks, like Young Park Elementary in Norfolk, gave testimony to the South's effort to resolve the disparities of segregation "in its own way."[12] Between 1950 and 1955 Norfolk completed four new elementary schools for blacks planned during the People's reform era (Young Park, Bowling Park, Lindenwood, and Diggs Park), three of which were built with federal redevelopment funds, and transferred a newly constructed junior high (Jacox) to the black school system. In addition, it completed a major building program to modernize most of the aging black facilities with new classroom wings, libraries, cafeterias, auditoriums, and other badly needed improvements. Teacher salaries had been equalized in 1941 as a result of a lawsuit,[13] and by 1951, Norfolk was reporting that it spent more to educate its black children than its white, due to the fact that black teachers had more seniority and degrees than their white counterparts.

Thus, the local record of attention to the fiscal and physical aspects of making separate-race schools more equal is in full keeping with efforts all across the South to maintain segregation in a more equitable setting. While the *Brown* cases were under consideration, most of the states where schools were segregated by law (*de jure*) began a deliberate effort to upgrade black schools, provide additional funding resources, equalize teacher salaries, and otherwise preserve segregation "on a voluntary basis."[14] During this same era, Norfolk made similar attempts to build other new facilities for blacks and to bring public services in black neighborhoods more into line with those that existed for whites. This effort, however, may have been more of an outgrowth of the People's reform movement than an indicator of a national trend. Thus when the Norfolk Redevelopment and Housing Authority acquired title to military housing projects in the postwar era, it quickly moved to turn a large percentage of these into public housing units for blacks, partly as a way to ease the crush of individuals crowding into traditional black neighborhoods. N.R.H.A. Project One, in addition to building new schools for blacks, also provided modern streets, parks, playgrounds, sidewalks, streetlights, curbs, gutters, and other public services that were almost nonexistent in most black areas.

2. **A Transition Period, 1955-1956: from Calm to Hostility.** A confrontation over school desegregation was not necessarily inevitable; the initial announcement of the Supreme Court's decision outlawing separate-race schools was greeted calmly by most Southern leaders. Indeed, they had expected some such determination. Only the reversal of the longstanding legal tradition under attack in the title case, *Brown* v. *Board of Education*, really caused much consternation. If federal courts followed the letter of the decision in *Brown*, as it became increasingly obvious they would, then it meant that traditional school attendance patterns in the South would have to be revised so that every child would attend the school closest to his or her home. This doctrine of proximity represented a much greater threat to segregated schools in the South than in the rest of the country, for it meant that not only would

blacks be admitted in fairly large numbers to formerly white schools—a situation that was rare enough elsewhere—in many Southern communities, because of the high percentage of blacks, whites would have to attend nearby black schools, a circumstance not found anywhere else in the world.[15] Part of the reason for the initial calm of most Southern leaders was the feeling that their efforts to achieve equal school facilities had been successful, and that "voluntary" segregation could continue. It was only when litigation was initiated in their own community, and they realized the problems posed by the doctrine of proximity, that there was first panic, and then wholesale opposition to the Court.

Norfolk in 1950, like Orlando,[16] Charleston, Washington, New Orleans, Baltimore, and a number of other older, more established Southern cities, had in addition to a large central slum, a half-dozen or so other black housing areas scattered around town; newer Southern cities, those that boomed after the Civil War (i.e., Atlanta, Birmingham, Memphis, and Augusta) were more like their Northern and midwestern counterparts in that black families were concentrated almost exclusively in a single downtown "ghetto." The newer cities could thus adopt the Northern model of *de facto* segregation without undue hardship; it was only in the older Southern cities, where the black population was more dispersed, that the doctrine of proximity meant that large scale integration would be required. Karl and Alma Taueber surmised that the "backyard" or "alley-dwelling" type of housing arrangement found in most older Southern cities, like Norfolk, was due to the fact that almost every white middle-class neighborhood had its own black residential area nearby which served as a source of domestic laborers.[17] Residential integration in Norfolk may have been even more pronounced than elsewhere, because navy housing, desegregated since 1948, presented additional pockets of black population in former white areas. Moreover, the fact that blacks were spread across the city meant that there were transition areas, blocks where housing was shifting from white to black, in a number of neighborhoods; it was these areas that posed the greatest threat to efforts to preserve segregated schools on a "voluntary" basis.

The calm reaction of the school board in Norfolk to the *Brown v. Board of Education* decision was praised as a model for the rest of the South. The board was confident that the schools could be desegregated with a "minimum of integration"—"so little you'd hardly notice it"[18]—without major disruption or problem. Catholic schools, including Norfolk Catholic High, had been desegregated without incident at the start of the 1954-1955 school year,[19] and the board felt that the same results could be achieved in the public schools. Not until they actually faced desegregation litigation did the city's leaders realize the explosive potential of the issue. Politics and events quickly overtook this initial calmness: Virginia's Governor Thomas Stanley and many of the state's urban political leaders at first expressed sentiments that paralleled those of the Norfolk School Board, but the ferocity of the resistance building in the rural Southside counties that formed the core of the Byrd Organization's voting strength soon forced a retreat from moderation. Hostility to school segregation was fed by the fact that the city's bus system, state park, and other recreation facilities had desegregated under either court mandate or the threat of litigation. The change is most apparent in the sentiments of the city's legislative delegation, which at first supported the board, but by 1956 was in full retreat as it faced opposition from the Defenders of State Sovereignty and Individual Liberty, Virginia's well-organized, and for the most part, well-heeled, staunchly segregationist, pressure group.

The school board's calm, "wait and see" attitude soon gave way to a quiet reappraisal of its own building effort: Additions scheduled for black schools were delayed, and the board began to evaluate the locations of proposed buildings in light of the critical issue of residential proximity. Plans to replace the aging Lafayette School were scrapped, as were at least four prospective sites for a badly needed (white) junior high. Some of these were rejected because they were too close to black neighborhoods to avoid desegregation under the *Brown* precedent, but the issue was clouded by the fact that Norfolk had also just annexed new areas where new facilities were also required. A similar situation appears to have existed in other aspects of municipal planning and development. Two major projects, the Cultural Center and Waterfront Quay, initiated during the waning days of the People's administration, were put on hold and finally discarded as the new leaders quietly assessed the impact of desegregation. It may well have been that with the prospect of political crisis facing Norfolk, its leaders were reluctant to commit precious funding for business development projects when the stability of its schools and neighborhoods was threatened.

The school board found itself increasingly isolated in both spirit and approach from the rest of Norfolk's political leaders. Public reaction to the possibility of school desegregation was stiffening, partly because the city was finding that it would not be given much of a transition period to shift from segregated to desegregated schools. Any hope that local blacks would be content with newly improved facilities was quickly dashed: The N.A.A.C.P. filed a petition seeking desegregated schools shortly after the *Brown* decision was rendered, and once its administrative remedies were exhausted, proceeded directly to federal court. U.S. District Judge Walter Hoffman was also not inclined to grant the sort of delay customary elsewhere in the South, and was preparing to order several elementary schools desegregated in 1957, an event that would have put Norfolk on the same collision course as Little Rock. The reaction in Norfolk was much like that in other parts of the South,[20] and indeed much of the rest of the nation:[21] When legal challenges to segregation began to emerge in their own community, white leaders tended to blame this "interference" on the work of "outsiders," and failed to see it as a legitimate expression of local black hostility to segregation. At first the N.A.A.C.P. bore the brunt of these attacks, and all across the South state legislatures focused their wrath through anti-N.A.A.C.P. laws designed to intimidate its membership. The reaction of the white community to the N.A.A.C.P. spilled over into other community activities, and Norfolkians, just like others in areas thought to be racially moderate, had their own experience with hate mail, racist literature, and racial turmoil. Events were particularly intense in Coronado, a formerly white section of the city where the color line had been successfully breached amid the threat of firebombs, vandalism, and hostile mobs. The crisis of housing in the black community, in part exacerbated by redevelopment activity, was forcing racial change in a few other neighborhoods as well. Coronado was but one symptom of the problem; similar hostilities were evident in the Brambleton and Berkley sections of the city, both of which by the mid-1950s had nearly completed their transition to predominantly black housing areas, and in the Atlantic City, Lambert's Point, and Broad Creek areas on the fringe of the downtown section, which were just beginning to tip. Just as in Coronado, efforts by the black community to develop new homes in the Broad Creek Shores subdivision were met with strong opposition from whites in the surrounding areas. In fact, the pattern of housing in Norfolk and older Southern cities, where whites and blacks lived in closer proximity to one another, may have been in part responsible for some of the growing animosity between the races.

By 1956 race relations in the city, which had been at their highest peak a few years earlier, had deteriorated badly. No longer were blacks consulted on major planning or development initiatives, and even when controversies arose, like that faced in the Broad Creek Shores development, black leaders had so few contacts in city government that they had to turn to the banking and financial community for help. One black leader characterized the situation: "In Norfolk, there are no relations between the races."[22] The school board, too, found itself just as isolated. In spite of the strong personal commitment of its members to continue public education in Norfolk at all cost, they saw that state and local political leaders were more than willing to let public schools evolve into some sort of state-sponsored private educational system in order to preserve segregation. Although its members had been willing to do their part in carefully planning the location of new facilities, increasingly the school board was being called upon to go even farther in holding the line against desegregation. As members of the middle class, all of whom had benefitted enormously from public education, the Norfolk School Board, like hundreds of others across the South, was not willing to participate in the demise of public education in the city. Partly because they recognized this difference, political leaders in Virginia and a half-dozen other Southern states moved to take from the local boards a certain amount of the administrative powers necessary to maintain public schools. Instead they created a melange of state pupil-placement agencies designed to "interpose" the authority of the states between black litigants and local school boards.[23]

Thus, by 1956, the school board and political leaders in Norfolk found themselves in the midst of a firestorm of public unrest. The community seemed headed towards court-ordered desegregation of its public schools, yet Virginia's political leaders were indicating that they would not permit even the most minimal form of integration. Also, public opposition to the courts had, by this time, reached a fever pitch. Neither situation was unique to Norfolk, although the particular circumstance of its dispersed black population may have lent an extra air of urgency to its deliberations. Since the established political order cannot long endure this level of public unrest, the leadership in Norfolk, and indeed much of the rest of the South, felt obligated to take every legal step possible to delay the eventuality of desegregated schools; in doing so, they were following the lead of their counterparts in Congress and the state legislatures who were beginning to move beyond rhetoric to open defiance.

3. **Overt Attempts to Move from *De Jure* to *De Facto* Segregation, 1956-1960.** The doctrine of "interposition" that began to emerge in the rhetoric of the politicians found its outlet in a host of special state laws designed to interpose the authority of the state between the federal courts and local school officials. Most of these laws dealt with pupil placement, student transfer policies, attendance,[24] and financial control of the schools, but it is just as logical to assume that local officials followed these same legislative trends in their own enactments. Gradually the realization began to dawn on municipal officials that, because public education was much more a community than even a state responsibility, the powers of local school boards and city councils to manipulate public school policies were even greater than those of the state

government. By extending the interposition logic already being advanced by numerous state leaders, local officials discovered that their own inherent powers to assign pupils, rule on transfer applications, build schools, utilize space, draw attendance zones, and otherwise administer the day to day operations of the public schools could be judiciously applied to preventing, or at least delaying, the eventuality of court-ordered desegregation. Norfolk officials quickly seized on these powers and began to take the drastic steps that would be necessary to delay desegregation by closing threatened schools, demolishing mixed-race neighborhoods, isolating pockets of black population, and otherwise replacing the elaborate system of *de jure* segregation with the type of single-race schools zones already approved by the courts in northern and midwestern cities. Indeed, it is both the speed and the extent of the interposition activities in Norfolk that makes these events so exemplary of the larger process followed in most other cities all across the country to prevent the possibility integrated schools and neighborhoods.

Even though data on the 1950s attendance zones in Norfolk no longer exists, the application of the interposition philosophy at the local level may still be tracked by studying the fate of the school buildings most directly threatened by court-ordered integration. Since the first round of litigation followed almost exactly the proximity precedent established in *Brown* v. *Board*, by the winter of 1956-1957 Norfolk faced the certainty that at least two white elementary schools, Patrick Henry and Gatewood, would have to be integrated under the proximity doctrine.[25] Before the 1957-1958 school year ever began, however, the school board initiated its first real experiment with applying its inherent powers of school administration to block the court order. As Judge Hoffman had indicated, the two elementary schools most threatened by court-ordered integration were both in transition areas of the city. Patrick Henry was located in the Atlantic City area, a once proud working-class neighborhood that had always maintained some black housing near the cotton mill and seafood packing houses. In recent years blacks had begun to move into other portions of the neighborhood, and, by 1957, 50 blacks would have been eligible to attend Patrick Henry under the doctrine of proximity.[26] Even though whites would have outnumbered blacks by more than four to one, the school was closed and converted to administrative offices. Two other elementary schools, Benmoreell and Broad Creek Village, which served integrated navy housing projects, were also closed, even though both were little more than a decade old, and Pineridge Elementary, which also served the Broad Creek area, was closed for a few years.

Gatewood Elementary School was located in Berkley, another working-class neighborhood that was isolated from the rest of the city by the Elizabeth River. The black population, which had once been confined to areas around the shipyards, had begun in the previous decade to expand into other parts of Berkley. Gatewood remained the last white school in the area, but it, too, was threatened by desegregation, although Judge Hoffman indicated that the ratio of whites to blacks would have been only eight to one. Just as it had with Patrick Henry, the school board closed the school to its white clientele, and transferred it instead to the black school system. Whites in Berkley would have to commute to some other school across the river. In addition to Gatewood, the school board also transferred John Marshall Elementary on the edge of the downtown area from the white to black school systems, since it, too, was too close to nearby black housing to withstand a legal challenge. Since Judge Hoffman had already approved a similar shift two years earlier when blacks sought to enroll in Thomas Jefferson Elementary in Newport News,[27] the Norfolk School Board had every reason to feel he would approve the same tactic in the current instance. Indeed, Judge Hoffman all but suggested a repeat of the strategy to the Newport News School Board in an opinion written at the same time that the fate of Patrick Henry and Gatewood was being decided.[28]

In addition to the power to determine the attendance zone and the actual use of buildings, the Norfolk School Board found that it also had discretionary authority over the size, location, and grade composition of new schools as well. The most telling evidence that these powers were used to forestall school segregation may be found in the creation of the Rosemont and Coronado schools in the newly annexed Norview area. Rosemont, which early press accounts indicate was designed to serve as a combination elementary/junior/senior high school (the only such combination school in the city), was hastily erected to serve the black population threatening to integrate the schools in Norview. Not only did the papers speculate that the purpose of the school was to forestall school desegregation,[29] but the black community also fiercely resisted both the project and fact that the hastily erected building would lack many of the support facilities present in all the newer white structures. A school in the Coronado section was not planned until after the school board had been given the names and addresses of the black litigants seeking to integrate Norview Elementary. After examining the documents, the board discovered that, in spite of Rosemont, which was then under construction, the color lines in the Norview section had continued to shift, and some of the litigants still lived closer to a white school. When first conceived, Coronado was nothing more than six mobile classrooms pushed off the back of a truck onto a vacant lot,[30] which, like Rosemont, was designed almost entirely to place a black school in closer proximity to black litigants than the white school they sought to attend. Again, blacks complained bitterly that this "vest-pocket" school lacked appropriate facilities, and was only being built to counter their litigation.[31] Although Judge Hoffman discussed the situation in his review of the suit, he nevertheless felt powerless to intervene as long as the school board could point to a sound pedagogical reason (overcrowding) for creating the school.[32]

The strategy was even further refined, with the help of the more political mayor and city council, in the spring of 1959, just after the city's previously closed white schools had reopened. At that time Mayor Duckworth proposed building three-room schoolhouses all across the city, indicating that these mini-schools could better serve "their neighborhoods." In spite of his subtlety, the newspapers,[33] the school board,[34] and the city council[35] all knew that the ploy was aimed at maintaining single-race schools. Even though the school board had strong pedagogical reasons to oppose these minischools as impractical,[36] it nevertheless bowed to the mayor, and erected five buildings that met his specifications (Easton, Fairlawn, East Ocean View, Poplar Halls, and Pretty Lake) in the newly annexed eastern section of the city: "We had to build them . . . it was the only way we could get any schools at all . . . [although] they weren't quite as small as the ones Fred [Duckworth] wanted to build." Years later School Boardmember Frank Crenshaw would indicate that he thought these schools were partly responsible for the fact that the eastern portion of the city felt underserved for decades, a grievance that he sensed underlay much of the later pressure for its push for a ward system of elections.[37]

One other finding of this research is that city councils and other local officials, just like their colleagues on the school boards, state legislatures, and the Congress, used the powers at their disposal to frustrate and delay court-ordered integration. The minischool controversy in the spring of 1959 serves as a good introduction to the application of municipal powers to dictate school policies. The school system in Norfolk, like all of those in Virginia and most of the systems in other large cities, was a dependent district which relied upon the city government for a portion of its taxing and spending powers. Financing new construction is but one element of that financial power. Although normally unwilling to risk the political outcry of involving itself in school affairs, a city council nevertheless has the power to appropriate funds, and thus dictate many of the spending policies of the school district. Because it feared independent action by the more educationally—as opposed to politically—oriented school boards, Virginia passed special legislation that allowed municipal governments the power to cut off school funds on a 30-day notice, and several rural localities availed themselves of this power.[38] The Norfolk City Council applied the leverage of this tactic when it voted to appropriate school funds on a 30-day basis in the midst of the school closing crisis.[39] Another aspect of financial control may be found in the size of the local appropriation: After the school closing controversy, the city council intimated that it would cut local school funding because of the way the school board and the teachers had opposed it during the crisis.[40] Later the Council made good on a portion of its threat by substantially reducing the school board's budget, thereby effectively blocking raises for the teachers who had defeated Massive Resistance.[41] Finally, the city council sought legislation allowing it to replace the incumbent board members in a thinly veiled move to enlarge the membership and reduce their term of office.[42]

In addition to the ability to influence the operation of the schools directly through their powers of appointment, financial control, and capital funding, local governments also have considerable heretofore unrecognized authority to dictate the size and shape of school districts and attendance zones through their powers of urban renewal. The Broad Creek Shores controversy provides an interesting example: By the time the area had been annexed (January 1, 1955), a group of black developers had already platted the Broad Creek Shores subdivision and had a number of houses under construction. Although faced with a *fait accompli*, the City of Norfolk nevertheless moved through its powers of eminent domain to seize a large tract on the northern edge of the property, thereby isolating the black development from nearby white neighborhoods. Even though the stated purpose of the purchase was to buy up land for a park and possible school expansion, neither was ever built on the site; the land was eventually used for the National Guard Armory and an industrial park. Much later councilman (and later mayor) Roy Martin would indicate that the armory was placed there "in order to block the black development,"[43] a theory that confirms reports in the black press of the era.[44] Even though there is no other direct testimony to the fact, appearances at least suggest that Norfolk similarly used the placement of Old Dominion University, interstate highways, recreation areas, and industrial parks to act as a natural barrier between racially diverse neighborhoods and to maintain separate race school districts. Although confirmation of such a theory must be left to others, use of the powers of city planning and eminent domain to block desegregation has long been hypothesized.[45]

Perhaps the most damning indictment of the use of municipal powers to achieve *de facto* segregation comes from the former head of Housing and Home Finance Agency (H.H.F.A.) in the 1950s, who accused Southern cities of using their powers of urban renewal to break up integrated low-income neighborhoods in order to draw the color lines more clearly:

> Where, in a few Southern cities, there had been a protest against this, a compromise was sometimes reached involving proposed reuse for other than residential purposes. Thus a slum formerly housing both Negro and white families was proposed as the location for industry or a public institution. Urban renewal too often seemed to be an instrument for wiping out racially integrated living.[46]

Although he did not mention any city by name, Mr. Weaver could well have had in mind many of the projects undertaken in

Conclusion

Norfolk during its second phase of redevelopment. In spite of the fact that N.R.H.A. Project One had been carefully conceived, thoroughly planned, and meticulously implemented, Norfolk's second phase of redevelopment, begun after 1956, was rushed, haphazard, and poorly planned. Humanitarian concerns had been foremost in the minds of the planners of N.R.H.A. Project One: Public housing in the form of modern garden apartments in well designed neighborhoods replaced some of the worst slums in the nation, and development was implemented in carefully conceived stages so that residents were moved first to public housing units away from the site during demolition, and then moved back to their old neighborhood, once it had been rebuilt. In spite of its size and scope, the entire project took only five years to complete from the time the bulldozers first began to roll. The Atlantic City, Downtown, Broad Creek, and Old Dominion projects stand in sharp contrast to the careful planning and precision of N.R.H.A. Project One. Under either a remarkable coincidence, or as part of a much larger deliberate plan of action, at almost exactly the same time that federal Judge Walter Hoffman was ordering the desegregation of Patrick Henry Elementary School in the Atlantic City portion of the city, the Norfolk Redevelopment and Housing Authority was announcing that it planned to demolish the entire neighborhood. The coincidence theory is hard to accept, especially since closing Patrick Henry Elementary, an action already taken by the school board, did not remove the threat to segregated schools posed by the mixed-race neighborhood: 13 of the 24 black plaintiffs in the school desegregation suit lived in Atlantic City.[47] Even though Patrick Henry Elementary was removed from the challenge, these plaintiffs, as well as other black citizens in the area, still lived closer to the white schools in the Ghent portion of the city than to the black institutions further downtown. Although the N.R.H.A. indicated that it had been planning the Atlantic City project since 1954, announcement of it did not come until December 7, 1956,[48] and the bulldozers began to roll seven months later. According to former mayor and N.R.H.A. Commissioner Pretlow Darden, the second phase of Norfolk's redevelopment was initiated by Mayor Duckworth, who promoted the Atlantic City project as a way to "rid Ghent of the cancerous growth approximate to it," although there is little evidence that the "blight" would have spread beyond the natural geographic barriers that isolated Atlantic City from the rest of the city.

Atlantic City was not a slum, at least in the eyes of those who had the most professional knowledge of housing conditions in the neighborhood. The 1950 census revealed that more than half of the houses had central heat and indoor plumbing—both still rarities in many parts of town—were in adequate repair, and commanded moderate rents twice those of the areas demolished in Project One and the Downtown Project.[49] In spite of complaints of residents that persistent rumors of redevelopment had driven down real estate values and hastened its decline,[50] the new black families moving in were apparently willing to pay even higher rents than their white neighbors due to the housing crisis in the black community.[51] Because federal law required cities to rehabilitate one housing unit for each one torn down under redevelopment, the Health Department's housing inspection division had just completed a major code enforcement initiative in the area, one of the first major attempts in the nation to salvage a neighborhood by concentrated enforcement efforts. Atlantic City was chosen precisely because it was salvageable: It was "not so good that we couldn't rehabilitate it, and not so bad that we were wasting our time."[52] Because of the link between the rehabilitation project and redevelopment, there was close cooperation between the Health Department and the Housing Authority. When queried about future plans for the area, N.R.H.A. executive director Larry Cox reportedly indicated that it would be at least "five to ten years" before the Housing Authority would initiate a project in Atlantic City. That was why Health Department officials were so surprised to read the sudden announcement of the Atlantic City project; they had been present for months at the cabinet meetings of the N.R.H.A., and there had been no mention of such a plan. They were doubly upset when they found that their own surveys were used to declare the area a slum.[53]

The code-enforcement project had been a major success, and almost every residential unit had been brought up to the standard of the city's minimum housing code. Although there was a two-block wide strip of deterioration in a mixed-use area of commercial, residential, and light industrial structures that ran along the present site of Brambleton Avenue, these buildings could have been demolished in the highway project, and the rest of the neighborhood saved, the course urged by the Health Department. According to the head of the code-enforcement project, Atlantic City, even in 1956, had a "surprisingly large number of owner-occupied dwellings" that should never have been demolished as slum housing. Although a structure could pass the city's minimum housing code and still have major structural defects under federal standards, a number of blocks in Atlantic City had only one or two such defects. These blocks could have been included for demolition only by carefully designing the project boundaries so that the overall project area could meet the federal requirement of five defects per dwelling. This accounts for the odd shape of the project, and why it zigged around some blocks and then zagged to pick up others.

In short, there was much that was worth saving in the Atlantic City area: Many of its brownstones, row houses, and turn-of-the-century dwellings were clearly salvageable, and would have commanded a premium price when urban pioneers rediscovered the charm of in-town neighborhoods little more than a decade later. Although parts along the present site of Brambleton Avenue were dilapidated, some of the blocks closer to the downtown area exuded a "Greenwich Village flavor" and a "Bohemian and cosmopolitan character."[54] The perception that Health Department officials were working with the N.R.H.A. to help it find new slums dealt a severe blow to the city's code-enforcement efforts. The Health Department was so upset at how its services and its surveys had been used, that a major rift developed between it and the Norfolk Redevelopment and Housing Authority, a division that could still be seen decades later in the overlapping of housing inspection and enforcement authorities between the city and the N.R.H.A. In spite of its arguments and its expertise, the Department was powerless to help Atlantic City residents, many of whom were doubly bitter when they learned that the N.R.H.A. would pay less for their houses than they had spent in bringing them up to code.[55]

Neither was Broad Creek Village a slum. Built during World War II, all of the units were freestanding dwellings with central heat, and modern plumbing and electrical systems. The 2,598 units each had two to three bedrooms, hardwood floors, deep sash windows, and sturdy interior construction; many, in fact, were moved by their owners before they could be torn down, and still survive in other parts of the city. Moreover, residents were proud of the community, and especially pointed to its warmth, compassion, friendliness, lack of crime, and sense of positive spirit, hardly signs of deterioration.[56] Nevertheless, the N.R.H.A. was in a hurry to take possession of the property from the federal government so that it could be torn down. Since the Authority owned the housing as a result of the federal government's gift, demolition of the project did not have to meet redevelopment standards. Although there was some discussion of maintaining the area as residential, the city council was adamantly opposed to having low-rent housing in that portion of the city. Mayor Duckworth suggested using the land, which had rail service as well as a prime location between Virginia Beach Boulevard and Princess Anne Road, the two major thoroughfares into the downtown, as an industrial park, and its fate was sealed.[57] Once the N.R.H.A. took over in November 1954, the area was doomed. The Authority never maintained the structures properly and had no interest in renting the vacant units, so it was not long before neglect and vandalism took their toll on both the structures and the Broad Creek community. By the time bulldozers started to roll, the N.R.H.A. had been successful in creating a *bona fide* slum out of a once decent and even modern, low-rent housing development.[58]

These two new redevelopment projects share another common element: Both were rushed into the demolition phase so quickly that portions of the cleared land sat vacant for close to three decades. Atlantic City, especially, was poorly conceived as an industrial park: Although it had more than a 140 acres, it was long and narrow, and badly cut up by Brambleton Avenue, the new superhighway that crossed its spine. Why would an industry choose to be in this somewhat isolated spot on the edge of the downtown area when the city was also developing almost 500 acres in the Broad Creek Village Project closer to major thoroughfares and the population heart of the area? Not until the 1980s, when the Red Cross moved into the industrial park and the hospital complex eventually expanded to fill the western corner, did Atlantic City look like anything more than an urban desert. Even forty years later, most of the land in the project was dedicated to parking and governmental use by the U.S. Commerce Department, state highway projects, a largely unused waterfront park, city health department, medical school, and hospital authority facilities. If the project had been designed with more care, the city would have seized the last two blocks to the waterfront as well, and the area could have blossomed with highrise housing developments, a use it eventually discovered somewhat tenuously. In fact, Atlantic City has much that would recommend it to upscale apartment buildings, condos, and highrise residences: Partly because it is cut off from the rest of the city by both natural geographic barriers and major transportation facilities, it is much more conducive to residential than industrial uses. Even though it is bounded on very nearly all four sides by waterfront with spectacular vistas, the planners seemed to do everything possible to destroy its future use as a residential area. Brambleton Avenue cuts across it in such a way that only the two corner pieces of property on Smith Creek (the Hague), one of the city's premiere real estate assets, could be used for highrise apartment houses; the small commercial area, with its quaint shops and artsy flavor, was demolished; and the failure to seize its rotting wharves and crumbling factory district has made it difficult for all but the most persistent developer to realize any of the great potential of the area.

In 1957, when the two projects were planned and executed, the governing elites of the city appeared to be violently opposed to residential use of either site. There was no talk of demolition in phases, as had been done in N.R.H.A. Project One, to minimize hardships or plan for orderly expansion. In spite of the fact that Norfolk was also clearing almost 200 more acres in the downtown business district and starting another project near the present site of Old Dominion University, it was just more than a year between the time the projects were announced and most of the demolition had been completed. In just 16 months Norfolk appears to have torn down the homes of almost twenty thousand people—roughly ten percent of its population—but these were not the substandard dwellings of its poorest residents. Instead these were the homes of working-class white families and a few black residents attracted to decent housing. It was these latter residents, because of the threat they posed to school segregation, that the city wanted to remove, but in the process, it embarked upon a terribly destructive course.

The black families in Atlantic City and Broad Creek Village posed more than just an academic threat to school segregation. Because they represented the upwardly mobile black middle class, they held high aspirations for their children. For this reason, many had taken the lead in initiating the lawsuit that challenged the status of *de jure* segregation in the city. Because the N.A.A.C.P. had wished to follow the *Brown* precedent as closely as possible, the original 24 plaintiffs, and others like them, were probably sought out precisely because they lived closer to white elementary schools than the black institutions to which their children were assigned. Nevertheless, they were willing to enlist and take a very prominent and somewhat risky role in the effort. Thirteen of the original plaintiffs lived in Atlantic City; another five lived in Berkley section of the city and would have gone to the Gatewood Elementary. Instead, the school board transferred Gatewood to the black school system, thereby leaving the remaining whites in Berkley without a school, and speeding the departure of white families from the area. Although the other six plaintiffs resided closer to a black school than a white institution, they lived in the black section of Lambert's Point[59] that was just then in the process of expanding further towards the nearby white neighborhoods. Even though Smallwood Elementary (black) stood in the center of the area (the Old Dominion University Library now stands on the site), the city initiated a small redevelopment project in the area to provide land for expansion of the then two-year junior college that was to become Old Dominion University. The project had the effect of bulldozing the transition areas, stabilizing racial lines, and interposing a large barrier of public land (the university) between the black Lambert's Point section and the white neighborhoods of Larchmont and Edgewater, a result that is still obvious. Moreover, Lambert's Point, Atlantic City, and Broad Creek were all integrating fairly peacefully,[60] and experienced none of the violence or intimidation found in Brambleton and Coronado when the color lines were first crossed there. Instead, all three of these areas had supported a few black families for a number of years. Because of the critical housing shortage in the black community, in part created by redevelopment activity, landlords could command higher rents from blacks, and this helped smooth the transition of black residents into additional parts of these neighborhoods.

Thus, just as school boards could tear down or close schools directly threatened by court-ordered integration, cities had the power, through redevelopment, to tear down mixed-race or transition areas where the racial composition of the neighborhood schools would have been equally mixed. Parallel to the power to size schools in order to maintain single-race districts, is the authority, through redevelopment, to adjust the size of the neighborhoods to meet the racial designation of the schools. School boards could alter attendance zones, but cities could achieve the same effect by seizing land, demolishing housing, or erecting barriers between neighborhoods that would force resizing of the attendance zones. The evidence that Norfolk took this route and directly employed its powers of school administration and urban renewal to move the status of its segregated school system from *de jure* to *de facto* is overwhelming.

In spite of the monumental effort of its political leaders, the effort to forestall school desegregation by applying the city's powers of redevelopment, planning, and school plant planning worked for only a single year.

The schools that would have been integrated in the fall of 1957 were either torn down or removed from service, and in many cases, the neighborhoods, too, were demolished. But for the quick use of its urban renewal powers, Norfolk may have joined Little Rock, Arkansas, as the first major battleground over court-ordered school integration. Judge Hoffman was obviously cognizant that the city was working to counter his authority. Writing before either the fate of the school or the full boundaries of the Atlantic City project were known, he indicated that redevelopment there could "substantially reduce" the number of children he would have to assign to Patrick Henry Elementary.[61] Norfolk had both the motive and the opportunity to use its powers of urban renewal to forestall school desegregation. That it did so, and with a vengeance, seems obvious. Even so, any assessment of motive and municipal power would be incomplete without some discussion of possible rival hypotheses for the observed events. Although several alternate explanations are offered by other authors, the research supporting their conclusions comes from the 1960s or 1970s, and not the era under consideration.

Karl and Alma Taueber, in their study of residential segregation and neighborhood change, noted that in Southern cities, in sharp contrast to the rest of the country, residential segregation generally increased between 1950 and 1960. In their comments on this trend, they attribute this difference more to a number of market forces than to deliberate government policy. In a more detailed study of several selected cities, however, the Tauebers note that governmental action may have been a factor in maintaining segregated neighborhoods.

They found that Charleston, South Carolina, for instance, deliberately used separate-race public housing projects to maintain segregated neighborhoods. Also, the pattern of backyard residences for black domestics in white neighborhoods that was evident before 1940, was almost nonexistent by 1960, but they were unsure whether this was caused by voluntary housing changes or official zoning and housing-code enforcement initiatives. They note that in Memphis the planning commission blocked expansion of black housing into white areas, a pattern that the Tauebers felt was quite common: "In some Southern cities informal political agreements permitting 'zoning' portions of the city for white or black occupancy may have played a part in making available the requisite land for building new housing for blacks." They also indicate that Southern cities were much more aggressive in their annexation efforts in order to "capture new areas of white population." Although Norfolk was not one of the cities selected for in-depth study, the Tauebers' index of racial segregation indicates that it had one of the highest indexes of residential segregation in the country in both 1950 and 1960. By 1960 only Richmond, two cities in Louisiana (Monroe and Shreveport), and six cities in Florida (Daytona Beach, Fort Lauderdale, Jacksonville, St. Petersburg, West Palm Beach, and Miami), out of more than 200 studied, had a higher index.[62]

In his major work on the history of urban America, Kenneth T. Jackson notes many of the same trends as the Tauebers, but he points to deliberate government action as one of the primary causes of the increasing segregation of America's cities. The government he blames, however, is not municipal, but rather federal. Professor Jackson provides a stunning indictment of how the federal Home Owners Loan Corporation (H.O.L.C.) of the 1930s invented "redlining" of urban, black, and racially mixed neighborhoods—a practice that was later followed by both the Federal Housing Administration (F.H.A.) and the Veterans Administration (V.A.). According to Jackson, realtors knew that with these red-lining practices in effect, the sale of homes in a white community to black buyers meant that future loans would be denied, and they worked to steer buyers into single-race neighborhoods and away from transition areas. In addition, since the loan standards of these federal agencies specified minimum lot sizes, set-backs, and other standards, they favored newer suburban housing over older, intown neighborhoods. Because of these rigid standards, inner-city housing was difficult to sell, thereby hastening the decline of the cities. Potential new property owners could not get federally-backed loans in mixed-race or declining neighborhoods, and this increased absentee ownership, property abandonment, and the development of slums. By the time the federal government finally reversed its red-lining practices in 1966, the switch only helped the remaining white homeowners escape to the suburbs, thereby furthering the segregation of America.

The federal government's role in forcing housing segregation was more than just adherence to discriminatory lending practices. Jackson also documents how federal policies pushed public housing units into existing slum areas, thereby reinforcing segregated housing patterns and leading to the further decline of the surrounding neighborhoods. Although public housing had originally been intended for the "working poor" and the "deserving poor," by 1960 federal policies had forced it to become housing of last resort for welfare clients, thereby relegating it to a permanent home for the nation's underclass. Although cities are partly to blame for the design and location of public housing, nevertheless it appears that a number of national polices (e.g., subsidized highways, mortgage investment, and expansion of military and government facilities) also helped to isolate blacks in central cities, while their white former neighbors moved to the suburbs. The only direct role attributed to municipalities is the use of zoning powers by Southern cities to enforce racial segregation of neighborhoods.[63]

Even though Professor Jackson's treatment does not deal directly with this issue, his thesis lends some support to the premise that Norfolk's post-*Brown* redevelopment activity was prompted as much by racial as economic considerations. Atlantic City and Broad Creek Village were not slums, but the fact that they were integrated communities on the edge of the downtown area meant that, according to Jackson's research, they were red-lined and in great danger of tipping rapidly into slums. Thus, even though the structures themselves were sound, the fact that they could not be sold with government-backed loans in a navy town like Norfolk was a fatal flaw that doomed them to continued decline. At the time of its demise, the N.R.H.A. labored mightily to prove to the skeptics that Atlantic City was in danger of becoming a slum because of its increasing crime and public health problems.[64] Later, it would argue that the project was initiated to give the medical center room to grow.[65] This justification is a little hard to accept, especially since the entire medical complex even today occupies only a corner of the sprawling project. The idea of a medical school was not advanced until well after the entire 145-acre area had been swept bare,[66] and much of the land used for this and other medical purposes could have been acquired by eminent domain without tearing down the rest of the community. N.R.H.A. Commissioner Pretlow Darden, who was also on the board of Norfolk General Hospital, indicated that Atlantic City was torn down more to protect Ghent than to help the hospital.[67] The "white flight" theories advanced by James Coleman[68] and David Armour[69] are equally inadequate in explaining events in Norfolk, where whites were pushed out of transition areas like Atlantic City and Broad Creek Village by municipal redevelopment activity. Moreover, most of the research on "white flight" was developed in the late 1960s and early 1970s, and shows that whites left areas when school integration efforts were at their maximum and crosstown busing plans were being implemented. These same concepts are not appropriate in the analysis of an era in which schools were not yet desegregated: Norfolk's redevelopment projects appear to have been initiated more to prevent "white flight" by keeping the schools segregated, than because of it. Similarly, the "tipping theory" advanced by Charles Willie and Susan Greenblatt deals with events once large-scale integration had begun under court orders. In their study of ten school systems, only four of which were in the South (Richmond, Dallas, Mobile, and Corpus Christi), they found several instances where federal courts cited direct municipal actions to preserve desegregated schools: The Boston School Committee, for instance, manipulated school district boundaries and used student attendance patterns to reinforce residential segregation. They also found that discriminatory actions by the state government and the real estate community contributed to residential segregation in Wilmington, Delaware. In their examination of school desegregation in Mobile, the authors describe how that city appeared to place its interstate highway so that it would serve as a dividing line between the races, allowing it to zone the school districts accordingly. In Richmond, Virginia, which faced some of the same harsh political restraints as Norfolk, they discovered that the city entered into a racially motivated merger with its surrounding counties in order to redraw attendance zones for white schools. In addition, there was some evidence of "blockbusting" by the Richmond real estate community, especially in areas on the north side of town. The Richmond School Board also appears to have established two distinct feeder system of schools with different grade organizations to minimize transfers between the majority black and white schools: White schools operated on a grades 1-5, 6-8, and 9-12 organization, while black schools had grades 1-6, 7-9, and 10-12.[70] Another researcher found that the Richmond School Board, under the leadership of its chairman, Lewis Powell, later a U.S. Supreme Court Justice, deliberately built new schools to forestall school desegregation. This building plan appears to have been in response to the advice of James J. Kilpatrick, then editor of the *Richmond News-Leader*, that the desegregation problem, "especially in the cities, could be handled by the relocation of school buildings and the gerrymandering of enrollment lines"[71]—advice that Norfolk followed as well.

Gary Orfield, perhaps the premier researcher in the field, offers an amalgam of all of these explanations in his description of the "ghettoization" of Chicago and other Northern cities in the late 1960s and early 1970s. His research documents both "white flight" and the rise of private and parochial schools as alternatives to extensive court-ordered integration. Like Jackson, he lays much of the blame for the failure of mixed-race neighborhoods on the federal government and its discriminatory lending practices. His indictment goes even farther, however, and accuses federal officials of permitting segregation in housing constructed with federal funds. He also blames federal urban renewal policies for allowing cities to demolish black neighborhoods without building adequate public housing or other low-income replacement units. Unlike Norfolk, very few public housing units were apparently built in Northern cities for the residents of redeveloped areas, and Orfield believes that this factor tended to accelerate the ghettoization of the neighborhoods adjoining renewal areas.[72]

His thesis is particularly applicable to a city like Norfolk, where there was both extensive urban renewal activity and a large-scale commitment to public housing, that, unfortunately, were not always coordinated. In the city's first phase of redevelopment, 1950 to 1955, begun under the leadership of the Silkstocking reformers, urban renewal and public housing were marvelously woven together as integral parts of the same overall plan. The city's business leaders worked closely with officials in Washington to convert many of its wartime housing projects into public housing in the postwar period. N.R.H.A. Project One, which was the first redevelopment project in the nation, was so carefully planned that residents of the renewal area were relocated to offsite public housing units, their neighborhood demolished, and new public housing units built in the project area, so that the former residents could be moved back before the next area was demolished. Since black areas were torn down and new public housing for blacks rebuilt on the same site, the action had little impact upon the segregation of the city, and, in fact, expanded the number of black housing units.

Norfolk's second phase of redevelopment, from 1956 to 1959, initiated under the leadership of Mayor Duckworth, stood in sharp contrast to Project One. First, the scope of the projects was enormous: The city proposed to bulldoze more than 800 acres, destroying the homes of almost a tenth of its population in less than a year and a half. Not only were no new public housing units planned, none of the areas being redeveloped would return to residential use. Except for the tiny (44 acres) project around what would eventually become Old Dominion University and a portion of the Downtown Project, which was more commercial and industrial than residential, most of the housing torn down belonged to white working-class residents who would not have been eligible for relocation to public housing. This phase of redevelopment confirms part of Orfield's theory on the expansion of slums, but with a twist. Since the private real estate market could not absorb this enormous movement of people with any combination of new construction or existing units, the sudden, mass migration of residents out of the project areas put tremendous pressure on the rest of the city's housing. Private homes and apartment buildings on the fringe of the downtown area were badly cut up and expanded to accommodate some of this influx. The end result was that the enormous scope of the four projects and the speed of demolition contributed to the deterioration of East Ghent, Park Place, and other established in-town neighborhoods, and raised questions in the minds of realtors, bankers, and the residents themselves about their future viability, especially when the burden of increasing school desegregation over the next few years fell disproportionately upon their schools. Because the projects had also displaced black residents and equally burdened the black real estate market, it was not long before many of these same neighborhoods, once they became overcrowded, began to decline, integrate, and then "tip" as whites sought housing choices in the suburbs. This type of "chain reaction effect," whereby destruction of one slum only creates new slums, is more fully explained by other critics of redevelopment.[73] The difference in Norfolk is that its redevelopment effort, because it tore down housing in areas that were still salvageable, only created slums where pleasant neighborhoods once stood.

Although Orfield's work deals with a later era, well after federal courts had ordered school desegregation in the cities under study, he reports that federal courts in a number of school desegregation cases found that the combination of federal and municipal housing policies increased school segregation in Charlotte, Wilmington, Cleveland, New York and other cities, although the focus of these findings was more on racially segregated public housing than other redevelopment and planning activities of the cities.[74] This finding is echoed by the research of Karl Taueber, who similarly reports that federal courts all across the South found that, once they were ordered to integrate schools, Southern school boards used their powers to delay the impact of the orders by closing school buildings directly threatened by integration, building new "vest-pocket" schools to minimize integration, redrawing attendance zones, and establishing liberal transfer policies.[75] Although both researchers deal with events that occurred in the 1960s, they nevertheless form an important part of the theoretical framework of this work, namely that cities took similar action in the 1950s, well before they actually faced the threat of large-scale school integration, to defer or delay court-ordered desegregation. The only difference in this work is the inference that in addition to relying upon school administrative and housing policies to achieve *de facto* segregation, cities also used their extensive powers of redevelopment and urban renewal to block the encroachment of blacks into white housing areas and to remove mixed-race neighborhoods that posed a threat to the continuation of a segregated school system. The effort of the school board in Norfolk to close schools, redesignate their racial composition, redraw attendance zones, and even demolish buildings in an era in which enrollment was expanding so rapidly that many schools were operating on double shifts,[76] seems to have had little to do with rapid changes in the white population explained by these approaches. Thus, even though "white flight" fails as an alternate explanation, especially when applied to a time before schools were actually integrated, it may be useful in understanding the process of neighborhood change that precipitated such dramatic redevelopment activity.

Even though the advocates of redevelopment enterprises have always claimed a purely economic motive for their initiatives, the critics, and there have been many who disapproved of the way urban renewal was handled by cities in the 1950s, have indicated that the economies of redevelopment have been false and even counterproductive.[77] In essence, the argument of the critics is that redevelopment has been a concerted attack upon the poor, those least able to cope with the hardship of relocation and loss of neighborhood ties; that many of the areas torn down were still salvageable and served a useful purpose by providing housing for the poor that was never replaced; and that much of the land actually developed was put to uses that could have been accomplished without the wholesale destruction of neighborhoods and such massive clearance efforts.

Norfolk provides both a fascinating counter and overwhelming confirmation of these critical approaches: Project One, because it tore down vast tracks of what was generally recognized as some of the worst slum housing in the country and replaced them with both well-designed public housing developments and badly needed industrial space, represents a triumph of the planners' art, especially since the entire 127-acre area was cleared and rebuilt in about five years. On the other hand, the Atlantic City and Broad Creek Village projects, initiated suddenly in Norfolk's second phase of redevelopment, provide confirmation of the worst nightmares of the critics. Not only did these projects clear away vast acres of decent, even modern, homes, they left the city's working-class poor without recourse in the housing market, thereby creating future slums by overburdening the surrounding neighborhoods. In their rebuilding phases, the projects provided a subsidy to governmental agencies, industries, and corporate developers who required no such assistance. Most of the uses for which the cleared land was eventually developed—hospitals, universities, highways, medical schools, government buildings, high-rise apartments, and industrial expansion—could have been achieved gradually and without the awesome destruction of redevelopment.

Part of the tragedy of Norfolk's second phase of redevelopment

Conclusion 213

is that most of the land, once cleared, sat vacant for so very long: It took 20 to 30 years before portions of Atlantic City and Broad Creek Village were developed, and Norfolk's downtown area sat for 40 years without any real prospects for development. Norfolk's second phase of redevelopment provided the acid test of the "land bank" concept, whereby vast tracts of urban land are cleared and "saved" in their vacant state, ready for the day when a prospective developer is ready to make a withdrawal. Indeed, Larry Cox, Director of the N.R.H.A. and later Under-Secretary of Housing and Urban Development, was one of the nation's greatest proponents of the land bank concept:

> Delays and land lying idle are inevitable if urban renewal is going to do what it should do in downtown areas. Projects involving great investments do not spring full-blown upon the scene in the average-size American community. Delay counseled by realistic appraisal of land potential is worthwhile delay. So my thesis is have worthwhile delay introduced into urban renewal, particularly in central city areas.[78]

Unfortunately, Norfolk's experience provides a stunning rebuttal to Mr. Cox's thesis: Except for a strip shopping center on the edge of the downtown area, a few high-rise bank buildings and office towers that would have been built anyway, and several small residential developments that are still underway in the Freemason Harbor area, almost all of the "full-blown" or major developments in downtown Norfolk—the Scope arena and concert complex, the municipal center, Waterside marina and urban marketplace, Town Point Park, baseball stadium, Nauticus maritime center, and the new convention hotel center—have all been public, not private, facilities that could have been built without redevelopment. Similarly, there was no need to "bank" vast tracts of land in the Atlantic City, Broad Creek Village, and Old Dominion project areas; all of the public and private investments there could have been achieved by timely destruction and phased development of the projects. Except for the unstated purpose of achieving *de facto* school segregation, the vast scope and destruction of these areas was both unnecessary and ill-advised. According to one contemporary of Cox:

> Technical skills relating to land use design have today [1960] reached the point where . . . existing improvements need not be demolished before replacement can proceed. . . . Even those structures bad enough to be the subject of a clearance project contribute significantly to the local tax revenues. The demolition of these structures not only takes the value off of the tax roll, but also burdens the tax structure with payment of the city's share of the clearance cost, together with interest on money borrowed in order to accomplish this. . . . Analyzed in terms of planning future land use, the prudent course of action for the city is to plan first and undertake the execution of urban renewal projects only when it is apparent that the land can be advantageously put to use immediately upon completion of the clearance. Therefore, the only situation which would justify creation of a "land bank" would be the one in which the project area was so bad that the city would be better off without it, even if nothing arose in its place.[79]

All four of the projects initiated in Norfolk's second phase of redevelopment have unquestionably contributed handsomely to Norfolk's tax base; upgrading land use from low- or moderate-income residences to predominantly industrial or commercial properties almost always greatly expands the real estate tax base, provides new jobs, and generates revenue from other tax sources. The economic assessment of redevelopment is not whether it has been profitable or even moderately successful in its stated aim of providing vacant land for development, it is rather whether these successes, most of which could have been achieved without the massive scale of destruction, the disruption of human lives, and the adverse impact on the rest of the city's housing stock, were worth the trauma and the social cost. In spite of the fact that downtown Norfolk eventually underwent a tremendous renaissance (largely at public expense), the economic argument for major portions of the other redevelopment projects pales, especially when one considers that the second, unspoken motive of preserving segregated schools was the prime reason for the rush to demolish housing and "bank" the vacant land.

In spite of the pros and cons of the economic argument, however, there has been an undercurrent that redevelopment activities have been guided more by political than developmental considerations.[80] Martin Anderson coined the phrase "black removal" to characterize what he saw as municipal efforts across the country to get rid of unwanted elements of the community; by "black," however, he meant not a racial designation, but rather areas of blight, crime infestation, and unprofitable business uses.[81] N.R.H.A. Project One provides a prime example of black removal at its best: A horribly blighted section of housing, with its massive attendant problems of crime, infestation, juvenile delinquency, disease, and public health menace, was removed and then replaced with modern public housing, designed as garden apartments and arranged to provide a continued sense of community. Demolition of the city's notorious East Main Street "sin district," which brought such ill repute to Norfolk during the war years, also represents another element of black removal, even though the area was still commercially viable.

Cities may be able to make a strong case for using redevelopment to clear areas of extensive blight, but there can be little justification for demolishing the "gray areas"[82]—neighborhoods like Atlantic City and Broad Creek Village—which were contributing and salvageable. If Anderson's thesis of black removal can be applied to these projects, and perhaps to other Southern redevelopment initiatives undertaken at the same time, one explanation is that the unwanted elements in these projects were in neighborhoods where blacks and whites lived too close together to be served by separate schools.

This is precisely what the plaintiffs in a number of school desegregation suits have claimed, that is, that urban renewal powers were used to create segregated neighborhoods, strictly enforce well-defined color barriers, isolate black populations, relocate integrated schools, and otherwise frustrate efforts to desegregate the public school system.[83] Although this claim has been in part supported by demographic researchers[84] and other social scientists,[85] they have chosen to blame school boards, rather than city councils, redevelopment authorities, or planning commissions, for efforts to replace *de jure* with *de facto* segregation. Even though Norfolk provides the perfect case history for all of these charges, far from being the villain, the school board played only a bit part in the effort to divide the city into racially distinct school districts. In fact, it is only through the somewhat heroic actions of its school board that Norfolk still had some semblance of an operational school system left after its political leaders finally gave up their fight to preserve segregated schools.

In Norfolk, at least, the fight to preserve segregated education clearly went much farther than the school board's efforts to close affected schools, select racially "safe" sites, redraw attendance zones, and manipulate the other factors of school plant planning and student attendance, transfer, and grade organization. In several instances (Atlantic City and Broad Creek Village), the school board's action to close a threatened school came after the city had committed to demolishing the entire school zone. In other cases (Easton, Poplar Halls, Fairlawn, Pretty Lake, and East Ocean View), the school board went along with the city council's desire to build tiny, "vest-pocket" schools, even though it opposed the structures; the financial control of the city council over capital expenditures was such that, because the city was desperately short of classroom space, the board had to take whatever new buildings it could get. In several other areas, interstate highways (Coronado, Broad Creek Shores, Brambleton, Ingleside), parks (Titustown and Benmoreell), and other major public facilities (Old Dominion University and the National Guard Armory) appear to have been used, along with natural geographic barriers, to provide both a clear-cut color line between school districts and a logical limitation to the size of their attendance zones. These same barriers would make it even more difficult to provide racially balanced neighborhood schools once the effort to preserve segregation was abandoned.

Although the actions in Norfolk to preserve segregated schools were dramatic, they do not appear to be unique. Norfolk, as well as many other communities in the South, had a strong motive to preserve segregation: Public reaction to the dictates of the U.S. Supreme Court were overwhelmingly negative, and large portions of the populace indicated that they may have been prepared to engage in disruptive, even illegal, activity to block court-ordered integration. Political leaders all across the South were attempting to interpose the authority of state governments between the courts and the local schools in a legal jury rig of hastily enacted legislation controlling pupil assignment, transfer, and attendance policies.

Southern senators and congressmen had banded together in the "Southern Manifesto" to urge their constituencies to use every legal means at their disposal to oppose integration. In addition to this element of motive, which may actually have been tempered in Norfolk by the leadership of the school board, the editorial writers of the *Virginian-Pilot*, and the Norfolk Committee for Public Schools, an urgency of the situation also existed, because so many areas of the city appeared to run afoul of the Supreme Court's doctrine of proximity in maintaining school attendance zones. Because it had extensive areas of integrated navy housing, a few mixed-race neighborhoods in various stages of transition, and several communities where there were pockets of black population too small to be served by their own school, Norfolk faced the prospect that it would be among the first cities in the South to face widespread school integration. In Virginia that meant political death, and the fear of being cut off from state funding was very real; for two decades after it had finally integrated its schools, local residents referred to the Norfolk area as "Tollwater," an ironic allusion to the fact that the state was punishing it for killing Massive Resistance by refusing to provide funding for the bridges, tunnels, and highways so necessary for economic growth.

In addition to the strength of opposition to school desegregation and urgency of situation, as measured by areas of mixed-race housing, the third variable determining the power of the relationship between school desegregation and urban renewal activities is an opportunity to employ the powers of redevelopment and planning unchecked by normal political constraints. All three variables were present in Norfolk to their maximum extent—that is why the story in this one city is so instructive—but Norfolk, as well as other communities across the South, had numerous occasions to bend the powers of school administration, planning, and urban renewal to serve both the cause of preserving segregation and providing economic development. Southern cities faced a period of rapid growth in population, school enrollment, industry, land area, and economic base. This meant that they could use the opportunity already available in this expansion to build new schools or change school zones so that school districts would remain segregated, and therefore acceptable to the public. This at least was the course urged by James J. Kilpatrick, editor of the *Richmond News Leader* and chief publicist for the doctrine of interposition.[86] They could go a step further and use the opportunity to close schools, redesignate their use, or reallocate their grade composition as another way to defer or delay integration in a couple of areas of the city. Or they could go the final step proposed by this work and make sure that the schools in threatened areas of the city remained segregated by using their urban renewal and municipal planning powers to carefully position parks, highways, or other public facilities so they posed a barrier to blacks living near a white school; municipalities could control land-use policies so that black housing could move no closer to white schools; and cities could use their powers of redevelopment to tear down mixed-race areas that proved threatening under the court's doctrine of proximity. Norfolk was not alone in taking these extra steps; there is strong evidence to suggest that Richmond, Mobile, Memphis, Charleston, Boston, Wilmington (Delaware) and others used at least some of these techniques. Only in Norfolk is the record complete enough to project a concerted use of urban renewal to preserve segregated schools.

This interpretation is not meant, however, to discredit the economic argument made for annexation, urban renewal, industrial development, and city planning. For most of these cities, growth in both land area and tax base was absolutely essential for survival, and every element of municipal government was concerned with the effort to plan for and sustain that growth. The suggestion that the effort to preserve school segregation was also involved in these planning, development, and redevelopment decisions is not meant to denigrate the purely economic considerations of such activities; it is only meant to infer that the powers of urban renewal in many cities in the 1950s was meant to serve two masters, the publicly avowed one of growth, and the privately held determination to stay the same, at least as far as segregated schools were concerned. The irony in Norfolk is that the powers of redevelopment pioneered with such pride during the People's era to create equal facilities for blacks, were now transformed and manipulated as political weapons during the school desegregation crisis.

Finally, some larger historical context is necessary to fully understand the events and actions herein described. Other contemporaneous researchers[87] found that appointed school boards were far more adept at handling the controversies surrounding school desegregation than their elected counterparts. This is definitely the case in Norfolk: All six appointed members of the school board responded to the crisis in admirable, even heroic, fashion, and their calm and deliberate approach, coupled with their overriding devotion to the concept of public education, was largely responsible for the peaceful resumption of classes, the sense of continuity and control, and the fact that quality schools continued in Norfolk once the legal issues were settled. Their courage and devotion to duty brought them into constant conflict with the elected leaders of their day. None of its members had sought appointment to the board,[88] and, for the most part, they were not the sort of individuals who seek election to office. All had been chosen because of their record of involvement in volunteer, not political, community service, and it was this experience that served them well when the clamor of the constituency of the day demanded short-term approaches. There was unanimity on the board, the kind of calm consensus that rarely is seen in elected bodies in times of such violent social upheaval and conflicting values. The Norfolk School Board had the long-term interest of public education in mind throughout the controversy; their judgement was not clouded by political expediency or the need to seek reelection. Their calm reaction to crisis and their devotion to the future of public education should give pause to all those who think that urban school systems, especially those beset with major problems and diverse clientele, would be better served by elected, rather than appointed, boards.

Although school boards all across the South were vilified for their efforts to delay or defer court-ordered desegregation efforts, in Norfolk, at least, the school board was but one actor in a larger cast that included the mayor, the city council, the N.R.H.A., and other municipal officials responsible for planning and development. While this larger relationship has been the source of some speculation, it is the major contribution of this work that the interplay between school desegregation and urban renewal in one community has been more completely analyzed. The response to court-ordered desegregation did not begin with the first local court case, the traditional starting date of other histories of the process; instead, it began with a realization in the South that predates even the *Brown* decision that, in order to pass court review, "separate" school facilities for the two races must be made more nearly equal. Later, when it became clear that the courts would not accept separate facilities as equal when the pupils lived in close geographic proximity to one another, a much larger cast of characters than just Southern school boards followed the dictates of their state and national political leaders, as well as their voting constituencies, to do everything in their power to prevent school integration. The powers of urban renewal, school-plant planning, redevelopment, and school administration appear to have been used liberally to create separate-race neighborhoods and school attendance zones, thereby replacing segregation by law (*de jure*) with the type of *de facto* separation of races already approved by the courts in Northern and Midwestern cities. Although a temptation exists to fix blame or criticism for actions that turn out now, by modern standards, to be misdirected, judging the motives of the 1950s by the mores of the present is just as unfair as requiring the citizens of that era to share the advantage of our own more modern perspective to receive fair treatment. Enough time has passed to gain both the advantage of historical hindsight and a passionless examination of the events and issues; few cities could withstand the judgement of a serious local history if viewed from the high ground of both hindsight and moral certainty. Norfolk is no better or worse than other cities; if it is proud of its accomplishments, and it has every right to boast, then it should not be afraid to face its failures. Judgement is not intended by this critical examination of the era; indeed, one has to marvel at both the competence and the devotion to cause depicted here. Mayor Duckworth and the other members of the city council, the school board, the N.R.H.A., and other public officials were responding to a public mandate to do everything legally possible to preserve what was considered by the city's (white) voters to be a sacrosanct way of life. Not only did they respond with vigor and ingenuity, they received close counsel and guidance from others in the state and national government who shared their sentiment. That all of these officials enjoyed the overwhelming support of their constituencies is evident in the voting patterns of the era. In a democratic society we must be prepared to accept the fact that powerful and passionate elected leaders will do everything possible to respond to such a mandate without condemning their actions or criticizing their motives.

Partly because Norfolk encountered its desegregation crisis early and faced it so precipitously, the city has been able to achieve and maintain a level of racial and political harmony that exists in few other areas of the country. Norfolk emerged from its school crisis with an intensity of support for public education that has never diminished. Even when faced with the prospect of court-ordered crosstown busing that was more extensive than almost anywhere else in the country, community support remained strong. Partly because of this support and because it continued to offer quality interracial education, Norfolk did not experience the level of white flight found in a number of other central cities. Also, the new leadership of the city that emerged from the crisis determined that they, and not the federal courts, should ultimately determine the pattern and extent of school segregation. Thus, each time the school board was faced with a new round of court-ordered integration, it followed the lead of the 1958-1959 School Board, drew the lines itself, and endured the outcry. By doing so, Norfolk's School Boards have helped it escape the fate of Boston and numerous other cities where the federal courts had to take a more direct role of intervention. In Norfolk, school desegregation has been "voluntary," albeit under pressure from the courts. Partly because of this higher level of cooperation with the courts, only a decade later Judge Hoffman declared that Norfolk operated a truly "unitary" school system, a step that paved the way for it to be among the first major school systems in the country to leave the phase of court-ordered busing behind and return to neighborhood schools at the elementary level. Today the Norfolk Public Schools continue to win accolades as one of the nation's few effective urban school systems: test scores are up, dropout rates are down, white enrollment seems stable, and community support remains strong.

The Norfolk story is not a deviant case; instead, the history of its desegregation crisis exemplifies the level of the struggle that took place in cities all across the South in the 1950s and then moved to the North, Midwest, and border states in the 1960s when they, too, were faced with the prospect of massive court-ordered school integration initiatives. Although perhaps more compelling than events in other cities, partly because of the collapsed time frame and the fact that Norfolk was among the first cities in the South to desegregate, the actions of its public officials to preserve racially identifiable schools were not unique. Only the scale of the battle was larger than elsewhere, but that is why the story of this struggle is so instructive.

※ ※ ※

ABBREVIATIONS

F.H.A.	Federal Housing Administration (U.S. Government)
H.H.F.A.	Housing & Home Finance Agency (U.S. Government)
H.O.L.C.	Home Owners Loan Corporation (U.S. Government)
N.A.A.C.P.	National Association for the Advancement of Colored People
N.A.T.O.	North Atlantic Treaty Organization
N.C.P.S.	Norfolk Committee for Public Schools
N.E.A.	Norfolk Education Association
N.R.H.A.	Norfolk Redevelopment and Housing Authority
O.D.U.	Old Dominion University (Norfolk)
P.T.A.	Parent Teacher Association
T.E.F.	Tidewater Education Association
U.S.O.	United Serviceman's Organization
W.C.I.C.	Women's Council for Interracial Cooperation
V.A.	Veteran's Administration (U.S. Government)

※

Glossary

Atlantic City—an older middle-class neighborhood and industrial area on the edge of downtown Norfolk that contained about 50 black families at the time it was slated for a major redevelopment project.

Brambleton—an older middle-class and industrial area south of downtown Norfolk that was shifting from white to black by the mid-1950s.

Broad Creek Shores—a subdivision for blacks that was under development at the time of the U.S. Supreme Court's *Brown v. Board* decision. Completion of the subdivision was blocked when it was found to be too close to white schools under the doctrine of proximity.

Broad Creek Village—a large U. S. Navy housing project developed at the close of World War II, integrated as the military desegregated following the war, and torn down to make room for industrial expansion.

Byrd Organization—the dominant statewide political machine in Virginia run by U.S. Senator Harry F. Byrd, Sr. (D-VA); also referred to simply as the "Organization."

Committee of One Hundred—the name chosen by an informal group of business, financial, and community leaders in Norfolk who petitioned Mayor Duckworth and the city council to end the City's opposition to court-ordered integration in the city.

Coronado—a small middle-class community in the Norview section of Norfolk that was the scene of racial turmoil in 1954 when blacks first began moving into the area.

Glossary

de facto segregation—the type of legal housing and school segregation found most commonly in northern and midwestern cites where blacks and whites choose to live in separate-race neighborhoods.

Defenders of State Sovereignty and Individual Liberties—a statewide political pressure group formed to prevent the integration of public schools in Virginia; also referred to as the "Defenders."

de jure segregation—the type of "Jim Crow" segregation found in the South before 1954 where blacks and whites were forced by state laws to live in separate-race areas and attend separate-race schools.

doctrine of proximity—the essence of the precedent set by the U.S. Supreme Court in its 1954 *Brown* v. *Board of Education* decision. The Court held that Linda Brown and other black students who lived closer to a white school than the black school could not be denied the right to attend the school nearest their home.

Gray Plan—a "moderate" approach in the Virginia legislature to comply with court-ordered school desegregation by limiting the impact of integration. The Gray Plan was defeated, and Virginia turned instead to Massive Resistance (the Stanley Plan).

Harmony Ticket—the name given to Mayor Duckworth's city council slate in 1950 because it represented a forced union between the People's (or Silkstocking) business reformers and the Prieur Machine politicians.

Interposition—the centuries-old doctrine that individual states have an obligation to interject their own authority between their citizens and an unjust action of the federal courts. James J. Kilpatrick and the leaders of the Byrd Organization used the logic of interposition to justify Massive Resistance in Virginia.

Lambert's Point—an integrated housing area near Old Dominion University that was the site of Norfolk Redevelopment and Housing Authority Project Two, also referred to as the Old Dominion Project.

Land (or Kaufman) Committee—a group of high-level business, community and planning leaders chosen in 1954 to limit housing integration problems and select new sites for redevelopment activity.

Massive Resistance—the name given to the Byrd Organization's attempt to prevent school integration by closing school buildings that were under court orders to admit black pupils. Under Massive Resistance, the closed buildings could be sold to private groups, who would then operate them as whites-only private schools using tuition grants for the students and other state support.

Norfolk Committee for Public Schools—a group of progressive white parents who at first formed a lobby to support public schools, and then filed lawsuits crucial to the effort to reopen the closed schools.

People's Ticket or People's administration—a businessmen's reform movement that took control of Norfolk's municipal government in 1946 and then led the revitalization of the whole area. Also called the Silkstocking Ticket by its detractors.

Prieur Machine—the local affiliate of the statewide Byrd Organization that controlled politics and planning in Norfolk prior to 1946 and then experienced a rejuvenation during the 1950s.

Silkstocking Takeover—the process begun under the People's administration of replacing partisan considerations in city government with business, planning, and professional expertise.

Southside (Virginia)—the rural counties and small cities south of Richmond that formed the base of support for both the Byrd Organization and the Defenders of State Sovereignty and Individual Liberties.

Stanley Plan—the legal structure behind Virginia's effort to resist public school desegregation through Massive Resistance.

Summers' Plan—a local effort proposed by City Councilman Ezra Summers to preserve segregated schools by giving students a "choice" between attending segregated or integrated schools.

Tidewater Education Foundation—a private corporation established by the Defenders of State Sovereignty and Individual Liberties to operate "white flight" private academies in Norfolk as a replacement for integrated public schools.

White Citizen's Councils—the name adopted by several racist groups in the Deep South that opposed integration through violence, intimidation, protest, and political action.

Young Turks—the name given to a group of younger, mostly urban Virginia legislators, who, although part of the Byrd political Machine, frequently opposed the Organization and instead supported racial moderation, public education, governmental reform, and urban development issues.

❋

NOTES

Introduction

1 Wertenbaker 1962
2 Hunter 1953

Prologue – Norfolk Before 1950

1 *Norfolk Virginian-Pilot* 8/15/45)
2 Ibid., 8/16/45
3 Schlegel 1951, 361
4 Curtin 1969, 130-49
5 Darden

Chapter 1 – Planning the New Norfolk

1 *Norfolk Virginian-Pilot* 7/23/61
2 Ibid., 12/12/51
3 Ibid., 6/11/46
4 Ibid., 6/5/46
5 *Norfolk Ledger-Dispatch* 2/21/46
6 Darden; Gornto
7 *Norfolk Virginian-Pilot* 6/12/46
8 Ibid., 6/12/46
9 Darden
10 Ibid.
11 Ibid.
12 *Norfolk Virginian-Pilot* 12/3/48
13 Ibid., 12/4/48
14 Ibid., 3/13/49
15 Stinchcombe 1968, 129-50
16 Darden
17 *Norfolk Virginian-Pilot* 7/23/61
18 Curtin 1969, 140
19 Norfolk Redevelopment and Housing Authority, 1946: 30, 47-8
20 *Norfolk Virginian-Pilot*
21 Ibid., 11/29/48
22 Schlegel 1951
23 *Norfolk Journal and Guide* 6/8/46
24 *Norfolk Virginian-Pilot* 6/1/46
25 *Norfolk Journal and Guide* 6/1/46
26 *Norfolk Virginian-Pilot* 11/28/48
27 Ibid., 12/4/38
28 Ibid., 11/28/48
29 Darden
30 Curtin 1969
31 N.R.H.A. 1946, 8
32 *Architectural Forum* 1950, 137
33 *Norfolk Virginian-Pilot* 7/26/61
34 *Architectural Forum* 1950, 135
35 Beall, Price and Locke 1950, 7
36 Norfolk City Planning Commission 1950, 5-15
37 *Architectural Forum* 1950, 136-37
38 *Norfolk Virginian-Pilot* 7/26/61
39 *Architectural Forum* 1950, 137
40 *Norfolk Virginian-Pilot* 7/26/61
41 N.R.H.A. 1957, 5-6
42 *Norfolk Virginian-Pilot* 8/15/50
43 Ibid., 8/22/51
44 Ibid., 3/22/56
45 Ibid., 7/26/61
46 Hebert 1950, 10
47 *Architectural Forum* 1950, 132
48 N.R.H.A. 1974, 46; *Architectural Forum* 1950, 132; Hanna 1967, 92
49 *Architectural Forum* 1950, 132
50 Ibid., 1950, 134
51 Agle 1956, 79
52 Harrell 1949, 9
53 *Architectural Forum* 1950, 135
54 *Norfolk Virginian-Pilot* 4/16/52
55 Housing and Home Finance Agency 1950

Notes

56 Taueber and Taueber 1965, 35-96
57 N.R.H.A. 1957
58 *Architectural Forum* 1950, 134
59 Ervin 1956, 32-3
60 *Architectural Forum* 1950, 134
61 Ibid., 1950, 136
62 Ibid., 1950, 136-7
63 *Norfolk Virginian-Pilot* 10/11/56
64 Harrell 1950b, 9-14
65 *Architectural Forum* 1950, 137
66 Stinchcombe 1968, 129-50
67 Darden
68 Stinchcombe 1968, 129-50
69 *Architectural Forum* 1950, 136
70 Mason

Chapter 2 – Premonitions of Crisis

1 Darden
2 Sugg 1967, 368
3 Darden
4 *Norfolk Virginian-Pilot* 7/23/61
5 Darden; Mason
6 *Norfolk Virginian-Pilot* 6/10/42; 6/14/50
7 Darden
8 *Norfolk Virginian-Pilot* 7/25/61
9 Ibid., 7/4/75
10 Ibid., 6/4/50
11 Staylor
12 *Norfolk Virginian-Pilot* 7/25/61
13 Sugg 1967, 368
14 Reif 1960, 1
15 *Norfolk Journal and Guide* 6/1/46
16 Ibid., 6/1/46
17 Rorer 1968, 207
18 *Norfolk Journal and Guide* 4/19/58
19 Taueber and Taueber 1965, 35-96
20 U.S. Census 1952:11
21 *Norfolk Virginian-Pilot* 5/29/46
22 Reif 1960, 1
23 *Norfolk Virginian-Pilot* 3/15/54
24 Ibid., 8/22/54
25 *Norfolk Journal and Guide* 8/6/55
26 *Norfolk Virginian-Pilot* 8/22/54
27 Ibid., 8/31/54
28 Ibid., 8/22/54
29 *Norfolk Ledger-Dispatch* 8/30/54
30 *Norfolk Virginian-Pilot* 8/19/54, 8/25/54, 9/11/54, 9/20/54, and 8/22/54
31 *Norfolk Ledger-Dispatch* 8/30/54
32 *Norfolk Virginian-Pilot* 8/19/54
33 Ibid., 9/12/54
34 Ibid., 9/11/54
35 *Norfolk Journal and Guide* 1/7/56
36 *Norfolk Virginian-Pilot* 8/31/54
37 *Norfolk Journal and Guide* 8/6/55
38 *Norfolk Virginian-Pilot* 7/6/55
39 Ibid., 9/19/55; Roy B. Martin
40 Ibid., 4/29/56
41 *Norfolk Journal and Guide* 8/6/55
42 Ibid., 8/6/ 55
43 *Norfolk Virginian-Pilot* 4/29/56
44 *Norfolk Journal and Guide* 8/6/55
45 *Norfolk Virginian-Pilot* 4/29/56
46 *Norfolk Journal and Guide* 8/6/55
47 *Norfolk Virginian-Pilot* 4/29/56
48 Ibid., 4/29/56
49 *Norfolk Journal and Guide* 3/31/ 56
50 *Norfolk Virginian-Pilot* 4/29/56
51 Suggs 1988, 186

Chapter 3 – First Reactions to *Brown*

1 *Norfolk Virginian-Pilot* 5/18/54
2 Ibid., 5/18/54
3 Dabney 1971, 528-31
4 Women's Council for Interracial Cooperation 1955
5 Dabney 1971, 522-24

6 *Norfolk Ledger-Dispatch* 1/28/55
7 *Norfolk Journal and Guide* 4/19/58
8 Sullivan 1956
9 *Norfolk Ledger-Dispatch* 1/28/55
10 Brewbaker 11/11/54
11 Brewbaker 11/11/54
12 *Norfolk Ledger-Dispatch* 10/13/54
13 Brewbaker 8/8/55
14 School Board 7/1/55
15 School Board 9/14/56
16 Pentecost and Courtney 1957
17 School Board 3/25/58
18 *Norfolk Virginian-Pilot* 9/17/55
19 Ibid., 2/10/56
20 Rorer 1968, 346
21 Brewbaker 2/13/57
22 *Norfolk Virginian-Pilot* 10/24/56
23 Ibid., 1/26/57
24 Ibid., 10/24/56
25 *Norfolk Ledger-Dispatch* 8/21/53
26 *Norfolk Ledger-Dispatch* 12/13/51
27 Ervin 1956, 32-3
28 *Norfolk Ledger-Dispatch* 10/13/54
29 *Norfolk Virginian-Pilot* 1/16/55
30 *Norfolk Ledger-Dispatch* 10/13/54
31 *Norfolk Virginian-Pilot* 6/3/55
32 Ibid., 6/18/55
32 Ibid., 6/18/55
33 *Norfolk Ledger-Dispatch* 7/11/55
34 *Norfolk Virginian-Pilot* 6/3/55
35 *Norfolk Ledger-Dispatch* 7/11/55
36 Dabney 1971, 532-39
37 *Norfolk Virginian-Pilot* 3/6/ 56
38 Ibid., 7/27/55
39 Reif 1960, 2
40 *Norfolk Virginian-Pilot* 9/19/55
41 Ibid., 9/15/55
42 Ibid., 1/5/56
43 Reif 1960, 2
44 *Norfolk Virginian-Pilot* 7/14/55
45 Ibid., 5/11/56
46 Ibid., 7/14/55
47 Ibid., 8/29/56
48 Ibid., 4/25/56
49 Ibid., 5/13/56
50 Reif 1960, 1
51 *Norfolk Virginian-Pilot* 5/13/56
52 Ibid., 5/13/56
53 Crain 1968, 339
54 *Norfolk Virginian-Pilot* 6/22/56
55 *Norfolk Ledger-Dispatch* 7/3/56
56 *Norfolk Virginian-Pilot* 10/24/56
57 Ibid., 1/26/57
58 Ibid., 3/8/57
59 Ibid., 10/24/56
60 Ibid., 5/11/56
61 *Norfolk Ledger-Dispatch* 12/19/56
62 Ibid., 2/15/57
63 Ibid., 12/17/56
64 *Norfolk Virginian-Pilot* 7/24/56
65 *Norfolk Ledger-Dispatch* 6/8/57
66 Ibid., 3/10/58
67 Dabney 1971, 531-3
68 *Norfolk Virginian-Pilot* 10/25/56
69 Ibid., 10/13/56

Chapter 4 –
The Bulldozer Era

1 *Norfolk Virginian-Pilot* 4/14/58
2 Ibid., 6/11/58
3 Darden; Mason; Sugg
4 Darden
5 *Norfolk Virginian-Pilot* 9/3/56
6 Darden
7 *Norfolk Virginian-Pilot* 9/3/56
8 Mason; Sugg; Gregory
9 *Norfolk Virginian-Pilot* 3/6/56
10 Ibid., 7/23/61
11 Ibid., 3/6/56
12 Agle 1956, 19-20
13 *Norfolk Virginian-Pilot* 5/28/56
14 Housing and Home Finance Agency 1949
15 Agle 1956, 19-20
16 *Norfolk Virginian-Pilot* 12/23/51

17 Ibid., 12/23/51
18 Ibid., 7/9/52
19 Ibid., 8/14/56
20 Ibid., 5/28/56
21 Ibid., 5/28/56
22 *Norfolk Ledger-Dispatch* 8/22/56
23 *Norfolk Virginian-Pilot* 2/9/56
24 *Norfolk Ledger-Dispatch* 6/26/57
25 *Norfolk Virginian-Pilot* 2/9/56
26 Mason; Sugg; Gregory
27 Staylor; Sugg; Mason; Gregory
28 Staylor; Estes
29 Mason; Sugg; Staylor
30 Dillon 1970, 17-19
31 Sugg
32 *Norfolk Virginian-Pilot* 3/22/56
33 Darden
34 N.R.H.A. 1974, 39
35 *Norfolk Virginian-Pilot* 12/8/56
36 Ibid., 6/11/54
37 N.R.H.A. 1974, 39
38 *Norfolk Virginian-Pilot* 7/26/61
39 Darden
40 Architectural Forum 1950, 132
41 *Norfolk Virginian-Pilot* 7/6/55
42 Ibid., 4/24/55
43 Ibid., 6/19/58
44 Ibid., 5/21/55
45 Ibid., 6/19/58
46 Ibid., 7/15/79
47 Ibid., 10/4/49
48 Ibid., 10/11/56
49 U.S. Census 1952 III, 38: 22
50 U.S. Census 1952, III, 38: 21-2
51 Schlegel 1951, 20-60
52 Monola
53 Ibid.
54 Ibid.
55 *Norfolk Virginian-Pilot* 6/23/57
56 Ibid., 7/1/57
57 Ibid., 1/5/57
58 Norfolk City Planning Commission 1950; Agle 1956
59 Monola
60 N.R.H.A. 1957, 12
61 Schmidt 1959, 6

Chapter 5 – Redevelopment Rationales

1 Darden; Martin; Crenshaw
2 Darden
3 Norfolk City Planning Commission 1950
4 *Norfolk Virginian-Pilot* 3/22/56
5 Ibid., 12/8/56
6 *Norfolk Ledger-Dispatch* 2/17/57
7 N.R.H.A. 1974, 39
8 *Norfolk Virginian-Pilot* 1/5/57
9 Dillon 1970
10 *Norfolk Virginian-Pilot* 4/24/55
11 Ibid., 7/1/57
12 Caro 1975, 880-4
13 *Norfolk Virginian-Pilot* 8/9/57
14 Conrad; Smith
15 Dillon 1970, 18
16 N.R.H.A. 1974, 47
17 *Norfolk Virginian-Pilot* 9/11/56
18 Ibid., 6/11/54
19 Ibid., 5/20/53
20 *Norfolk Ledger-Dispatch* 7/23/57
21 *Norfolk Virginian-Pilot* 7/23/57
22 Mason
23 H.H.F.A. 1950, 7
24 *Norfolk Ledger-Dispatch* 12/21/57
25 Brewbaker 5/7/56
26 *Norfolk Virginian-Pilot* 2/10/56
27 Ibid., 8/19/60
28 Ibid., 9/19/55
29 Ibid., 8/9/57
30 Brewbaker 8/8/55
31 U.S. Census 1952 III, 38; Norfolk Chamber of Commerce 1954, 10-20
32 *Norfolk Virginian-Pilot* 3/10/57
33 Norfolk Chamber of Commerce 1954
34 *Norfolk Virginian-Pilot* 1/3/58
35 U.S. Census 1952 III, 38, tracts 9 and 11
36 *Norfolk Virginian-Pilot* 10/24/56
37 Ibid., 1/3/58
38 Leflar 1957; Stephan 1980, 11-7

39 *Norfolk Ledger-Dispatch* 12/13/51
40 *Beckett v. Norfolk* 1957, 3 38
41 *Norfolk Virginian-Pilot* 3/10/57
42 Ibid., 5/21/58
43 *Beckett v. Norfolk* 1957, 339
44 *Norfolk Virginian-Pilot* 8/9/57
45 Ibid., 5/21/58
46 Ibid., 3/10/57
47 Ibid., 3/10/57
48 Ibid., 5/21/58
49 Ibid., 2/10/56
50 Ibid., 1/3/58
51 Ibid., 12/21/57
52 Ibid., 3/28/58
53 Ibid., 1/14/59
54 Ibid., 5/21/58
55 Ibid., 2/13/57
56 Ibid., 3/16/57
57 Ibid., 3/26/57
58 Ibid., 2/13/57
59 Ibid., 3/26/57
60 Ibid., 10/22/57
61 Ibid., 10/22/57
62 Ibid., 8/19/58
63 Carter
64 Mason

Chapter 6 –
Prelude to Confrontation

1 White 1959
2 Hagan
3 Dabney 1971, 538-40
4 *Norfolk Ledger-Dispatch* 3/10/58
5 Ibid., 3/10/58
6 Hoffman; Mason
7 *Norfolk Virginian-Pilot* 6/11/58
8 Ibid., 6/12/58
9 Ibid., 6/12/58
10 Ibid., 6/12/58
11 Ibid., 6/19/58
12 Ibid., 6/13/58
13 Ibid., 8/19/58
14 Ibid., 6/13/58
15 Ibid., 8/30/58
16 Ibid., 7/25/58
17 Muse 1961
18 *Norfolk Virginian-Pilot* 6/13/58
19 Mason
20 *Norfolk Virginian-Pilot* 6/20/58
21 Ibid., 8/19/58
22 Ibid., 5/14/56
23 Ibid., 6/13/58
24 Ibid., 1/25/59
25 Ibid., 3/8/57
26 Ibid., 1/25/59
27 Ibid., 8/19/58
28 Ibid., 8/30/58
29 Crenshaw
30 *Norfolk Virginian-Pilot* 8/30/58
31 Crenshaw
32 *Norfolk Virginian-Pilot* 9/3/58
33 Ibid., 9/5/58
34 *Norfolk Ledger-Dispatch* 2/16/60; *Norfolk Ledger-Dispatch* 5/29/61; *Norfolk Ledger-Star* 12/22/72; *Richmond Times-Dispatch* 2/3/63
35 *Norfolk Ledger-Dispatch* 5/19/60
36 *Norfolk Journal and Guide* 8/30/58
37 Stern
38 White 1959b, 3
39 Reif 1959, 9
40 *Norfolk Virginian-Pilot* 9/19/58
41 Stern; White 1959b, 4
42 *Norfolk Virginian-Pilot* 9/19/58
43 Ibid., 10/25/59
44 Stern; White 1959b, 4-5
45 *Norfolk Virginian-Pilot* 9/26/58
46 Mason
47 *Norfolk Virginian-Pilot* 5/18/54

Chapter 7 –
In Pursuit of a Mandate

1 For details about Massive Resistance elsewhere in Virginia see Muse 1961; Smith 1965; Eley 1976
2 U.S. Census 1952 II 46 B, 46-7
3 *Norfolk Virginian-Pilot* 12/5/58

4   *Norfolk Ledger-Dispatch* 1/22/59
5   *Norfolk Virginian-Pilot* 10/19/58
6   Ibid., 9/12/58
7   Ibid., 9/25/58
8   Duckworth 10/6/58
9   Christian Science *Monitor* 10/8/ 58
10 Reif 1960, 1, 9
11 *Norfolk Virginian-Pilot* 8/7/58
12 *Norfolk Ledger-Dispatch* 10/1/58
13 Ibid., 10/3/58
14 Ibid., 10/13/58
15 *Norfolk Virginian-Pilot* 10/2/58
16 Ibid., 11/6/58
17 Ibid., 10/26/58
18 Ibid., 1/25/59
19 Ibid., 10/12/58
20 Reif 1960, 6
21 *Norfolk Virginian-Pilot* 1/25/59
22 Ibid., 10/26/58
23 Mason
24 *Norfolk Virginian-Pilot* 10/16/58
25 *Norfolk Ledger-Dispatch* 10/22/58
26 *Norfolk Virginian-Pilot* 10/23/58
27 Ibid., 1/16/59
28 Ibid., 10/24/58
29 Campbell and Boswell 1959
30 Reif 1960, 6
31 *Norfolk Ledger-Dispatch* 10/1/58
32 Ibid., 10/1/ 58
33 Reif 1960, 25
34 *Norfolk Virginian-Pilot* 10/23/58
35 Ibid., 10/19/58
36 Ibid., 10/19/58
37 Ibid., 10/19/58
38 Reif 1960, 17
39 *Norfolk Virginian-Pilot* 11/6/58
40 Ibid., 11/15/58
41 *Norfolk Ledger-Dispatch* 10/22/58
42 *Norfolk Virginian-Pilot* 10/22/58
43 Reif 1960, 19
44 *Norfolk Ledger-Dispatch* 3/30/60
45 Ibid., 3/30/60
46 *Norfolk Virginian-Pilot* 1/25/59
47 *Norfolk Ledger-Dispatch* 2/16/60
48 Crenshaw; *Norfolk Ledger-Dispatch* 5/29/61
49 *Norfolk Ledger-Star* 12/22/72
50 Ibid., 9/1/64
51 *Richmond Times-Dispatch* 2/3/63
52 *Norfolk Virginian-Pilot* 11/15/58
53 *Norfolk Ledger-Dispatch* 11/19/58
54 *Norfolk Virginian-Pilot* 11/19/58

Chapter 8 –
A Very Massive Resister

1   *Norfolk Virginian-Pilot* 11/20/58
2   Ibid., 1/11/59
3   Ibid., 9/5/60
4   Ibid., 1/11/59
5   Darden; Mason
6   *Norfolk Virginian-Pilot* 11/26/58
7   Ibid., 1/25/59
8   Ibid., 11/8/58
9   Smith 1965
10 *Norfolk Virginian-Pilot* 11/26/58
11 Ibid., 1/14/59
12 Ibid., 11/13/58
13 Ibid., 10/26/58
14 Ibid., 1/25/59
15 Ibid., 10/19/58
16 Reif 1960, 11-22
17 *Norfolk Virginian-Pilot* 1/1/59; 1/4/59
18 Ibid., 10/13/58; 1/17/59
19 Ibid., 1/1/59; 1/17/59
20 *Norfolk Virginian-Pilot* 12/7/59; Dabney 1971, 537
21 *Norfolk Virginian-Pilot* 9/3/90
22 Ibid., 12/11/58
23 Ibid., 1/14/59
24 Ibid., 1/14/59
25 Martin
26 *Norfolk Virginian-Pilot* 1/16/59
27 Ibid., 1/16/59
28 Ibid., 1/18/59
29 Ibid., 1/20/59

30 Ibid., 1/25/59
31 Ibid., 1/25/59
32 Ibid., 1/28/59
33 Ibid., 1/20/59
34 Ibid., 1/24/59
35 Hoffman
36 Dabney 1971, 542
37 *Norfolk Virginian-Pilot* 1/21/59
38 *Norfolk Ledger-Dispatch* 1/22/59
39 Reif 1960, 22
40 Darden
41 Reif 1960, 21-2
42 *Norfolk Virginian-Pilot* 1/30/59
43 Ibid., 1/27/59
44 Reif 1960, 21-2
45 *Norfolk Virginian-Pilot* 1/27/59
46 Ibid., 1/27/59
47 Darden
48 *Norfolk Virginian-Pilot* 1/28/59
49 Ibid., 1/27/59
50 Hoffman
51 *Norfolk Virginian-Pilot* 1/28/59
52 Ibid., 1/28/59
53 *Richmond Times-Dispatch* 2/10/80
54 *Norfolk Virginian-Pilot* 6/9/64
55 Ibid., 1/27/59
56 *Richmond Times-Dispatch* 8/4/74
57 *Norfolk Virginian-Pilot* 1/30/59
58 Dabney 1970, 539
59 Dabney 1970, 542-3
60 *Norfolk Virginian-Pilot* 1/29/59
61 Dabney 1970, 543
62 *Norfolk Virginian-Pilot* 1/30/59
63 Dabney 1970, 543
64 *New York Times* 2/1/59
65 Reif 1960, 15
66 Darden; Mason
67 *New York Times* 2/1/59

4 Ibid., 2/1/59
5 Stern; White 1959b
6 Crain et al. 1968, 231
7 Darden
8 *Norfolk Virginian-Pilot* 6/9/64
9 Darden
10 Campbell et al. 1960, 56-61
11 *New York Times* 2/8/59
12 *Norfolk Virginian-Pilot* 2/22/59
13 Campbell 1959
14 *Norfolk Virginian-Pilot* 3/13/59
15 Brewbaker 5/21/59; 5/29/59
16 *Norfolk Virginian-Pilot* 7/8/59
17 Ibid., 7/21/59
18 *Norfolk Ledger-Dispatch* 8/20/59
19 *Norfolk Virginian-Pilot* 5/13/59
20 Ibid., 10/25/59
21 Ibid., 6/6/58
22 Ibid., 8/8/59
23 Ibid., 1/3/58
24 Martin
25 *Norfolk Virginian-Pilot* 11/11/59
26 Ibid., 5/2/59
27 Ibid., 4/23/59
28 Ibid., 4/22/59
29 Ibid., 4/22/59
30 Ibid., 4/24-7/59
31 Ibid., 4/15/59
32 Ibid., 7/15/59
33 Ibid., 7/19/59
34 Ibid., 10/30/59
35 *Norfolk Ledger-Dispatch* 11/23/59
36 *Norfolk Virginian-Pilot* 10/25/59; 12/8/59
37 *Norfolk Ledger-Dispatch* 2/16/60
38 Ibid., 6/15/60
39 Ibid., 6/10/60
40 Ibid., 6/15/60

Chapter 9 – A Second School Crisis

1 Hoffman
2 *Norfolk Virginian-Pilot* 2/3/59
3 *New York Times* 2/1/59

Chapter 10 – Conclusion

1 Darden; Crenshaw
2 *Southern School News* 9/3/54
3 Williams and Ryan 1954, 45, 57, 102, 240-2, 443

4 Williams and Ryan 1954, 40, 80-110
5 Metcalf 1983, 3
6 Stephan and Feagin 1980, 3-9
7 Williams and Ryan 1954
8 *Heywood* v. *P.H.A.* 1956, 347
9 *Norfolk Virginian-Pilot* 8/31/54
10 Anderson 1964; Bellush and Hausknecht 1967
11 *Beckett* v. *Norfolk* 1957
12 Ervin 1956, 32-33
13 Rorer 1968, 69
14 Workman 1957, 92
15 Williams and Ryan 1954
16 Abbott 1981, 93
17 Taueber and Taueber 1965, 23, 48
18 *Norfolk Virginian-Pilot* 5/18/54
19 *Southern School News* 10/1/54
20 Ibid., 1/6/55
21 Williams and Ryan 1954, 237
22 *Norfolk Virginian-Pilot* 6/15/58
23 *Southern School News* 2/57
24 McCauley 1957, 132
25 *Beckett* v. *Norfolk* 1957
26 *Norfolk Virginian-Pilot* 3/10/57
27 *Southern School News* 10/55
28 Ibid., 3/57
29 *Norfolk Virginian-Pilot* 7/8/59
30 Ibid., 7/21/59
31 *Norfolk Ledger-Dispatch* 8/20/59
32 *Beckett* v. *Norfolk* 1958
33 *Norfolk Virginian-Pilot* 2/22/59
34 Crenshaw
35 Martin
36 Campbell 1959
37 Crenshaw
38 *Southern School News* 8/55
39 *Norfolk Virginian-Pilot* 11/26/58
40 Ibid., 2/21/59
41 Ibid., 10/25/59
42 Ibid., 4/23/59
43 Martin
44 *Norfolk Journal and Guide* 8/6/55
45 Willie and Greenblatt 1981, 189
46 Weaver 1967, 94
47 *Norfolk Virginian-Pilot* 3/10/57
48 Ibid., 12/8/56
49 U.S. Census 1952 III, 38, 22
50 *Norfolk Virginian-Pilot* 7/1/57
51 Ibid., 3/10/57
52 Monola
53 Monola
54 *Norfolk Virginian-Pilot* 1/31/59
55 Monola
56 *Norfolk Virginian-Pilot* 7/15/79
57 Martin
58 Monola
59 *Norfolk Virginian-Pilot* 3/10/57
60 Monola
61 *Beckett* v. *Norfolk* 1957, 339
62 Taueber and Taueber 1965, 33-41, 49, 191, 124, 240
63 Jackson 1987, 190-218, 227, 242
64 *Norfolk Virginian-Pilot* 6/23/57
65 Martin
66 Darden
67 Darden
68 Coleman et al. 1975
69 Armour 1980, 187-225
70 Willie and Greenblatt 1981, 33, 101, 189, 220-31
71 Eley 1976, 134, 36
72 Orfield 1978, 80-1
73 Greer 1965, 56; Frieden and Morris 1968, 130; Rothenberg 1967, 68-9
74 Orfield 1978, 84
75 Taueber 1990, 18-24
76 *Norfolk Virginian-Pilot* 2/10/56
77 Wilson 1966; Gans 1966, 540-5; Barron and Barron 1965
78 Cox, as quoted in Brownfield 1960, 760
79 Brownfield 1960, 761
80 Greer and Miner 1967, 152-63
81 Anderson 1964
82 Frieden 1966, 585-623
83 Taueber 1990, 18-24
84 Orfield 1985, 161-96
85 Taueber 1989
86 Eley 1976, 36
87 Crain et al. 1968
88 Crenshaw

Bibliography

Abbott, Carl. 1981. *The New Urban America: Growth and Politics in Sunbelt Cities*. Chapel Hill: University of North Carolina Press.

Anderson, Martin. 1964. *The Federal Bulldozer: A Critical Analysis of Urban Renewal, 1949-1962*. Cambridge: M.I.T. Press.

Agle, Charles K. 1956. *A Master Plan For The Central Business And Financial District*. Norfolk: Planning Commission, 19-20. Norfolk City Planning Department files.

Architectural Forum. 1950. "Federal Slum Clearance Gets Its First Full Scale Tryout in Norfolk, Va." May:132-138.

Armour, David J. 1980. "White Flight and the Future of School Desegregation." In *School Desegregation: Past, Present, and Future*, edited by Walter G. Stephan and Joe R. Feagin, 187-225. New York: Plenum Press.

Barron, Bryton, and Ella Barron. 1965. *The Inhumanity of Urban Renewal*. Arlington, Va.: Crestwood Books.

Beall, E. T., George W. Price, and Donald R. Locke. 1950. "Face Lifting for Better Urban Living," Norfolk XII, 1 (February):6-10.

Beckett, Leola Pearl, et al. v. School Board of the City of Norfolk, Va., et al. 1957. In *Race Relations Law Reporter* 2: no. 2 (April):334-340.

Beckett, Leola Pearl, et al. v. School Board of the City of Norfolk, Va., et al. 1958. In *Race Relations Law Reporter* 3: no. 5 (October):953-954.

Bellush, Jewell, and Murry Hausknecht, editors. 1967. *Urban Renewal: People, Politics, and Planning*. New York: Doubleday.

Brewbaker, J. J., Norfolk School Superintendent. 11 November 1954. Letter to H. H. George, Norfolk City Manager. Norfolk Public Schools files.

___. 8 August 1955. Letter to Sherwood Reeder, Norfolk City Manager. Norfolk Public Schools files.

___. 7 May 1956. Letter to John Corbell, Clerk of the City of Norfolk. Norfolk Public Schools Files.

___. 13 February 1957. Letter to Thomas F. Maxwell, Norfolk City Manager. Norfolk Public Schools files.

___. 21 May 1959. Letter to Thomas F. Maxwell, Norfolk City Manager. Norfolk Public Schools files.

___. 29 May 1959. Letter to Thomas F. Maxwell, Norfolk City Manager. Norfolk Public Schools files.

Bibliography

Brown, Oliver, et al. v. Board of Education of Topeka, Shawnee County, Kansas, et al. 1956. In *Race Relations Law Reporter* 1: no. 8 (February):6-20.

Brownfield, Lyman. 1960. "The Disposition Problem in Urban Renewal," *Journal of Law and Contemporary Problems*, XXV:4 (Autumn):736-740.

Campbell, Edmund D., and Archie L. Boswell. 1959. Brief for Appellee, United States Court of Appeals, Fourth Circuit, No. 7848 (*James* v. *Almond*), Norfolk Committee for Public Schools files, Old Dominion University archives.

Campbell, Ernest Q., et al. 1960. *When a City Closes Its Schools*. Chapel Hill: University of North Carolina Press.

Campbell, W. E., Assistant Superintendent of Schools. 1959. "Report of the Committee Relegated By the School Board of the City of Norfolk to Study the Proposal for Construction of Small Primary Schools." Norfolk Public Schools files.

Caro, Robert A. 1975. *The Power Broker: Robert Moses and the Fall of New York*. New York: Random House.

Carter, Luther J., former reporter for the *Norfolk Virginian-Pilot*. Interview with author, 12 January 1991. Tape Recording, Washington, D.C.

Coleman, James S., Sara P. Kelly, and John A. Moore. 1975. *Trends in School Segregation, 1968-1973*. Washington, D.C: Urban Institute.

Community Builders of Norfolk, Virginia. 1942. Norfolk: Community Builders.

Conrad, Lewis, Assistant Norfolk City Auditor. Interview with author, 13 August 1979. Norfolk.

Crain, Robert L. et al. 1968. *The Politics of School Desegregation: Comparative Case Studies of Community Structure and Policy-Making*. Chicago: Aldine Press.

Crenshaw, Francis N., former Norfolk School Board member and legal counsel for Norfolk Redevelopment and Housing Authority. Interview with author, 7 February 1991. Tape recording, Norfolk.

Curtin, Theodore A. 1969. "A Marriage of Convenience: Norfolk and the Navy, 1917-1967." Masters thesis, Old Dominion University.

Dabney, Virginius. 1971. *Virginia: The New Dominion*. Garden City, N.Y.: Doubleday.

Darden, Pretlow, former mayor and commissioner of the Norfolk Redevelopment and Housing Authority. Interview with author, 13 August 1975. Tape recording, Norfolk.

Dillon, Gordon. 1970. "An Exceptionally Talented Lad," Article One I:ii (May): 17-19.

Duckworth, W. Fred, Mayor of Norfolk. 6 October 1958. Letter to J. Lindsay Almond, Governor of Virginia. Box 136 papers of Governor J. Lindsay Almond, Virginia State Archives.

Eley, James W., Jr. 1976. *The Crisis of Conservative Virginia: The Byrd Organization and the Politics of Massive Resistance*, Twentieth-Century America Series. Knoxville: University of Tennessee Press.

Ervin, Sam, Jr. 1956. "The Case for Segregation," *LOOK* 20, no. 7 (April 3):32-33.

Estes, John F., former Police Sargeant. Interview with author, 20 September 1979. Tape Recording, Norfolk.

Frieden, Bernard 1966. "Policies for Rebuilding." In *Urban Renewal: The Record and the Controversy*, edited by James Q. Wilson, 585-623. Cambridge: M.I.T. Press.

Frieden, Bernard J., and Robert Morris. 1968. *Urban Planning and Social Policy*. New York: Basic Books.

Gans, Herbert J. 1966. "The Failure of Urban Renewal." In *Urban Renewal: The Record and the Controversy*, edited by James Q. Wilson, 540-545. Cambridge: M.I.T. Press.

Gragila, Lino A. 1980. "From Prohibiting Segregation to Requiring Integration." In *School Desegregation: Past, Present, and Future*, edited by Walter G. Stephan, and Joe R. Feagin, 69-96. New York: Plenum Press.

Greer, Scott. 1965. *Urban Renewal and American Cities: The Dilemma of Democratic Intervention*. New York: Bobbs-Merrill Co.

Greer, Scott, and David W. Miner. 1967. "The Political Side of Urban Development and Redevelopment." In *Urban Renewal: People, Politics, and Planning*, edited by Jewel Bellush and Murray Hausknect, 152-163. New York: Doubleday.

Gregory, L. Cameron, former reporter for the *Norfolk Virginian-Pilot*. Interview with author, 20 July 1979. Tape recording, Norfolk.

Gornto, Vernon, former campaign manager of the People's Ticket of 1946. Interview with author, 17 August 1975. Norfolk.

Hagan, J. Addison, former candidate for Norfolk City Council. Interview with James Sweeney, 25 January 1977. Transcript, Old Dominion University Archives.

Hanna, Ira R. 1967. "The Growth of the Norfolk Naval Air Station and the Norfolk-Portsmouth Metropolitan Area Economy in the Twentieth Century." Masters thesis, Old Dominion University

Harrell, Charles A. 1949. *The Norfolk Story: Annual Report for 1948*, Norfolk. Sargeant Collection, Kirn Library.

___. 1950a. "The Role of the City in America," Norfolk XXI:1 (February):12-14. Sargeant Collection, Kirn Library.

___. 1950b. "Norfolk—A Progress Report," Norfolk XII:2 (November):9-14. Sargeant Collection, Kirn Library.

Harrison, Albertis S., Jr., Attorney General of Virginia, v. Sidney C. Day, Jr., Comptroller of Virginia. 1959. Race Relations Law Reporter 4: no. 1 (Spring): 65-78.

Hebert, George J. 1950. "Downtown Norfolk: Commercial and Municipal Progress," Norfolk XXI:1 (February): 10-13. Sargeant Collection, Kirn Library.

Heywood, et al. v. Public Housing Administration. 1956. In *Race Relations Law Reporter* 1, no. 2 (April):347.

The History of Lower Tidewater, Virginia. 1954. *Family and Personal History*, vol III. New York: Lewis Historical Publishing Co.

Hoffman, Walter E. Hoffman, U.S. federal district judge. Interview with author, 8 March 1991. Tape recording, Norfolk.

Housing and Home Finance Agency. 1949. *Slum Clearance Under The Housing Act of 1949: A Preliminary Statement To American Cities.* Washington, D.C.: U.S. Government.

___. 1950. *A Guide to Slum Clearance and Urban Development.* Washington, D.C.: U.S. Government.

___. 1966. "The Operation and Achievements of the Urban Renewal Program." In *Urban Renewal: The Record and the Controversy*, edited by James Q. Wilson, 189-229. Cambridge: M.I.T. Press.

Hunter, Floyd W. 1953. *Community Power Structure*. Chapel Hill: University of North Carolina Press Press.

Jackson, Kenneth T. 1987. *Crabgrass Frontier: The Suburbanization of the United States*. New York: Oxford University Press.

James, Ruth Pendleton, et. al. v. J. Lindsay Almond, Governor of Virginia, et al. 1959. In *Race Relations Law Reporter* 4: no. 1 (Spring):46-54.

James, Ruth Pendleton, et. al. v. W. Fred Duckworth, et al. 1959. In *Race Relations Law Reporter* 4: no. 1 (Spring):55-57.

Leflar, Robert A. 1957. "Law of the Land: The Courts and the Schools." In *With All Deliberate Speed*, edited by Don Shoemaker, 1-14. New York: Harper & Brothers.

Martin, Roy B., Jr., former Norfolk mayor. Interview with author, 18 February 1991. Tape Recording, Norfolk.

Mason, Robert H., former editor of the *Norfolk Virginian-Pilot*. Interview with author, 27 September 1979. Tape recording, Norfolk.

McCauley, Patrick E. 1957. "Be It Enacted," In *With All Deliberate Speed*, edited by Don Shoemaker, 130-146. New York: Harper & Brothers.

Metcalf, George R. 1983. *From Little Rock to Boston: The History of School Desegregation*. Westport, Conn.: Greenwood Press.

Monola, G. D., former Director of Environmental Health and the Department of Community Improvement for Norfolk. Interview with author, 3 April 1991. Norfolk.

Muse, Benjamin T. 1964. *Ten Years of Prelude: The Story of Integration Since the Supreme Court's 1954 Decision*. New York: Viking Press.

Muse, Benjamin T. 1961. *Virginia's Massive Resistance*. Bloomington, Ind.: Indiana University Press.

Norfolk Chamber of Commerce. 1954. "Population and Housing Survey," Norfolk XVI: 7 (November):10-20. Sargeant Collection, Kirn Library.

Norfolk City Planning Commission 1950. *Major Highway Plan, Part I, Major Highways and Collector Streets*. Norfolk, Norfolk City Planning Department files.

Norfolk Public Schools. 1959. General Fund Budget for the 1958-1959 school year, Norfolk Public Schools files.

___ . 1960. General Fund Budget for the 1959-1960 school year, Norfolk Public Schools files.

Norfolk Redevelopment and Housing Authority 1946. *This Is It*. Norfolk: Norfolk Redevelopment and Housing Authority.

___ . 1957. Report. Norfolk: Norfolk Redevelopment and Housing Authority.

___. 1975. Annual Report to the City Council (1974).

Orfield, Gary. 1978. *Must We Bus? Segregated Schools and National Policy*. Washington, D.C.: Brookings Institute.

___. 1985. "Ghettoization and Its Alternatives," In *The New Urban Reality*, edited by Paul E. Peterson, 161-96. Washington, D.C.: Brookings Institute.

Pentecost & Courtney (Architects) (1957). "Lakewood Junior High School (building plans)." Norfolk Public Schools.

Raffel, Jeffrey A. 1980. *The Politics of School Desegregation: The Metropolitan Remedy in Delaware*. Philadelphia: Temple University Press.

Reif, Jane. 1960. *Crisis in Norfolk*. Richmond: Virginia Council on Human Relations.

Rist, Ray. 1979. *Desegregated Schools: Appraisals of the American Experience*. New York: Academic Press.

Rorer, Henry S. 1968. *History of Norfolk Public Schools*. Norfolk: by the author. Special Collections, Old Dominion University.

Rothenberg, Jerome. 1967. *Economic Evaluation of Urban Renewal: Conceptual Foundation of Benefit-Cost Analysis*. Washington, D.C.: Brookings Institute.

Schlegel, Marvin W. 1951. *Conscripted City: Norfolk in World War II*. Norfolk: Norfolk War History Commission. Special Collections, Old Dominion University.

Schmidt, John C. 1969. "Norfolk: A City Remakes Itself," Baltimore, March. Reprinted by Norfolk Redevelopment and Housing Authority.

School Board of the City of Norfolk. 1 July 1955. Formal Minutes of the Board. Norfolk Public Schools files.

___ . 25 March 1958. "School Construction and Site Acquisition Program." Norfolk Public Schools files.

Shoemake, Don, editor. 1957. *With All Deliberate Speed*. New York: Harper & Brothers.

Smith, Bob. 1965. *They Closed Their Schools: Prince Edward County, Virginia, 1951-1964*. Chapel Hill: University of North Carolina Press.

Smith, James E., comptroller for the Norfolk Redevelopment and Housing Authority. Interview with author, 13 August 1979. Norfolk.

Staylor, Claude J., Jr., former chief of Police and Norfolk City Councilman. Interview with author, 25 July 1979. Tape recording, Norfolk.

Steadfast, Philip A., Director of the Norfolk Department of City Planning. 27 January 1976. *Memorandum to Paul Smith, Assistant Superintendent for Business and Finance*. Norfolk Public Schools files.

Stephan, Walter G. 1980. "A Brief Historical Overview of School Desegregation." In *School Desegregation: Past, Present, and Future*, edited by Walter G. Stephan and Joe R. Feagin, 11-17. New York: Plenum Press.

Stern, Robert L., board member of the Norfolk Committee for Public Schools. Interview with author, 22 April 1978. Norfolk.

Stinchcombe, Jean L. 1968. *Reform and Reaction: City Politics in Toledo*. Belmont, Calif.: Wadsworth.

Sugg, Harold. 1967. "1945-1965: Youth Takes Command," In *Saltwater and Printer's Ink: Norfolk and Its Newspapers, 1865-1965*, edited by Lenoir Chambers and Joseph E. Shank, 376-394. Chapel Hill: University of North Carolina Press Press.

___ , former reporter and editor, *Norfolk Virginian-Pilot*. Interview with author, 17 August 1979. Tape recording, Roanoke, Va.

Suggs, Henry Lewis. 1988. *P. B. Young, Newspaperman*. Charlottesville, Va.: University of Virginia.

Sullivan, Frank. 1954. "Norfolk's Redevelopment Story," Norfolk XVI: 7 (November): 4-25. Sargeant Collection, Kirn Library.

Sullivan, W. P., Director of Building and Grounds. 15 September 1956. "Cost Data, Outline Specifications, and Facilities in the New Schools in Norfolk, Virginia, Since 1951." Norfolk Public Schools files.

Taueber, Karl E. 1989. "Residence and Race: 1619 to 2019." In *Race: Twentieth Century Dilemmas—Twenty-First Century Prognoses*, edited by Winston A. Van Horne. Milwaukee: University of Wisconsin.

___ . 1990. "Desegregation of Public School Districts: Resistance and Change," Phi Delta Kappan 21, no. 1 (September):18-24.

Taueber, Karl E. and Alma Taueber. 1965. *Negroes in Cities: Residential Segregation and Neighborhood Change*. Chicago: Aldine.

U.S. Bureau of the Census. 1952. U.S. Census of Population, 1950, vol. II, Characteristics of the Population, Part 46, Virginia, Chapter B. Washington: U.S. Government.

___. 1952, v. Ill, Census Tract Studies, Chapter 38. Washington: U.S. Government.

Weaver, Robert C. 1967. "The Urban Complex." In *Urban Renewal: People, Politics, and Planning*, edited by Jewel Bellush and Murray Hausknecht, 90-101. Garden City, N.Y.: Doubleday.

Wertenbaker, Thomas J. 1962. *Norfolk: Historic Southern Port*. Durham, N.C.: Duke University Press.

White, Forrest P., M.D. 1959. "Will Norfolk Schools Stay Open?" *Atlantic Monthly* 204:iii (September):30.

___. 1959b. unpublished and untitled, Article, Norfolk Committee for Public Schools files, Old Dominion University Archives.

___. 1960. "Tuition Grants: Strange Fruit of Southern Integration," *South Atlantic Quarterly*, Autumn.

Williams, Robin M., and Margaret W. Ryan, editors. 1954. *Schools in Transition: Community Experiences in Desegregation*. Chapel Hill: University of North Carolina Press.

Willie, Charles V., and Susan L. Greenblatt. 1981. *Community Politics and Educational Change: Ten School Systems Under Court Order*. New York: Longman.

Wilson, James Q., editor. 1966. *Urban Renewal: The Record and the Controversy*. Cambridge: M.I.T. Press.

Women's Council for Inter-racial Cooperation. 1955. "Letters to the Press: A Sampling of Public Opinion on Desegregation." Women's Council for Inter-racial Cooperation News Sheet, March, Norfolk Committee for Public Schools files, Old Dominion University Archives.

___. 1959. "How Norfolk's Closed Schools Were Reopened." Norfolk Committee for Public Schools files, Old Dominion University Archives.

Workman, W. D., Jr. 1957. "The Deep South." In *With All Deliberate Speed*, edited by Don Shoemaker, 88-109. New York: Harper & Brothers.

NEWSPAPERS (in chronological order)

"Councilmanic Consensus on Norfolk Housing," editorial, *Norfolk Virginian-Pilot*, 4 December 1938. Sargeant Collection.

"City Administration Ticket Winners In Election," *Norfolk Virginian-Pilot*, 10 June 1942, 20.

Twiford, Warner, "Old Mother Norfolk Lets Her Hair Down," *Norfolk Virginian-Pilot*, 15 August 1945, 22.

Twiford, Warner, "The Night Before Is What Norfolk Remembers (Though Some Celebrants May Be Exception)," *Norfolk Virginian-Pilot*, 16 August 1945, 18.

Borland, Armistead (City Manager), "Defects at City Hall," guest editorial, *Norfolk Ledger-Dispatch*, 21 February 1946, 6.

"Halstead Asks City Committee to Solve White-Negro Problem," *Norfolk Virginian-Pilot*, 29 May 1946, 2-3.

"Council Asked to Stop Move to White Areas," *Norfolk Journal and Guide*, 1 June 1946, 1.

"Wrong Way to Solve the Housing Shortage Problem in Norfolk," *Norfolk Journal and Guide*, 1 June 1946, 1.

"Low Cost Housing a Paying Investment," editorial, *Norfolk Journal and Guide*, 1 June 1946, 10.

"Seven Seek Racial Answer in Brambleton," *Norfolk Virginian-Pilot*, 1 June 1946, 16.

"Ruffin Says Borland Resigned as City Manager 'In a Violent Temper'; Accuses Official of Attempting to Usurp Functions of Council," *Norfolk Virginian-Pilot*, 5 June 1946.

"Vote for Ashe," editorial, *Norfolk Journal and Guide*, 8 June 1946.

"Our 'Pig-in-a-Poke' Qualification System," editorial, *Norfolk Virginian-Pilot*, 11 June 1946, 6.

Lankford, G. Wright, "Cooke, Darden and Twohy Win City Council Election," *Norfolk Virginian-Pilot*, 12 June 1946, 1.

Sugg, Harold, "Time to Act on Housing, All 5 Councilmen Agree," *Norfolk Virginian-Pilot*, 28 November 1948. Sargeant Collection.

Sullivan, Frank, "New Norfolk Out of Old: Program Outlined," *Norfolk Virginian-Pilot*, 4 October 1949, 1.

"130 Arrested in 'Numbers' Raid; Tickets, $3,051 in Cash Taken," *Norfolk Virginian-Pilot*, 3 December 1948, 40.

Gregory, Cameron, "114 'Numbers' Defendants Fined; Total of $11,700, 16 Dismissed, 2 Continued," *Norfolk Virginian-Pilot*, 4 December 1948, 20.

"The Grand Jury's Report on the Police Department," *Norfolk Virginian-Pilot*, 13 March 1949, 6.

Kelley, George, "The Boys Don't Call Him 'Charley'," *Norfolk Virginian-Pilot*, 4 June 1950, V-1.

"The New Councilmen," an editorial, *Norfolk Virginian-Pilot*, 14 June 1950. Sargeant Collection.

"Redevelopment Project Will Start Next Month," *Norfolk Virginian-Pilot*, 15 August 1950, 1. Sargeant Collection.

"Slum Project Approved By Council," *Norfolk Virginian-Pilot*, 22 August 1951, A-17. Sargeant Collection.

Sullivan, Frank, "Rumble of First Slum House to Be Razed Echoes 15 Years of Planning," *Norfolk Virginian-Pilot*, 12 December 1951, 1.

"New School Districts Are Formed," *Norfolk Ledger-Dispatch*, 13 December 1951. Sargeant Collection.

Kelley, George, "City Culture United under Center Plans," *Norfolk Virginian-Pilot*, 23 December 1951. Sargeant Collection.

Sullivan, Frank, "$10.9 Million Loan-Grant Executed for Redevelopment Project Number 1," *Norfolk Virginian-Pilot*, 16 April 1952. Sargeant Collection.

"A Half-Century's Blueprint," editorial, *Norfolk Virginian-Pilot*, 9 July 1952. Sargeant Collection.

"Segregation's Summing Up—Living and Evolving Law," editorial, *Norfolk Virginian-Pilot*, 13 December 1952, 5.

"Housing Authority Powers Should Not Be Abused," editorial, *Norfolk Virginian-Pilot*, 20 May 1953. Sargeant Collection.

"Cost of Negro Schooling Hits $217.55 Per Pupil," *Norfolk Ledger-Dispatch*, 21 August 1953. Sargeant Collection.

"City Council Divided on Annexation As Costs Soar Beyond Expectations," *Norfolk Virginian-Pilot*, 15 March 1954, 2-1.

"The Decision on Segregation," editorial, *Norfolk Virginian-Pilot*, 18 May 1954, 6.

Marcus, Clare, "'Keep Calm' Is Plea of Brewbaker," *Norfolk Virginian-Pilot*, 18 May 1954, back page.

"Norfolk's Dual School System," map, *Norfolk Virginian-Pilot*, 18 May 1954, back page.

Sullivan, Frank, "Kiland Asks Retention of War Housing," *Norfolk Virginian-Pilot*, 11 June 1954. Sargeant Collection.

"Negro Agent Holds Firm on Coronado Home Sales," *Norfolk Virginian-Pilot*, 30 July 1954. Sargeant Collection.

"Norfolk Will Begin to Operate Broad Creek Village October 1," *Norfolk Virginian-Pilot*, 11 August 1954, 32.

Cahill, Carl, "Home Owners of Both Races Seek Solution to Problem," *Norfolk Ledger-Dispatch*, 16 August 1954. Sargeant Collection.

"Coronado Still County Matter in Eyes of City," *Norfolk Virginian-Pilot*, 19 August 1954. Sargeant Collection.

Rodeffer, Charles C., "Home of Whites Threatened Says Resident of Coronado," *Norfolk Virginian-Pilot*, 19 August 1954. Sargeant Collection.

Smith, Robert C., "Coronado: Where Mixed Housing, through Sales, Has Generated Tensions," *Norfolk Virginian-Pilot*, 22 August 1954. Sargeant Collection.

"Newly Occupied House Shaken, Panes Broken," *Norfolk Virginian-Pilot*, 25 August 1954. Sargeant Collection.

Cahill, Carl, "State and County Police Probe Blast in Coronado," *Norfolk Ledger-Dispatch*, 30 August 1954. Sargeant Collection.

Young, P. B., Sr., "Negroes in Coronado," guest editorial, *Norfolk Virginian-Pilot*, 31 August 1954. Sargeant Collection.

McKnight, C. A., "Reporting Service to Tell School Story," *Southern School News*, 3 September 1954, 1.

"Reaction to Supreme Court Decision Calm, Resigned," *Southern School News*, 3 September 1954, 1-2.

"Coronado and the Law," an editorial, *Norfolk Virginian-Pilot*, 11 September 1954. Sargeant Collection.

"Porch, Interior of Coronado Home, Sold in June, Damaged by Explosion," *Norfolk Virginian-Pilot*, 11 September 1954. Sargeant Collection.

May, Ronald, "Blast-Ravaged House in Coronado Looted; Action by Governor Asked," *Norfolk Virginian-Pilot*, 12 September 1954.

Smith, Robert C., "Bullets Fired into Coronado Home; Two Negro Residents Are Uninjured," *Norfolk Virginian-Pilot*, 20 September 1954. Sargeant Collection.

"Virginia: Parochial Schools Integrated Calmly," *Southern School News*, 1 October 1954, 14.

"The Segregation Decision Curbs School Construction," editorial, *Norfolk Ledger-Dispatch*, 13 October 1954, 6.

"Leaders Blame Racial Communications Problems on Pressures to Integrate," *Southern School News*, 1 December 1954, 7.

"School-Building Arithmetic—It's the Hardest Subject," editorial, *Norfolk Virginian-Pilot*, 16 January 1955. Sargeant Collection.

Hopkins, Mary, "Norfolk Keeps Pace with Growing Need for Schools," *Norfolk Ledger-Dispatch*, 28 January 1955. Sargeant Collection.

Smith, Robert C., "Apprehension about the Future Seizes Broad Creek Villagers," *Norfolk Virginian-Pilot*, 24 April 1955. Sargeant Collection.

Kelley, George M., "Broad Creek Rezoning for Industry Approved With Residents' Backing," *Norfolk Virginian-Pilot*, 21 May 1955. Sargeant Collection.

"Group Study of Integration Rapidly Gains Adherents," *Norfolk Virginian-Pilot*, 3 June 1955. Sargeant Collection.

"Study Group Wins Backing," *Norfolk Virginian-Pilot*, 18 June 1955. Sargeant Collection.

Kelley, George M. "Study Seeking New Basis for Referendums Ordered," *Norfolk Virginian-Pilot*, 6 July 1955. Sargeant Collection.

"Virginia: Norfolk Board Votes 'Approval in Principle' of Integration," *Southern School News*, 6 July 1955, 10.

"Schools Lauded for Racial Stand," *Norfolk Ledger-Dispatch*, 11 July 1955. Sargeant Collection.

Phillips, Joseph V., "End to School Segregation Petition Handed to Board," *Norfolk Virginian-Pilot*, 14 July 1955. Sargeant Collection.

Kelley, George M., "Parent Could Pick School under 'Integration' Plan Summers Offers to Council," *Norfolk Virginian-Pilot*, 27 July 1955. Sargeant Collection.

"City 'Compromises' on Shores Property," *Norfolk Journal and Guide*, 6 August 1955, 1.

"Group Reports on Race Home Sites," *Norfolk Journal and Guide*, 6 August 1955, 17.

"The Kaufman Committee Report," editorial, *Norfolk Journal and Guide*, 6 August 1955, 1-2.

"Virginia: More Counties Choose to Vote School Funds Month by Month," *Southern School News*, August, 1955, 10.

"Rising Pressure for School Space," editorial, *Norfolk Virginian-Pilot*, 17 September 1955. Sargeant Collection.

"A Broad Creek Shores Plan Replaces an Issue There," editorial, *Norfolk Virginian-Pilot*, 19 September 1955. Sargeant Collection.

"The City School Program and How It May Grow," editorial, *Norfolk Virginian-Pilot*, 19 September 1955. Sargeant Collection.

"Virginia: Newport News Board Turns School over to Negroes Rather Than Integrate," *Southern School News*, October 1955, 6.

Smith, Robert C., "Integration Effect Minimized; Circumvention Effort Denied," *Norfolk Virginian-Pilot*, 5 January 1956. Sargeant Collection.

Holloway, Lin, "Progress Was By-Word in Norfolk in '55," *Norfolk Journal and Guide*, 7 January 1956. Sargeant Collection.

"From Ripley to Layton on the City Council," *Norfolk Virginian-Pilot*, 9 February 1956. Sargeant Collection.

"City Schools Fast Reducing Shift Classes," *Norfolk Virginian-Pilot*, 10 February 1956. Sargeant Collection.

"Abbott-Summers-Layton—Administration Ticket," editorial, *Norfolk Virginian-Pilot*, 6 March 1956. Sargeant Collection.

Sullivan, Frank, "Bids on Final Housing Project Opened; $2,625,982 Low Figure," *Norfolk Virginian-Pilot*, 22 March 1956. Sargeant Collection.

"Tidewater Drive Building Booms," *Norfolk Virginian-Pilot*, 22 March 1956. Sargeant Collection.

"Views on Oakwood Plan Aired," *Norfolk Journal and Guide*, 31 March 1956, 2-1. Sargeant Collection.

"Segregation on Buses Officially Discontinued," *Norfolk Virginian-Pilot*, 25 April 1956. Sargeant Collection.

Carter, Luther J., "Oakwood's Redevelopment Hangs Fire Pending Appeal," *Norfolk Virginian-Pilot*, 29 April 1956, C-1.

"Segregation Supported By Summers," *Norfolk Virginian-Pilot*, 11 May 1956. Sargeant Collection.

Henderson, Jim, "Negroes Ask for Injunction Ending School Segregation in Norfolk; Claim 'Injury,'" *Norfolk Virginian-Pilot*, 11 May 1956. Sargeant Collection.

Kelley, George M., "Norfolk Request for Special Session Includes Any Ideas Beyond Gray Plan," *Norfolk Virginian-Pilot*, 13 May 1956. Sargeant Collection.

"Norfolk School Board 'Unable to Act' Alone on Desegregation," *Norfolk Virginian-Pilot*, 14 May 1956. Sargeant Collection.

"Downtown Waterfront Priority," an editorial, *Norfolk Virginian-Pilot*, 28 May 1956. Sargeant Collection.

"Segregation Policy and Laws 'Valid,' School Board Answers," *Norfolk Virginian-Pilot*, 22 June 1956. Sargeant Collection.

"Racial Status in Schools of Norfolk May Continue through '56-57 Terms," *Norfolk Ledger-Dispatch*, 3 July 1956. Sargeant Collection.

Kelley, George M., "Continued School Operation Norfolk's First Aim," *Norfolk Virginian-Pilot*, 24 July 1956, 1.

Phillips, Joseph V., "Integration Study Group Is Launched," *Norfolk Virginian-Pilot*, 6 August 1956. Sargeant Collection.

"Bold, Imaginative Agle Report," editorial, *Norfolk Virginian-Pilot*, 14 August 1956. Sargeant Collection.

"Norfolk's Other 'Center'," editorial, *Norfolk Ledger-Dispatch*, 22 August 1956. Sargeant Collection.

Stein, Tony, "Negroes Granted Free Use of Portsmouth Golf Course," *Norfolk Ledger-Dispatch*, 29 August 1956. Sargeant Collection.

"Some History Making on the Council," editorial, *Norfolk Virginian-Pilot*, 3 September 1956. Sargeant Collection.

Leslie, Joseph A., III, "City's Master Plan Opposed and Praised during Hearing," *Norfolk Virginian-Pilot*, 11 September 1956. Sargeant Collection.

Sullivan, Frank, "1,000 Dwelling Units Due for Rehabilitation," *Norfolk Virginian-Pilot*, 11 October 1956. Sargeant Collection.

"Third Party Is Operating in Quarters," *Norfolk Virginian-Pilot*, 13 October 1956. Sargeant Collection.

Carter, Luther J., "$15 Million Revised School Plan Set," *Norfolk Virginian-Pilot*, 24 October 1956. Sargeant Collection.

Smith, Robert C., "Origin of 'Hate' Pamphlets Is Exposed After 'Sneak Attacks' on Chest Drives," *Norfolk Virginian-Pilot*, 25 October 1956.

Sullivan, Frank, "Atlantic City Redevelopment Hearing Scheduled January 4," *Norfolk Virginian-Pilot*, 8 December 1956. Sargeant Collection.

"Norfolk's Deferred Projects," editorial, *Norfolk Ledger-Dispatch*, 17 December 1956. Sargeant Collection.

Williams, Paul, "Cloud over Future of New School Seen," *Norfolk Ledger-Dispatch*, 19 December 1956. Sargeant Collection.

Sullivan, Frank, "Atlantic City Redevelopment Fought by Property Owners," *Norfolk Virginian-Pilot*, 5 January 1957, 24.

"New Negro Elementary School Plans Pressed," *Norfolk Virginian-Pilot*, 26 January 1957, 27.

"Background: Power to Assign Pupils Is Studied in 7 States," *Southern Schools News*, February, 1957, 1.

Henderson, Jim, "Norfolk Schools Ordered to Integrate in Fall," *Norfolk Virginian-Pilot*, 13 February 1957, 1.

"13 Schools Affected by Integration," *Norfolk Virginian-Pilot*, 13 February 1957, A-8.

Porter, Jean Bishop, "Parents Favor More City Funds to Better Schools," *Norfolk Ledger-Dispatch*, 15 February 1957. Sargeant Collection.

Dodson, Bob, "Atlantic City Development to Cost City $7,700,000," *Norfolk Ledger-Dispatch*, 17 February 1957. Sargeant Collection.

"Court's Ruling in Newport News Case," *Southern School News*, March 1957, 14.

Carter, Luther J., "Elementary-Junior High for Oakwood-Rosemont Studied by School Officials," *Norfolk Virginian-Pilot*, 8 March 1957. Sargeant Collection.

Smith, Robert C., "Aging Atlantic City is Next on the List," *Norfolk Virginian-Pilot*, 10 March 1957. Sargeant Collection.

Kelley, George M., "Usual Operation until Crisis Rises," *Norfolk Virginian-Pilot*, 16 March 1957. Sargeant Collection.

Kelley, George M., "In Virginia 'All of Us in Same Boat,'" *Norfolk Virginian-Pilot*, 26 March 1957. Sargeant Collection.

Carter, Luther J., "Integration Opposed By P.T.A. Council," *Norfolk Virginian-Pilot*, 30 March 1957, 28.

"Hagan, Ford, and White File for Primary Race," *Norfolk Virginian-Pilot*, 10 April 1957. Sargeant Collection.

"Two Views of 'Resistance,'" editorial, *Norfolk Ledger-Dispatch*, 8 June 1957. Sargeant Collection.

Smith, Robert C., "Atlantic City Plan Would Erase Dangers to Health, Safety, Morals," *Norfolk Virginian-Pilot*, 23 June 1957.

"Norfolk's New Councilman," editorial, *Norfolk Virginian-Pilot*, 26 June 1957. Sargeant Collection.

"A Resident," "Talk of Slums—Not the Facts—Injured Atlantic City," letter to the editor, *Norfolk Virginian-Pilot*, 1 July 1957. Sargeant Collection.

Carter, Luther J., "Old School Considered for Offices," *Norfolk Virginian-Pilot*, 9 August 1957. Sargeant Collection.

Blackford, Frank, "Mandate from Court Due Soon in Norfolk, " *Norfolk Virginian-Pilot*, 22 October 1957. Sargeant Collection.

"Old B C V School Will Be Removed," *Norfolk Ledger-Dispatch*, 21 December 1957. Sargeant Collection.

"Population Shift Will Hit School," *Norfolk Virginian-Pilot*, 3 January 1958. Sargeant Collection.

Dodson, Bob, "Local Legislators Moved Independently on Mixing," *Norfolk Ledger-Dispatch*, 10 March 1958. Sargeant Collection.

Carter, Luther J. "5.5 Million Program for Schools Drafted," *Norfolk Virginian-Pilot*, 28 March 1958. Sargeant Collection.

Bibliography

"1958 City Campaign and Its Obligations," *Norfolk Virginian-Pilot*, 14 April 1958. Sargeant Collection.

Holloway, Lin, "Building Shifts Indicate Norfolk Population Trends," *Norfolk Journal and Guide*, 19 April 1958, 17.

Carter, Luther J., "Integration May Close 6 Schools," *Norfolk Virginian-Pilot*, 21 May 1958. Sargeant Collection.

"Landsdale Junior High to be 'One of the City's Finest,'" *Norfolk Virginian-Pilot*, 6 June 1958. Sargeant Collection.

Kelley, George M., "Biracial Study Goal of Petition," *Norfolk Virginian-Pilot*, 11 June 1958, p. 1.

"At Tax Windows and Behind Bars," editorial, *Norfolk Virginian-Pilot*, 12 June 1958. Norfolk Committee for Public Schools files, Old Dominion University Archives.

Carter, Luther J., "'Frustrated' City School Board Looks for Collision of Authority," *Norfolk Virginian-Pilot*, 13 June 1958. Sargeant Collection.

"Negro Pupils' Applications by Schools," *Norfolk Virginian-Pilot*, 13 June 1958. Sargeant Collection.

"Inter-Racial Relations," *Norfolk Virginian-Pilot*, 15 June 1958, D-3.

"Bi-Racial 'Bargaining' Repudiated," *Norfolk Virginian-Pilot*, 19 June 1958. Norfolk Committee for Public Schools files, Old Dominion University Archives.

"The 'Black Eye' of Closed Schools," editorial, *Norfolk Virginian-Pilot*, 20 July 1958, D-2.

"Closing School's Doors Is 'Small Sacrifice,'" *Norfolk Virginian-Pilot*, 25 July 1958, 60.

"Clergymen Rule Out Classes," *Norfolk Virginian-Pilot*, 7 August 1958. Sargeant Collection.

Carter, Luther J., "City School Board Denies Negro Applications," *Norfolk Virginian-Pilot*, 19 August 1958, 1.

Young, P. Bernard, Jr., "Key Participants in Norfolk School Integration Suit," *Norfolk Journal and Guide*, 30 August 1958.

Brooks, John I., "Six Norfolk Schools Facing Closing Threat as Board Agrees to Admit 17 Negro Students," *Norfolk Virginian-Pilot*, 30 August 1958, 1.

Carter, Luther J., "September 22 Date for Norfolk Schools," *Norfolk Virginian-Pilot*, 3 September 1958. Sargeant Collection.

Geary, James, "Don't Assign Negro Pupils, Almond Tells Norfolk Board," *Norfolk Virginian-Pilot*, 5 September 1958, 1.

Carter, Luther J., "Southside Classes Offered If 6 Norfolk Schools Close," *Norfolk Virginian-Pilot*, 12 September 1958, 1.

"Committee Is Formed to Keep Schools Open," *Norfolk Virginian-Pilot*, 19 September 1958, 1.

"What 'Progress,' Governor?" editorial, *Norfolk Virginian-Pilot*, 25 September 1958, 4.

"654 Norfolk Students Enrolled Outside City," *Norfolk Virginian-Pilot*, 26 September 1958. Sargeant Collection.

Williams, Paul, "Mayor Suggests Ministers Use Persuasion on Negroes," *Norfolk Ledger-Dispatch*, 1 October 1958. Sargeant Collection.

Carter, Luther J., "Closed City Schools' Cost Put at $172,000 Monthly," *Norfolk Virginian-Pilot*, 2 October 1958, 1.

"NEA Wants Schools Open with Mixing If Necessary," *Norfolk Ledger-Dispatch*, 3 October 1958. Sargeant Collection.

Ripley, Josephine, "Virginia's Massive Resistance Cracks Under Court Hammers," *Christian Science Monitor*, 8 October 1958, 3.

Brooks, John I., "Tidewater Educational Foundation: What Next?" *Norfolk Virginian-Pilot*, 12 October 1958. Sargeant Collection.

"3,000 to 3,500 Studying in Norfolk Tutor Groups," *Norfolk Ledger-Dispatch*, 13 October 1958. Sargeant Collection.

Carter, Luther J., "Norfolk Students in Area Schools," *Norfolk Virginian-Pilot*, 16 October 1958, 1.

"What 'Massive Resistance' Costs City," *Norfolk Virginian-Pilot*, 16 October 1958. Sargeant Collection.

Carter, Luther J., "Is Norfolk 'Complacent' Since Schools Closed?," *Norfolk Virginian-Pilot*, 19 October 1958, D-3.

Roberts, Gene, "The Hows and Whys of a Referendum," *Norfolk Virginian-Pilot*, 19 October 1958, D-1.

"Norfolk Citizens Request Almond to Return Schools," *Norfolk Ledger-Dispatch*, 22 October 1958, 19.

Roberts, Gene, "School Referendum Set; Board Rebuffed," *Norfolk Virginian-Pilot*, 22 October 1958. Sargeant Collection.

"Help Reopen Schools, Businessmen Urged," *Norfolk Virginian-Pilot*, 23 October 1958. Sargeant Collection.

"Little Hope Is Offered by Almond," *Norfolk Virginian-Pilot*, 23 October 1958. Norfolk Committee for Public Schools files, Old Dominion University Archives.

"Education," *Norfolk Virginian-Pilot*, 26 October 1958, D-3.

Carter, Luther J., "Teachers Paid Little as Tutors," *Norfolk Virginian-Pilot*, 6 November 1958. Sargeant Collection.

"State Obligation toward Schools Dead—Harrison," *Norfolk Virginian-Pilot*, 8 November 1958, A-1.

"If Norfolk Won't Stand with Us, I Say Make Them Stand—Tuck," *Norfolk Virginian-Pilot*, 13 November 1958, 1.

"Tuition Charges Allowed," *Norfolk Virginian-Pilot*, 15 November 1958. Sargeant Collection.

Bibliography

Dodson, Bob, "Integration Foes Win Norfolk Vote," *Norfolk Ledger-Dispatch*, 19 November 1958. Sargeant Collection.

"Vote by Precincts," *Norfolk Virginian-Pilot*, 19 November 1958, 8.

Brooks, John I., "Court Delays Its Decision in Test on Closed Schools," *Norfolk Virginian-Pilot*, 20 November 1958, 1.

Kelley, George M., "City Negro Schools in Line for Closing," *Norfolk Virginian-Pilot*, 26 November 1958, 1.

Roberts, Gene, "New Private School Going Up in Norfolk," *Norfolk Virginian-Pilot*, 5 December 1958. Sargeant Collection.

"Statewide Organization Set Up to Save Schools," *Norfolk Virginian-Pilot*, 7 December 1958. Sargeant Collection.

"Layton's School Plea Falls on Deaf Ears," *Norfolk Virginian-Pilot*, 11 December 1958. Sargeant Collection.

Sullivan, Frank, "Business and Industry Are Geared for Good Year," *Norfolk Virginian-Pilot*, 1 January 1959. "The Year Virginia Closed the Schools," editorial, *Norfolk Virginian-Pilot*, 1 January 1959. Sargeant Collection.

Kelley, George M., "Forced Integration in Norfolk Schools Foreseen by Almond," *Norfolk Virginian-Pilot*, 4 January 1959, 1.

Sofflin, Mike, "Virginia Business Recovers," *Norfolk Virginian-Pilot*, 4 January 1959, C-1.

Kelley, George M., "Southside's Suspicions toward Norfolk Change," *Norfolk Virginian-Pilot*, 11 January 1959, C-1.

"Committee on Schools Critical," *Norfolk Virginian-Pilot*, 14 January 1959, 8.

"The Council's Lock Out," editorial, *Norfolk Virginian-Pilot*, 14 January 1959, 4.

"Council Step Advances Rosemont School Plans," *Norfolk Virginian-Pilot*, 14 January 1959. Sargeant Collection.

Kelley, George M. and Gene Roberts, "Negro Secondary Schools Face Closing Along with All White Grades Over 6th," *Norfolk Virginian-Pilot*, 14 January 1959, 1.

Martin, (Councilman) Roy B., "Martin's Statement," *Norfolk Virginian-Pilot*, 14 January 1959, 8.

"Granby Scores Cut-Off," *Norfolk Virginian-Pilot*, 15 January 1959.

Carter, Luther J., "'Moral Right' to Limit Education Is Questioned By P.T.A. of Bay View," *Norfolk Virginian-Pilot*, 16 January 1959, 57.

"Do They Know What They Are Doing?," editorial, *Norfolk Virginian-Pilot*, 16 January 1959, 4.

"Bite the Hand That Feeds Us?," editorial, *Norfolk Virginian-Pilot*, 17 January 1959, 4.

"Chamber Voice on Schools Quiet After Committee Bid," *Norfolk Virginian-Pilot*, 17 January 1959, 15.

"Counter-Revolution among P.T.A.'s," editorial, *Norfolk Virginian-Pilot*, 18 January 1959, 3-B.

Henderson, Jim and John I. Brooks, "Massive Resistance Laws Ruled Void by Both Virginia and Federal Courts," *Norfolk Virginian-Pilot*, 20 January 1959, 1.

"Open Schools Soon, Schweitzer Advises," *Norfolk Virginian-Pilot*, 20 January 1959, 1.

Kelley, George M., "Stand Fast, Governor Pleads," *Norfolk Virginian-Pilot*, 21 January 1959, 1.

"Women's Boos Stop Council," *Norfolk Virginian-Pilot*, 21 January 1959, 1.

Mulfold, Ralph, "'Lost Class of '59' Called Objective by Observers," *Norfolk Ledger-Dispatch*, 22 January 1959, 21.

"Navy Has Plans for Own Schools," *Norfolk Ledger-Dispatch*, 22 January 1959, 1.

Kelley, George M., "Norfolk School Closings Permanently Banned," *Norfolk Virginian-Pilot*, 24 January 1959, 1.

Carter, Luther J., "History of a Norfolk Tiff," *Norfolk Virginian-Pilot*, 25 January 1959, C-1.

Mansfield, Richard M., "School Problem before Congress," *Norfolk Virginian-Pilot*, 25 January 1959, C-2.

Henderson, Jim, "Cut-Off Ruling Due Today at 4 P.M.," *Norfolk Virginian-Pilot*, 27 January 1959. 1.

"A New Clear Voice Speaks in Norfolk," editorial, *Norfolk Virginian-Pilot*, 27 January 1959, 4.

"A Public Petition to the Norfolk City Council," advertisement, *Norfolk Virginian-Pilot*, 27 January 1959, 11.

"Reopen Schools, Council Urged," *Norfolk Virginian-Pilot*, 27 January 1959, 1.

"Schools Could Operate Even with Funds Cut," *Norfolk Virginian-Pilot*, 27 January 1959, 5.

Henderson, Jim, "Way Cleared for Norfolk Integration," *Norfolk Virginian-Pilot*, 28 January 1959, 9.

"New School Plea Aimed at Council," *Norfolk Virginian-Pilot*, 28 January 1959, 13.

"T.E.F. Seeks City School Buildings," *Norfolk Virginian-Pilot*, 28 January 1959, 1.

Kelley, George M., "Gloomy Legislators Laud Governor But Still Seeking to Bar Integration," *Norfolk Virginian-Pilot*, 29 January 1959, 1.

"Ohioan Would Cut Federal Spending in Norfolk Area," *Norfolk Virginian-Pilot*, 29 January 1959, 48.

Carter, Luther J., "Norfolk Opening Set," *Norfolk Virginian-Pilot*, 30 January 1959, 1.

Kelley, George M., "Resisters Make Their Bid Today," *Norfolk Virginian-Pilot*, 30 January 1959, 1.

"Resurrection Morn on Botetourt Street," editorial, *Norfolk Virginian-Pilot*, 31 January 1959. Sargeant Collection.

Phillips, Cabell, "Norfolk Schools Aim to Avoid 'Little Rock,'" *New York Times*, 1 February 1959, 6-E.

Lewis, Anthony, "Virginia Viewed as Turning Point for Integration," *New York Times*, 1 February 1959, 1.

"The Opening of Schools," editorial, *Norfolk Virginian-Pilot*, 1 February 1959, B-2.

Carter, Luther J., "7 Schools Desegregated Peacefully," *Norfolk Virginian-Pilot*, 3 February 1959, A-l.

Bigart, Homer, "Virginia Integration Still Has Far to Go," *New York Times*, 8 February 1959, E-7.

"Schools Face Budget Cuts, Mayor Warns," *Norfolk Virginian-Pilot*, 21 February 1959, 28.

"Commission Invites Ideas on Schools," *Norfolk Virginian-Pilot*, 22 February 1959, 1.

Carter, Luther J., "Board Names Small-School Study Group," *Norfolk Virginian-Pilot*, 27 February 1959, 56.

"Small Primary Schools Approved by Committee," *Norfolk Virginian-Pilot*, 13 March 1959. Sargeant Collection.

Roberts, Gene, "Young Candidates Buck Resisters," *Norfolk Virginian-Pilot*, 15 April 1959. Sargeant Collection.

"School Board May Lose Two," *Norfolk Virginian-Pilot*, 22 April 1959. Norfolk Committee for Public Schools files, Old Dominion University Archives.

Crenshaw, Francis N., letter to the editor, *Norfolk Virginian-Pilot*, 22 April 1959. Norfolk Committee for Public Schools files, Old Dominion University Archives.

"Breeden Supports School Board Bill," *Norfolk Virginian-Pilot*, 23 April 1959, 60.

"Letters to the Editor," *Norfolk Virginian-Pilot*, April 23-26, 1959. Norfolk Committee for Public Schools files, Old Dominion University Archives.

"Committee Seeks School Suit Fee," *Norfolk Ledger-Dispatch*, 2 May 1959. Norfolk Committee for Public Schools files, Old Dominion University Archives.

"Schools Cut Opposed By Parents," *Norfolk Virginian-Pilot*, 13 May 1959. Norfolk Committee for Public Schools files, Old Dominion University Archives.

Carter, Luther J., "Demountable Classrooms for Coronado," *Norfolk Virginian-Pilot*, 8 July 1959. Sargeant Collection.

Kelley, George M., "Breeden Defeats Spencer; Howell, Childress Head to House," *Norfolk Virginian-Pilot*, 15 July 1959.

Kelley, George C., "How the Roof Fell In on Grover Outland," *Norfolk Virginian-Pilot*, 19 July 1959, C-l.

"School Board Firm on Oakwood Plans," *Norfolk Virginian-Pilot*, 21 July 1959. Sargeant Collection.

"New Junior High Indicated in Eastern Part of Norfolk," *Norfolk Virginian-Pilot*, 8 August 1959. Sargeant Collection.

Mulford, Ralph, "Negroes Make Move to Push Integration," *Norfolk Ledger-Dispatch*, 20 August 1959. Sargeant Collection.

"Little Creek to Get Junior High School," *Norfolk Virginian-Pilot*, 23 October 1959. Sargeant Collection.

Carter, Luther J., "The Politics of a Budget," *Norfolk Virginian-Pilot*, 25 October 1959, 3.

Kelley, George M., "Vote Solidly Democratic, Negroes Told," *Norfolk Virginian-Pilot*, 30 October 1959. Sargeant Collection.

"Council Acquires New School Site," *Norfolk Ledger-Dispatch*, 11 November 1959. Sargeant Collection.

"Larger School Outlay Demanded," *Norfolk Virginian-Pilot*, 8 December 1959. Sargeant Collection.

Kestner, Jack, "Paul Schweitzer Talked Over New Post with Whole Family Before Signing Up," *Norfolk Ledger-Dispatch*, 16 February 1960. Sargeant Collection.

Paschang, Chet, "Schweitzer Choice Appears Move for Harmony Slate," *Norfolk Ledger-Dispatch*, 16 February 1960. Sargeant Collection.

Stein, Tony, "He'll Work Hard and Lead Others," *Norfolk Ledger-Dispatch*, 30 March 1960. Sargeant Collection.

Stein, Tony, "Lewis Layton: Often a Compromise Is the Only Way," *Norfolk Ledger-Dispatch*, 19 May 1960. Sargeant Collection.

Dodson, Bob, "Opposition Guide Ballot to List Paul Schweitzer?" *Norfolk Ledger-Dispatch*, 10 June 1960. Sargeant Collection.

Dodson, Bob, "Sam Barfield Will Attend If 'Secret' Meetings Open," *Norfolk Ledger-Dispatch*, 15 June 1960. Sargeant Collection.

"Old School Faces Ax," *Norfolk Virginian-Pilot*, 19 August 1960. Sargeant Collection.

Carter, Luther J., "Political Change Breathes in City," *Norfolk Virginian-Pilot*, 5 September 1960, 29.

Richardson, Barrett, "Challenge Children Board Member Says," *Norfolk Ledger-Dispatch*, 29 May 1961. Sargeant Collection.

Tazewell, William L., "A New Norfolk Has Arisen Out of the Blight," *Norfolk Virginian-Pilot*, 23 July 1961. Norfolk Redevelopment and Housing Authority.

Tazewell, William L., "Businessmen Provide Push in Norfolk Development," *Norfolk Virginian-Pilot*, 25 July 1961. Norfolk Redevelopment and Housing Authority.

Tazewell, William L. "Renewal Men Spark City's Growth," *Norfolk Virginian-Pilot*, 26 July 1961. Norfolk Redevelopment and Housing Authority.

"Norfolk Man Got $6 A Week to Start," *Richmond Times-Dispatch*, 3 February 1963. Sargeant Collection.

Carter, Luther J., "'The Senator Couldn't Be Reached,'" *Norfolk Virginian-Pilot*, 9 June 1964, A-l.

Woodlief, Wayne, "Political and Social Polish Can't Smooth Ballard's Face," *Norfolk Ledger-Star*, 1 September 1964. Sargeant Collection.

Owen, Gene, "Hard Times Touched First Citizen in Heart," *Norfolk Ledger-Star*, 22 December 1972. Sargeant Collection.

Lattimer, James, "J. Lindsay Almond, Jr.: Ordeal of a Governor," *Richmond Times-Dispatch*, 4 August 1974. Sargeant Collection.

Mason, Robert, "City Government—People and Politics," editorial, *Norfolk Virginian-Pilot*, 4 July 1975, A-18.

Coit, John, "A Return To Broad Creek: The Way We Were," *Norfolk Virginian-Pilot*, 15 July 1979, G-1.

Lattimer, James, "Almond in '80: On Staying in Power in Virginia," *Richmond Times-Dispatch*, 10 February 1980. Sargeant Collection.

NOTE: The Sargeant Memorial Local History and Genealogy Collection of local history memorabilia is housed in the Slover Library, Norfolk, Virginia. The Archives section of the Old Dominion University Library houses the papers of the Norfolk Committee for Public Schools that were collected by the author for this work.

※

Index

Abbott, George, 65, 139, 158, 180
Agle, Charles K., 13-16
Alfriend, John, 164
Almond, J. Lindsay, 113-114, 123, 134-135, 138, 142, 147, 149-151, 159-160, 166-168, 170, 173; election, 113, 142, 147, 149; Massive Resistance, 113-114, 142, 151, 159, 166-170; school crisis, 123, 134-135, 138, 155, 168
Anderson, Martin, 215
Andrews, Dr. Mason C., 128, 181
annexation, 18, 21, 32, 34, 39, 46, 48, 64, 75, 77, 80, 178, 206, 218
Arlington, schools, 30, 107, 131
Atlantic City, 78, 81-83, 86, 95, 97-98, 104-108, 199, 201-203, 208, 215, 216; impact, 77, 91, 94, 96, 97, 194, 200; racial composition, 32, 53, 81, 83, 100, 104, 192, 203-205, 207; redevelopment, 77-78, 84, 86, 91, 94, 97, 105, 199-200, 212-213; rationale, 78, 79. *See also* Patrick Henry Elementary
Attaway, Dorothy, 179

"Back to School, Keep It Cool" movement, 168, 172
Ballard, William P., 125, 146
Ballentine, 46. *See also* Lafayette School
Barfield, Sam, 155, 180
Batten Frank, 155, 164
Battle, John, 44, 48
Bay View Elementary, 157
Benmoreell Elementary, 98, 101, 106, 195, 216
Berkley, 44, 48, 101, 104, 192, 195, 204. *See also* Gatewood Elementary

blacks, housing, 10-12, 18, 32, 35, 41, 46, 100-101, 117, 188-189, 192, 194-195, 200, 204, 206-207, 209-210, 218; leadership, 31, 40, 116-117, 125, 140, 181; schools, 44, 57, 59, 103-104, 106, 174, 184, 188-190, 209. *See also* race relations
black removal, 215
Blair, William F., 155
Blair Junior High School, 106, 121
Bollingbrook, 32, 106
Borland, Col. Charles K., 4, 16
Boston, schools, 208, 221
Boswell, Archie, 155
Bowling Park Elementary, 174, 187
Brambleton, 10-12, 31-32, 34, 64, 83, 192, 204, 216, 224
Breeden, Edward L., 753, 180
Brewbaker, J. J., 42, 47, 50, 52, 58, 122, 151
Brewer, Rev. James, 127
Broad Creek Shores, 37-39, 41, 46, 53, 64, 74
Broad Creek Village: racial composition, 37, 38, 53, 64, 101, 105; redevelopment, 37, 38, 77-81, 86, 95-96, 98, 100, 105
Brooks, Dr. Lyman, 47, 178
Brown v. Board of Education, xiii, 30, 44, 46-49, 51-52, 57, 101, 103, 112-114, 131, 135, 152, 182-185, 187-188, 190-191, 194, 201, 204, 207, 219
Burroughs, Charles, 164
business community, 4, 14, 16, 24, 61, 64, 92-94, 96, 110, 113, 119, 140-141, 145, 154-156, 162-163, 170, 180. *See also* People's reform movement
Byrd, Harry F., Sr., 28, 50, 63, 147,

256

150, 159, 167, 170, 173, 224
Byrd Organization, 27, 29-30, 43, 50, 60, 63, 72, 73, 112-113, 119, 123-124, 126, 129, 133, 137, 141, 144, 150, 153, 162, 166, 170, 173-174, 178-179, 190, 224
Campostella, 32, 44
Campostella Junior High School, 44, 46, 48, 58
Caro, Robert A., 95
Carter, Luther, 48, 58, 128, 175
Chambers, Lenoir, 120, 135, 154, 155, 173
Charleston, S.C., x, 189, 205, 218
Charlotte, North Carolina, schools, 129, 211
Charlottesville, schools, 30, 107, 131
Christian Nationalist Party, 61
churches, response to Massive Resistance, 135, 136
city government, powers of, 3, 23, 37, 67, 76, 125, 197
Coleman, James, 208
Committee of One Hundred, 164-166, 173
Community Fund, 7, 9, 60, 116
Cooke, Richard D., 4-5, 22, 26, 65, 164
Coronado: housing, 34-35, 37, 53; litigants, 115, 118, 121, 122, 125, 193, 196; racial turmoil, 34-36, 39, 41, 53, 64, 83, 168, 170, 191-192, 204, 216; school, 175, 195-196
council-manager form of government, 2, 3, 22-24, 65-66
Cox, Lawrence, 80, 83, 200, 213
Crenshaw, Francis, 122, 125, 146, 179, 196
Cultural Center, 68-71, 75, 86, 88, 191

Dallas, Mildred, 125, 146
Dalton, Theodore, 43, 113
Darden, Colgate, 155
Darden, Pretlow, 4, 22, 65; redevelopment, 199, 208; 164, 173

Davis, Leonard, 158
Defenders of State Sovereignty and Individual Liberties, 61, 63, 112-114, 117-119, 137-138, 141, 147, 148, 166, 172-173, 179-180, 190; formation, 43, 60, 131; logic, 43, 60, 112-113
Diggs Park Elementary, 44, 187
Downtown Redevelopment Project, 77-79, 82, 86, 91, 96, 98, 101, 105, 199, 200, 210
Duckworth, W. Fred: accomplishments, 64, 67, 75, 76; appearance, 149; background, 27; board-packing plan, 72, 121, 125; Committee of One Hundred, 164-166, 173; funds cut-off plan, 151-152, 168, 175; mini-schools plan, 187, 196, 211, 216; "None of Your Business," 179; People's group, 28, 29, 41; philosophy, 28-29, 62, 150; plan to sell off schools, 158; political aspirations, 29, 150; power, 28, 62, 65-67, 72, 75, 132; Prieur Organization, 29, 64, 73, 125, 141, 144, 150, 158; race relations, 31, 36, 37-38, 116-117, 139; redevelopment plan, 75-76, 78, 88, 90, 94, 101, 107, 110, 111, 114, 153; redevelopment powers, 101, 140, 165; relationship with teachers, 136, 137, 141, 145, 151-177, 197; school closing plan, 124, 138, 159, 164, 165, 170, 186, 197; school crisis, 56, 59, 76, 107, 111, 132, 136, 140-141, 145, 156, 173, 186, 197; school segregation plan, 56, 59, 61, 63, 76, 101, 106-107, 110, 122, 167, 173; style, 28, 64-65, 67, 74-75, 94, 149.
East Ocean View Elementary, 174, 196
Eggleston, John W., 159
Eisenhower, Dwight D., 154, 172
eminent domain, 198, 208

Ervin, Sam, 48, 187
Etheridge, N. B., 28

Fairlawn Elementary, 175, 196, 216
Federal Housing Administration, 206
Fishwick, John, 155
Foote, George, 164
Ford, Frank R., 152
Friendly, Ed, 160

Gatewood Elementary, 104-106, 108, 194-195, 204. *See also* Berkley
Ghent, 68-69, 71, 80, 85, 92, 122, 199, 208, 210
Godwin, Mills, 161, 168
Goode Elementary, 32, 98
Granby district, 32, 106
Granby High School, 121, 157
Grandy, C. W., 164
Gray, Garland, 50
Gray Plan, 50, 63, 225

Hagan, Col. J. A., 113
Harrell, C. A.: accomplishments, 5-6, 15, 18-20, 23, 34, 62; departure, 28, 29; management style, 6-7, 24-25, 44, 75; planning New Norfolk, 6-8, 19, 28, 29, 31, 48, 62
Harrison, Albertis S., 152
Harrison v. Day, 139, 151, 158-159
Health Department, 82-84, 92, 200-202
Henry Clay Elementary, 105
Hofheimer, Henry Clay, 39, 164
Hoffman, Walter, 20, 54, 103-104, 108, 122, 123, 165-166, 168, 187, 191, 194-195, 199, 201, 221: minimum housing code, 20; *James v. Almond*, 159; judge, 53, 196
Home Owners Loan Corporation, 206
housing, 8, 11, 15-19, 31, 34, 35, 56, 70, 75, 77, 79, 80, 86, 96, 98, 104, 198, 200, 202-203, 211, 215: black, 10-12, 18, 32, 35, 41, 46, 100-101, 117, 188-189, 192, 194-195, 200, 204, 206-207, 209-210, 218; code enforcement, 8, 20-22, 41, 82-84, 93, 200, 201; slum housing, 12, 15, 21, 34, 40, 76, 84, 92, 93, 97-98, 201, 212, 215; Southern cities, 82, 172, 185, 186, 189, 192, 206, 207, 211
Housing and Home Finance Agency, 198
Howell, Henry E., Jr., 180

Ingleside Elementary, 38, 46
interposition, 50, 55-56, 63, 123, 151, 193, 194, 217, 225

Jackson, Kenneth T., 206-209
Jacox Junior High, 48, 187
James, Ellis, 128, 138
James v. Almond, 139, 151-152, 157-159. *See also* Norfolk Committee for Public Schools
James v. Duckworth, 163
Jenkins, John S., 39, 164
Jordan, Joseph, 40-41
Journal and Guide, Norfolk, 37, 39-40, 125

Kaufman, Charles, 21, 39, 40, 164
Kaufman (Land) Committee, 38, 71, 226
Kidd, Mary, 128
Kilpatrick, James J., 50, 63, 209, 217, 225

Lafayette School, 46, 190
Lakewood Junior High School, 47, 178
Lambert's Point, 92; racial composition, 32, 100, 192, 204; redevelopment, 76, 98; schools, 106, 204
Land (Kaufman) Committee, 38, 71, 226
Landsdale Junior High School, 47, 178
Larchmont Elementary, 106, 204
Layton, Lewis, 72, 152

Ledger-Dispatch, Norfolk, 24, 48, 71, 97, 119, 155, 163
Lindenwood Elementary, 44, 174, 187
Lindsay, Harvey, Jr., 165
Little Rock, Ark., 54, 113-116, 118, 123, 129, 145, 168, 170, 172, 191, 205
Lott Cary School, 98

Madison, J. Hugo, 40-41, 53
Madison Elementary School, 106-107
Marshall Elementary School, 106, 195
Martin, James G., IV, 136
Martin, Roy, 38, 42, 177, 198: break with Duckworth, 156-158, 166; Broad Creek Shores, 38; on *Brown*, 42; selection, 38, 72, 180
Mason, Vivian (Mrs. W. T.), 140
Massive Resistance, 30, 50, 52, 58, 60, 112-114, 119-124, 128, 131-134, 138, 141-142, 145, 148-153, 158, 164, 166, 168-170, 173, 175, 178-180; resistance to, 50, 131-133, 135-137, 145, 156, 170, 173, 177, 179; end, 159, 161, 167-169, 173-174, 197, 217
Maury High School, 106, 121
Maxwell, Thomas, 47, 66
McKendree, William I., 157
Memphis, Tenn., 189, 206, 218
Miller, Col. Francis Pickens, 155
Mobile, Alabama, 172, 208, 218
Monola, G. D., 83-85
Morrow, Edward R., 160-161

Nashville, Tennessee, schools, 129
National Association for the Advancement of Colored People (N.A.A.C.P.), 61, 117, 140, 183; legal actions, 54, 57, 64, 105, 110, 139-140, 185, 191; legal strategy, 40, 53, 60, 114-115, 191; Norfolk cases, 54, 60, 151, 152, 203; plaintiffs, 47, 57, 59, 104, 106, 114; school crisis, 49, 57, 115, 117, 121, 141
National Bank of Commerce, 95
Newport News, schools, 107, 195
Norfolk: before World War II, xvi; during World War II, xx, 3, 82, 100, 201; 1945-1950, x, 12, 101; downtown, xx, xviii, 7, 13, 14, 16, 18-19, 67-71; housing patterns before 1954, xviii, 8-20, 32, 35; race relations before 1954, 34. *See also* Cultural Center; Downtown Redevelopment Project; waterfront development
Norfolk Catholic High School, 52, 135, 190
Norfolk Committee for Public Schools, 126, 128, 138-139, 217; *James v. Almond*, 139, 151-152, 157-159; *James v. Duckworth*, 163; members, 127, 179, 181
Norfolk Education Association, 136
Norfolk General Hospital, 77, 92, 208
Norfolk Redevelopment and Housing Authority (N.R.H.A.), 8, 11-13, 15, 40, 77, 78, 83, 86, 92, 104, 201; background, 8, 17, 22, 24; commissioners, 39, 83, 92, 95, 199, 200, 208, 213; management, 13, 16-17, 40, 79-83, 84, 94, 199, 201, 202, 207, 219. *See also* Lawrence M. Cox; Atlantic City; Broad Creek Village; Downtown; Lambert's Point; Project One; Oakwood
Norfolk School Board: on *Brown*, 49, 51, 221; budget cuts, 105, 151-158, 165, 177, 197; building plans, 46, 57, 58-59, 61, 106; members, 119, 122, 124, 144, 146, 155, 158, 180, 218; opposes Duckworth, 54, 61, 63, 121, 136, 140, 158, 174, 191; race relations, 48, 51, 52, 101, 171-175, 195, 196, 204, 215; relations with city council, 55, 56, 135, 174, 178-179; on Massive Resistance, 49, 54, 105,

120, 141-143, 167, 190, 194; on school closing referendum, 49, 59, 121, 122, 125, 138, 140, 144, 157, 158, 166, 216; vest-pocket schools, 178, 196, 211, 216
Norview, schools, 168-172, 175, 195-196, 224

Oakwood, 32, 35, 39, 41, 53; Elementary School, 47-48, 105-106, 175; Redevelopment Project, 39-41, 57-58, 71, 75, 77, 98
Oceanair Elementary School, 44
Old Dominion Redevelopment Project, 77-78, 92, 98, 106, 199, 213
Old Dominion University (O.D.U.), 93, 155, 198, 203-204, 210, 216
Orfield, Gary, 209-211

Paige, Walter, 73
Page, Lawrence C., 27-28, 38
Patrick Henry Elementary School, 98, 100, 104-106, 194-195, 199. *See also* Atlantic City
Parent Teacher Association (P.T.A.), 49, 127, 156-157
parlor schools, 136
People's reform movement: accomplishments, 28, 31, 48; "Back to School...," 168, 172; city planning, 28, 39, 41, 64, 67, 68, 70-71, 77, 188; Committee of One Hundred, 164; demise, 41, 61, 64, 69, 75; during school crisis, 155; initiation, 32, 61; takeover, 41, 65; redevelopment, 41, 71, 91; relations with Duckworth, 29, 62; search for successors, 26; school construction, 44, 48
Perkins, Linwood F., 72
Pilcher, Theodore, 73
Pineridge Elementary School, 100, 105, 195
planning, city, 67, 180, 198, 218

Planning Commission, 7, 37, 39, 46, 68-70, 92
Poplar Halls Elementary School, 175, 196, 216
Port Authority, 70, 71
Powell, Lewis F., 209
Powers, W. Farley, 49, 125, 146
Pretty Lake Elementary, 165, 196, 216
Prieur, William F. "Billy": before 1945, 9, 48; in 1950, 29, 63; 1958-1959, 65, 121; elections, control of, 113; relationship with Duckworth, 27-29, 37; Young Turks, 73
Prieur Organization, 5, 26, 27, 225: before 1945, 9, 48; 1946-1950, 22, 72-73; in 1950s, 6, 61, 73, 74; relationship with organized crime, 113; relationship with Duckworth, 29, 64, 73, 125, 141, 144, 150, 158
Prince Edward County schools, 30, 107, 131, 152, 183
Project One, 24-26, 35, 39, 75-78, 82-84, 93, 203; initiation, 15, 24, 78, 210; description, 15-19, 21, 40, 78-79, 91, 188, 199-200, 212, 215. *See also* Norfolk Redevelopment and Housing Authority
proximity doctrine, 101, 106, 188, 194, 217, 218
public schools: black schools, 44, 57, 59, 103-104, 106, 174, 184, 188-190, 209; building powers, 46, 58, 61-63, 100, 105, 106; construction, before 1954, 44-49, 106, 108, 110; construction, after 1954, 174; funding, 138, 144, 177; teachers, 48, 103, 117, 123, 134, 136-137, 141, 151, 158, 173, 177, 187, 197; vest-pocket mini-schools, 187, 196, 211, 216; in Virginia, 50-51, 55, 60, 107, 113, 117-118, 131, 134-137, 141, 147, 152, 192, 194, 215

race relations: Brambleton, 31-32, 34, 64, 192, 204; before 1954, 31, 34; in 1954-1956, 115-116, 192; in 1958-1959, 172; military, 31, 34, 186, 207; planning, 292. *See also* W. Fred Duckworth; Atlantic City; Broad Creek Shores; Coronado; Lambert's Point

redevelopment: black removal, 215; economic theories, 13, 14, 15, 19, 68, 91, 93-94, 172, 210, 212, 214; financing, 12, 44, 48, 82, 91, 187; powers, 16, 18, 21, 39, 68, 84, 90, 94-97, 101, 108, 111, 114, 204, 211, 217-218, 220; Housing Act of 1949, 14, 97-98

red-lining: 206-207

referendum, school closing, 144-147, 149-153, 161

Richmond, 116, 132, 162, 179, 206, 208, 209, 218

Ripley, Robert, 38, 72

Rixey, John F., 73

Robertson, Clarence, 164

Rosemont Junior High School, 35, 39, 48, 57, 58, 105, 122, 175, 195, 196

St. Louis, Mo. schools, 129

Savage, Toy, 73

school boards, powers of, building, 46, 58, 61-63, 100, 105, 106; elected v. appointed, 56, 106; financial, 48, 57, 105. *See also* Norfolk School Board; public schools

Schweitzer, Paul, 52, 119, 121, 125, 144-145, 155, 157, 180

Seashore State Park, 54

segregation, *de jure* v. *de facto*, 42, 101, 106-107, 122, 184-185, 188-189, 193-194, 198, 203, 205, 207, 211, 213, 215, 220

Sherwood Forest Elementary, 46-47

Smallwood Elementary, 106, 204

Smythe Elementary, 98

Southern Manifesto, 216

South Norfolk, schools, 134, 135

Southside (Campostella) Junior High School, 44, 46, 48, 58

Stanley, Thomas, 36, 43, 50, 63, 190

Staylor, Claude J., 6

Stern, Robert L., 127-128

Stonewall Jackson School, 32

Story, William J., 134

Straus, Nathan, 9

Suburban Park Elementary, 106

Summers, Ezra, 42, 51, 58, 63, 72;

Summers Plan, 51

Tanner's Creek District: annexation 46, 100; Oakwood, 32, 35, 39-40; schools, 47

Taueber, Karl, 189, 205-206, 211

Taylor Elementary School, 106

Thornton, Dan, 164

Thrasher, Mary, 128

Tidewater Academy, 137

Tidewater Education Foundation (T.E.F.), 118-119, 127, 133-137, 148; plan to buy schools, 119, 158; recruits teachers, 136. *See also* Defenders of State Sovereignty and Individual Liberties

Titustown, 32, 106, 216

Titustown Elementary School, 46

Tuck, William, 43, 153

Truitt, Irving F., 128

Twohy, John, 4-5, 22, 26

United Fund, 92

University of Virginia, 130, 132, 155

urban renewal, 40, 71, 81, 90, 115, 183, 186, 197-198, 205, 209-215, 217-220

Veterans Administration, 206

Virginian-Pilot, Norfolk, 71, 177; on Committee of One Hundred, 164-166; on Duckworth, 36, 72; on segregation, 11, 42, 50, 105, 106, 129, 138, 153, 176; on redevelopment, 97-98; on schools, 58, 104, 120, 128, 134, 138, 140-144, 153-157, 163, 172, 174, 217. *See also* Lenoir Chambers

Washington, D.C., schools, 129, 206
waterfront development, 38, 68, 70, 85-86, 91, 202-203
Weaver, Robert C., 198
Webb, Lewis W., Jr., 155
West Elementary, 174
White, Dr. Forrest P., M.D., 128
White, Harvey E., Jr., 113
White, Margaret, 128
white flight theories, 208-209, 212, 221
Wilcox, Thomas, 164
Willard Junior High School, 47
William and Mary, College of, 77, 92, 132
Willis, Benjamin, 57, 125, 144-146
Worsham, Rives, 22, 164

Young, P. B., Sr., 19
Young, P. B., Jr., 31, 36-37, 41, 64, 116
Young Park, 19, 174, 187
Young Park Elementary School, 19, 44, 48, 187
Young, Thomas, 40
Young Turks, 73

About the Author

Photo by Nate Duncan

FORREST R. "HAP" WHITE was reared in Norfolk in a family that for four generations was active in local church, civic and cultural affairs. When his father, pediatrician Dr. Forrest P. White, M.D., first introduced his hometown to his young wife, Edith (Edie), a twice-decorated World War II "code breaker" from New Jersey, he ended their tour at a bench in Norfolk City Park. There, Forrest told Edie of his dream for his hometown: a new children's specialty hospital, well-baby clinic, and medical school. Edie agreed, and she spoke of the need for expanded theater, symphony, and arts facilities. And then she turned, pointed to the "Whites Only" sign guarding the park's playground, and pleaded, "This also has to end. If Norfolk is going to be my city, you have help me push for quality schools, libraries, parks, and playgrounds that all its citizens can use." The bargain was struck: Dr. White set up one of the first fully integrated medical practices without "separate" waiting rooms. When the city's white public secondary schools were closed under Virginia's Massive Resistance laws, he reluctantly stepped into the limelight to help lead the Norfolk Committee for Public Schools, the citizens' group that successfully sued to re-open the schools and consequently desegregate them. In addition to leading numerous church, civic and cultural endeavors to promote library, literary, theatre, and orchestral activities, Mrs. White also served as head of the Women's Interracial Council and was active enough in other progressive causes to earn the epithet of "Comrade Edie" from her students and social peers. Eventually, and in part through their own efforts, they saw their dreams for Norfolk realized.

Thus, Hap White grew up fully aware of both the pride and the prejudice of his hometown: its public face of dynamic modernization and its more guarded side of intolerance, intimidation, and incivility. After graduating from college, the author worked to help Norfolk overcome this sad legacy by working in political campaigns and as a school teacher, municipal officer, and public school administrator, before retiring to Williamsburg, Virginia. He holds a bachelors degree from Bucknell University (1970) as well as a Masters (1987) and Ph.D. (1991) in Public Administration from Old Dominion University. His award-winning doctoral dissertation was the basis for *Pride and Prejudice: School Desegregation and Urban Renewal in Norfolk*, published by Praeger Press in 1991.

※

www.ingramcontent.com/pod-product-compliance
Lightning Source LLC
Chambersburg PA
CBHW020049170426
43199CB00009B/221